defending rights

defending rights

LAW, LABOR POLITICS, AND THE STATE IN CALIFORNIA, 1890–1925

THOMAS RALPH CLARK

WAYNE STATE UNIVERSITY PRESS
DETROIT

Library of Congress Cataloging-in-Publication Data

Clark, Thomas R., 1958–
Defending rights: law, labor politics, and the state
in California, 1890–1925 / Thomas Ralph Clark.
p. cm.
Includes bibliographical references and index.
ISBN 0-8143-3043-6 (cloth : alk. paper)
1. Labor unions—Law and legislation—California—History.   2. Labor
disputes—California—History.   3. Labor injunctions—California—History.
4. Labor movement—California—History.   5. Labor
movement—United States—States—History.   I. Title.
KFC557 .C58 2002
323'.2'0979409041—dc21
                                        2002010169

In Memory of

Ralph J. Clark

AND TO THE FUTURE OF

Samuel Matthew Clark

Contents

Preface

This study examines the political and ideological consequences of court and police intervention in labor disputes in Progressive-era America. Using California as a case study, my manuscript extends and revises recent works that investigate the impact of the law and legal discourse on the political development of the American labor movement. Most of these studies conclude that labor's encounters with a hostile legal system in the late nineteenth and early twentieth centuries pushed the American labor movement—especially the national leaders of the American Federation of Labor—in an "apolitical" and "antistatist" direction. While providing novel reinterpretations of the "exceptionalism" of the American labor movement, these studies too often focus on the federal courts and the national leadership of the American Federation of Labor. But when one turns to the state and local levels—the most likely sites of labor's legal encounters before the 1930s—the story is much more complex. My examination of law, labor politics, and the state in California shows how legal hostility pushed labor into politics with greater urgency, both to defend labor's rights of collective action and to sponsor an ambitious program of social reform.

Acknowledgments

It is with great pleasure that I finally thank the many people who assisted in the long process of turning my ideas into a book. Although it has undergone two major overhauls, this book began as a dissertation in the History Department at UCLA. My first debt, therefore, is to those who guided the dissertation: William Forbath, Karen Orren, John Laslett, and especially Eric Monkkonen. Willie Forbath and Karen Orren not only helped me shape the dissertation in the early stages, but their own provocative works on labor and the law provided inspiration and an engaging set of questions. John Laslett gave each chapter of the dissertation a careful and thoughtful reading and provided a model of historical craftsmanship. Finally, I thank Eric Monkkonen for guiding and encouraging the project from beginning to end. He is a mentor, a friend, and, above all, a fine human being.

My research was also aided by scores of librarians and archivists. I especially thank the staff of the Bancroft Library at the University of California, Berkeley. A Bancroft Library fellowship for the 1991–1992 academic year provided funds, a desk in the library, direct access to some of the richest sources available on California labor history, and a stimulating environment. I also thank the staffs of the following libraries or archival repositories: the California State Archives; the California State Library, especially the California History Room and the library's impressive collection of state newspapers on microfilm; UCLA Special Collections and University Research Library; the Labor History Archives at Sutro Library, San Francisco State University; the Los Angeles County Archives; and the California State Law Library. In addition to the Bancroft Fellowship, I reaped the benefits of several grants, especially a UCLA dissertation fellowship; the UCLA Rosecrans fellowship; and a Research Services Council grant from the University of Nebraska at Kearney.

During the process of revising a far too long dissertation into a much shorter but more focused book, I had the good fortune to have my first tenure-track teaching position at the University of Nebraska at Kearney. There, tucked away in a small town in the middle of the Great Plains, I found a stimulating community of scholars and, more importantly, good friends. I especially thank Jim German and Carol Lilly for years of friendship and support. They not only read and commented on countless drafts of the revised manuscript, but they were forced to hear about its progress over a few beers along the way. (Perhaps it was more than *a few*). I also thank UNK's Research Services Council (and especially Ken Nikels and Daryl Kelley) for providing a generous grant that allowed me to spend the summer of 1998 doing additional research at the Bancroft Library in Berkeley.

At Wayne State University Press, I would like to thank Jane Hoehner for her enthusiastic support. I also thank Michael Goldfield, Kevin Boyle, and one anonymous reader for comments that have made the final draft much better than it otherwise would have been.

My thanks and debts to my wife, Ann Vuletich, go beyond words. Since we first met as college students in Santa Cruz, California, twenty years ago, she has given me more love, support, friendship, and joy than anyone has a right to expect. Finally, during the last year and a half that I struggled with a second major revision of this manuscript, I lost a father and gained a son. With love, I dedicate this book to them.

T.R.C.
Sacramento, California

Introduction

On October 2, 1911, Los Angeles labor organizer W. A. Engle traveled north to Bakersfield to attend the annual convention of the California Federation of Labor (CFL). As the CFL's vice president for the Los Angeles district, Engle had prepared a report on conditions in Los Angeles. To say the least, the past year had been a trying one for the Los Angeles labor movement. The bombing of the *Los Angeles Times* building—which housed one of the most anti-union newspapers in the United States—brought charges, arrests, and eventually convictions against two trade unionists, James and John McNamara. As the McNamaras sat in a Los Angeles jail awaiting trial, on-going strikes by metal trades and brewery workers elicited a half-dozen court injunctions and hundreds of arrests under a recently enacted anti-picketing ordinance. Convinced that the McNamaras had been framed, and troubled by the hostile actions that local courts and police had taken against strikers, Los Angeles trade unionists abandoned their customary non-partisanship and endorsed a slate of Socialist Party candidates in the 1911 municipal campaign. With the election only a few weeks away, these political developments were much on the minds of Engle and his audience. "The events of the past year," Engle informed the convention

> have educated the working classes of Los Angeles to
> the absolute necessity of taking control of the powers of
> government so that they may receive justice at the hands
> of the officials. The imprisonment of union men without
> warrant and upon trumped-up charges . . . [and] the rigid

13

administering of the infamous, un-American Anti-Picketing
Ordinance, has forced a coalition of the workers onto the
political field, without regard to previous affiliations . . . It is
my belief that it is the handwriting on the wall, that . . . this
[political action] will place the power of the government in
the hands of the governed and will sound the death knell of
corporation control of court, police, and military.[1]

Engle's assessment that court and police hostility had forced
labor onto the political field does not square with the conclusions
reached in recent historical studies on labor and the law. These
studies, as I detail below, argue that late-nineteenth- and early-
twentieth-century legal hostility caused the American Federation
of Labor (AFL) to shun political action in favor of "pure and simple unionism." Confronted with a hostile state, Samuel Gompers
concluded that "the best thing the State can do for Labor is to
leave Labor alone."[2] Wanting less state rather than more, the AFL
rejected politics and state-sponsored reform in favor of building
strong unions and winning workplace concessions through private
collective bargaining agreements. While offering compelling reinterpretations of the American labor movement, these studies
have focused too much on federal courts or, when considering local and state developments, on how the law shaped the thinking of
Samuel Gompers and the national leadership of the AFL. Before
the 1930s, however, most labor disputes were local affairs. Legal
intervention came overwhelmingly from local institutions, and
it drew responses from local labor leaders more inclined toward
political activism than their national counterparts.[3]

When we shift our focus from the national to the state and
local level, we begin to understand how W. A. Engle could endorse political remedies so at odds with those of Samuel Gompers. If legal hostility caused the AFL to shun political action
and state-sponsored social reform, it had the opposite effect on
state and local labor leaders. Indeed, I argue that the need to defend rights of collective action pushed the California labor movement into politics with greater urgency. After initial forays into

third-party politics, California trade unionists took advantage of Progressive-era political changes that made interest group lobbying and coalition-building a more viable strategy than independent labor politics. Moreover, while trade unionists in California placed organizational rights at the center of labor's political agenda, once drawn into the political arena they pushed the state legislature to enact an array of progressive social reforms. Nothing in the demand that the state recognize a sphere of working-class collective action compelled California trade unionists to oppose state intervention more generally. Through the Progressive era and 1920s, labor's political efforts to curtail court and police hostility most often ended in failure. But in the process, state and local labor leaders fashioned a sophisticated defense of labor's rights and anticipated the New Deal transformation of both labor law and labor politics.

LAW AND LABOR POLITICS IN THE GOMPERS ERA: AN OVERVIEW

Labor historians have long noted the deleterious effect of the law on the American labor movement, especially from the 1890s through the 1920s, the so-called "era of the injunction." In fact, the first histories of labor and the law were written by Progressive-era labor lawyers and labor economists deeply involved in contemporary debates on the "labor problem" and the proper role of the state in responding to labor disputes.[4] With the New Deal transformation of American labor law in the 1930s, however, the preceding era was examined less for its own significance than as a gloomy preliminary to the triumphant Wagner Act of 1935, which at last guaranteed labor's right to organize free from employer interference and committed federal policy to the active promotion of trade unionism and collective bargaining.[5] But the history of labor law before the 1930s represents more than just a dark hour before the dawn. As historian Leon Fink observed, the "era of the injunction" saw the American labor movement abandon a broad politics of reform for a more conservative, relatively apolitical trade unionism. It was precisely during this period of "'exceptionalist' drift"—when the developmental trajectory of the American labor movement diverged from its European counterparts—that "legal issues took on their most determining historical role." Yet despite its obvious importance to the political development of the American labor movement, Fink observed, "the law in American labor history has yet to be fully explored."[6]

Fink's observation is less true today than when he made it more than a decade ago. Recent studies by Victoria Hattam and William Forbath, for example, argue that late-nineteenth- and early-twentieth-century legal hostility propelled the American labor movement in a uniquely conservative, apolitical, and "antistatist" direction.[7] Hattam sets out to explain the origins of "business unionism" or "voluntarism"—that is, the AFL's propensity to forgo politics and legislative reform in favor of building strong unions and winning concessions directly from employers. In the nineteenth century, Hattam argues, organized labor embraced political action in order to secure workplace reforms and shelter union activity from criminal conspiracy prosecution. But by the late nineteenth century the courts had struck down or otherwise eviscerated many of labor's legislative efforts. "It was only after a prolonged campaign to check judicial power," Hattam concludes, "that organized labor turned away from politics and developed an alternative strategy of antistatist voluntarism."[8] Hattam convincingly argues that the courts' power of judicial review often negated labor's political efforts to win legislative reforms. Unfortunately, Hattam does not take her study past the 1890s, when it became apparent that turning to "antistatist voluntarism" had still not freed labor from the burdens of judicial hostility; to the contrary, labor's decision to focus on economic action brought a new wave of judicial interference—in the form of the injunction—in the 1890s and beyond.

William Forbath, unlike Hattam, carries his study into the era of injunction, yet he reaches much the same conclusion. Less costly and more immediate than the conspiracy trial, the labor injunction provided employers a powerful weapon against strikes, especially sympathy strikes or those demanding the closed shop. In addition to breaking strikes, the harsh language of the injunction granted legitimacy to other forms of repression and evoked images of labor violence and lawlessness that often spilled over into general public discourse on the "labor problem." By the early 1900s, therefore, curbing the power of the courts became the AFL's foremost, and nearly exclusive, legislative goal. As Gompers and the AFL became increasingly preoccupied with this narrowed agenda, they moved the labor movement even farther away from a program of broad social reform and independent politics.[9]

Forbath tells another, perhaps more significant, story: as labor leaders embraced the language of the law as a matter of self-defense, they abandoned an older "republican" language of social reform for a more constricting "liberal" language of rights. Nineteenth century "labor republicanism," best exemplified in the program of the Knights of Labor, had advocated positive state action to promote the common good and create conditions for meaningful, participatory citizenship. Liberalism, by contrast, was essentially "negative and antistatist," limiting the state's role to the protection of private rights. While organized labor often found ways to turn the liberal language of rights to its advantage, Forbath argues, it had nonetheless adopted a "court-minted ideology" rooted in a commitment to property rights and liberty of contract. In the long run, such an ideology failed to provide much of a foundation for trade unionism, let alone for a class-based political challenge to capitalism.[10]

In short, Forbath and Hattam recast the problem of "American exceptionalism," seeking to explain why the American labor movement, especially after the 1890s, did not behave like its European counterparts and create an independent labor party or support social democratic reforms. Drawing upon studies of European labor movements and the few existing comparative studies, both scholars stress that the nineteenth-century American labor movement often mirrored its European counterparts in terms of organization, politics, and ideology.[11] Only in the late nineteenth and early twentieth centuries did the American labor movement begin its sharp divergence from European patterns. Taken together, Hattam and Forbath make a compelling case that the American legal order provides a key (if not *the* key) to understanding American exceptionalism. Unfortunately, the effort to understand "American exceptionalism" too often provides an explanation of what the American labor movement *failed* to do (develop an independent labor party or support socialism, for example), instead of an understanding of what it did do.[12]

When we consider what did happen as opposed to what did not, we begin to see that the labor movement's approach to politics and the state was neither pure nor simple before the 1920s. To be sure, by the 1890s Samuel Gompers and many of the AFL's national leaders began to question the value of political action and support a cautious "pure and simple unionism," but this approach did not go unchallenged. Before World War I, as many as one-third of the AFL unions endorsed the Socialist Party, official AFL policy notwithstanding. In the 1912 presidential election, Socialist candidate Eugene Debs, in a four-way race that included two progressive candidates, received six percent of the national vote and much higher percentages in working-class districts. By comparison, the British Labour Party received a quite comparable 6.4 percent in the British national elections of 1910. One contemporary study estimated that in 1911 some 600 socialists held municipal and state offices throughout the United States. Although precise estimates of rank-and-file support for political action are difficult to attain, there is considerable evidence in the labor press and the proceedings of state and national conventions that even those trade unionists who did not ally themselves with the Socialist Party were sympathetic to calls for greater political action, including support for independent labor parties.[13] As Sean Wilentz argues, rather than viewing the period from the 1890s to the 1920s as a period of uncontested "voluntarism," we would better understand it as "a continuing series of political readjustments and [internal] conflicts."[14]

In a recent and major reinterpretation of AFL politics, Julie Greene shows that Gompers and the AFL's national leadership "experimented with diverse political strategies, committing vast resources and generating passionate debates."[15] Not only did the AFL's official policy of "pure and simple unionism" face challenges from within and without, but in practice even Gompers deviated from the federation's official antistatist and nonpartisan rhetoric. While Gompers preferred that workers win gains through trade unions rather than through legislation, he was not above lobbying Congress for those things over which unions had no control, such as immigration restriction and judicial interference with labor's right to strike. Court hostility to labor legislation most certainly caused labor to place most of its eggs in the basket of economic action, as both Forbath and Hattam demonstrate. But the line of causality ran both ways: economic action in turn drew more judicial hostility (in the form of the injunction), and this judicial hostility drove the AFL into the political arena whether they liked it or not. By 1908 the AFL abandoned its official nonpartisanship in all but name to support Democratic presidential candidate, William Jennings Bryan, the only candidate to oppose federal injunctions in labor disputes. In 1910, after a coalition of Democrats and "progressive" or "insurgent" Republicans took control of the House, the AFL intensified its lobbying efforts— an effort that bore limited fruit with the passage of the Clayton Anti-Trust Act of 1914.[16]

Not only did legal hostility force Gompers and the AFL to ally with the Democratic Party, but in time that alliance led the AFL to reassess its commitment to a limited state. Perhaps initially the AFL's national leaders supported the Democratic Party as a means of limiting state (i.e., court) intervention, but, as Melvyn Dubofsky has argued, the Democratic alliance in turn pushed labor toward "a more positive opinion of state regulation of the economy and society," especially during the administration of Woodrow Wilson.[17] Both the *de facto* alliance with the Democrats and greater reliance upon the state were strengthened during World War I, when the Wilson Administration, in creating the National War Labor Board, gave official recognition to labor's right to organize and bargain collectively. The alliance with the Democrats became official and permanent in the 1930s, as organized labor became a pillar of the New Deal coalition. As had been the case during World War I, labor supported the New Deal Democrats in exchange for federal protection of labor's collective rights.[18]

If the AFL's approach to national politics was more complex and far-reaching than historians have typically assumed, labor politics at the state and local levels present an even greater challenge to traditional interpretations. Not only did local unionists pursue politics with greater vigor than did their national counterparts, they were less shy about relying upon state action. As Gary Fink argued nearly thirty years ago, the reform agendas pursued by state labor federations simply do not square with the usual definitions of "antistatist voluntarism."[19] While Fink's work is widely and dutifully cited, the implications of state and local political activism clearly frustrate efforts to create a "synthesis" for the history of American labor politics. It is not that scholars have failed to appreciate the significance of the state and local level. In his survey of federal labor policy in the United States, Melvyn Dubofsky explains that he omitted an analysis of the separate state and local governments not because he thought them unimportant. "Indeed," he admits, "before the era of the New Deal, state and local governments probably had a greater impact on workers and unions than the federal government did." Rather, Dubofsky confesses to excluding state and local governments "because a single scholar can only do so much."[20] Precisely because a single scholar can only do so much, this study examines labor's political reaction to court and police hostility within a single state, California, during a critical period in the political development of the American labor movement.

A TALE OF TWO CITIES: CALIFORNIA AS A CASE STUDY

Although California's rise to national prominence in the twentieth century makes it of obvious interest and importance, the state was neither typical nor unique. If the many labor community studies of the past few decades have taught us anything, it is the need to attend to our nation's uneven economic development, the peculiarities of regional political cultures, and the complex nature of American federalism. California makes for an attractive case study, not least of all because both the "new labor history" and the "new political history" focused so heavily on the industrial Northeast and upper Midwest.[21] Moreover, California has played an important role in national labor and political history throughout the twentieth century: California's Governor Hiram Johnson helped to define progressivism as a political movement in the United States; California labor leaders like Andrew Furuseth figured prominently in the national debate over labor's legal rights, while Tom Mooney and Warren Billings became national, and even international, celebrities among labor and the left; and events like the 1911 *Los Angeles Times* bombing and the 1934 San Francisco waterfront strike informed national dialogues on the proper remedies for labor unrest. But perhaps most importantly, California provides an unparalleled opportunity to examine, within a single state, the political impact of court and police intervention in two quite different environments—closed-shop, union-dense San Francisco and open-shop, union-sparse Los Angeles.

"Seldom if ever," California labor historian Ira Cross wrote in 1935, "have there been two communities of such contrasting types as San Francisco and Los Angeles."[22] Most of the contrasts, Cross and many subsequent historians contend, flowed from the nature and timing of population and industrial growth in each city. San Francisco's initial growth came in the four decades after the 1849 Gold Rush, with most newcomers coming from the Northeastern United States or foreign countries. Los Angeles, on the other hand, drew its populations much later and mostly from native-born migrants from the Midwest. By 1910 San Francisco was still a city of immigrants, with native-born whites of native-born parents comprising less than twenty-eight percent of the population; in Los Angeles, this demographic group made up more than fifty-three percent of the city's population.[23] Although population growth in both cities exceeded the national average, Los Angeles experienced exceptionally rapid growth in the late nineteenth and early twentieth centuries. Its population more than doubled in the 1890s, more than tripled in the early 1900s, and nearly doubled once again in the 1910s. Once ridiculed by San Franciscans as a "cow town," by 1920 Los Angeles claimed more residents than its sometimes condescending neighbor to the North.

California's diverse commercial and manufacturing base also grew at a much faster rate than the United States as a whole. Here, too, the greatest growth occurred in Los Angeles, which by 1920 had surpassed San Francisco in most economic measures (except banking and shipping). While California never acquired the mammoth enterprises that characterized the industrial cities of the Northeast and Great Lakes region, the growth of its manufacturing sector was still phenomenal, especially in Los Angeles and Southern California. For example, in 1899 San Francisco had six times as many wage-earners employed in manufacturing as Los Angeles, but twenty years later the figures for each city was about the same. In the 1880s and 1890s Chamber of Commerce promotional literature touted Los Angeles as a "bucolic" paradise where anyone with initiative could establish him- or herself as an independent producer. But as Los Angeles developed in the first two decades of the twentieth century, new arrivals to the city were more likely to become wage-earners than independent farmers, artisans, or small businessmen.[24]

But very few of these new Los Angeles wage-earners joined labor unions. While Los Angeles outpaced San Francisco in population and manufacturing growth, it lagged far behind when it came to union membership. Contemporaries noted, and sometimes exaggerated, the contrasting fates of the Los Angeles and San Francisco labor movements. San Francisco earned a national reputation as the ultimate "closed-shop town," where a "labor barony" held "undisputed sway." Los Angeles earned a reputation as the quintessential "open-shop town," a "militant anti-union citadel" where well-organized employers—and their mouthpiece,

the *Los Angeles Times*—frustrated union efforts and created a climate hostile to labor.[25] While rhetoric sometimes exceeded reality, the differences were real enough. In 1910 Los Angeles con-
tained fourteen percent of the state's population, but only eight
percent of its union members; by contrast, San Francisco held
seventeen percent of the state's population, but sixty-five percent
of the state's union members. In addition, San Francisco workers
enjoyed a strike success rate of about forty-five percent, while Los
Angeles had a strike success rate of only eight percent. In addition
to losing more strikes, or perhaps because of it, union workers in
Los Angeles earned less in wages and worked longer hours than did
workers in San Francisco.[26] Whether measured by union membership, strike victories, or wages and working conditions, workers in
Los Angeles fared far worse than their brethren in San Francisco.

Although a comprehensive comparative study of the Los Angeles and San Francisco labor movements has yet to be written,
implicit comparisons pervade the many works that focus on one
city or the other. Explanations for the weakness of the Los Angeles labor movement include its relatively late development of
industry and manufacturing; the larger number of native-born,
Midwestern migrants with little or no union experience; the presence of strong and well-organized employer associations; and a
strongly anti-union "public sentiment," attributable in part to the
editorial policies of the relentlessly anti-union *Los Angeles Times*.
Historians of the San Francisco labor movement, on the other
hand, point to the early development of the San Francisco labor
movement, which benefitted from labor shortages and geographic
isolation; a high percentage of Irish, German, and Scandinavian
immigrants with strong union experience and proclivities; a divided business community; and a relatively tolerant public opinion toward labor, attributable in part to the absence of a domi-
neering anti-union newspaper like the *Los Angeles Times*.[27] More
recent studies, while more or less accepting these explanations,
also point to the political and organizational consequences of labor's campaigns against Asian immigration. Whereas ethnic divisions between whites weakened organized labor in the East, in San

Francisco such divisions were mitigated by a common animosity among whites toward Chinese workers in the late nineteenth century and Korean and Japanese workers in the first two decades of the twentieth century.[28] Not only did the perceived presence of an Asian "menace" offset ethnic differences, but ethnic differences among whites were not as great in San Francisco as they were elsewhere. San Francisco's immigrant population came largely from Northern Europe, especially the British Isles, Germany, and Scandinavia; the city never had the large number of Southern and Eastern Europeans that inhabited the industrial cities of the Northeast and upper Midwest.[29]

However, as Michael Kazin points out, despite the frequently cited differences between San Francisco and Los Angeles—and the more or less convincing ways that California historians have explained them—"the basic *character* of unionism [in both cities] was essentially" the same.[30] Despite quite different degrees of success, that is, the general patterns of labor's political and organizational development were quite similar. The Los Angeles movement may have been smaller and less successful, but it was just as active as the San Francisco movement.[31] Furthermore, in both cities, strong central labor councils consolidated the activities of local unions and set the tempo for the labor movement throughout the state. Unlike the parent AFL, these local labor councils actively pursued trade union interests through political means, whether through pragmatic support of third parties or by supporting lobbying efforts at the state capital.[32] It is also important to recognize the common characteristics of organized employers in each city. Although California labor historians typically stress the ability of well-organized employers to thwart the efforts of labor in Los Angeles, Robert Cherny and William Issel contend that organized employers in San Francisco were just as well organized and just as determined to check union growth and, where possible, restore open-shop conditions.[33]

In both cities, therefore, *organized* labor confronted *organized* employers, and the law—as both an ideology and a set of institutions—profoundly shaped the patterns of conflict that emerged. As workers organized and struck at unprecedented rates in the late nineteenth and early twentieth centuries, employers organized to combat this heightened activism. Organized employers pressured peers to resist union demands, assisted those who faced strikes or boycotts, imported strikebreakers, and printed scores of pamphlets condemning union "lawlessness" and praising the virtues of the open shop. Not least of all, organized employers in both closed-shop San Francisco and open-shop Los Angeles turned to local courts and police to break strikes and protect imported strike-breakers. When they did, as this study demonstrates, organized labor in both cities turned to politics in order to defend rights of collective action.

The remainder of this book is divided into two parts. Part One (Chapters 1 to 3) examines how court and police intervention shaped labor's approach to politics and the state in the Progressive era. Through a comparison of events in San Francisco and Los Angeles, Chapter 1 describes how local court and police hostility pushed labor into periodic experiments with third-party politics. But even where these efforts gave labor a degree of control over the police—as they did in San Francisco—employers could still turn to the state courts for injunctions. Chapter 2, therefore, examines the rise of the labor injunction in California and its political and ideological consequences, while Chapter 3 looks at labor's efforts to curb the power of the courts through state anti-injunction legislation. In the anti-injunction campaign, organized labor abandoned third-party efforts in favor of interest group lobbying and building coalitions with Progressive reformers; but the abandonment of third-party politics by no means entailed a lessening of political activism. Neither did labor's preoccupation with restraining a hostile judiciary cause it to embrace an "antistatist" political philosophy; indeed, labor in California lobbied to expand the size and power of the state in ways that benefitted union and nonunion workers alike. In sum, Part One shows how court and police hostility created a much more politically active, pro-statist, and class-conscious labor movement than recent studies on labor and the law would suggest.

Part Two (Chapters 4–6) examines the impact of World War I and its aftermath on labor's approach to politics and the state. World War I marked the first time that the federal government formally recognized labor's right to organize and bargain collectively and set up machinery to systematically intervene in labor disputes. Though wartime agencies like the National War Labor Board did not always live up to their promises—and were at any rate disbanded at war's end—their very existence emboldened union activists, inspired more aggressive union demands, and helped to dramatically increase union membership. In California labor leaders understood both the achievements and the limits of federal wartime labor policy. While labor welcomed federal intervention in wartime labor disputes, it also learned that federal boards had little power to enforce their rulings. Employers who did not like a federal ruling could simply ignore it and turn to more reliable local courts and police in order to break strikes. In politics California labor leaders continued to seek legal protections and social reforms from the state legislature, though by war's end they found themselves largely bereft of political allies. In sum Part Two expands the arguments made in Part One in two ways: first, I show that despite an increase in *local* legal hostility and a loss of political allies during and after the war, labor continued to take a positive view of both politics and the state; second, reflecting the promise (if not always the concrete achievements) of wartime labor policies, organized labor increasingly looked to the federal government as the most likely guarantor of labor's rights.

A concluding chapter considers how my interpretation of a politically active, pro-statist labor movement at the state and local levels helps us to understand national developments in the 1930s. According to traditional chronologies of labor's long-term political development in the United States, the period from the 1890s through the 1920s serves as a conservative interlude between the more politically engaged "reform unionism" of the 1870s and

1880s and the militant "social unionism" of the 1930s. But if organized labor in the Gompers' era was as tenaciously apolitical
and antistatist as historians have claimed, how do we explain the
resurgence of political activism and social democratic sentiment
among trade unionists in the 1930s? My answer is that the political
activism and pro-statist outlook of labor in the 1930s did not mark
an entirely new departure. At the state and local levels, as my research shows, Progressive-era labor leaders had always looked to
politics and the state as a positive source of social reform and legal
protection.

Finally, this study focuses on the "mainstream" labor movement, and especially the political activities of urban labor councils
and the statewide California Federation of Labor, all affiliates of
the AFL. When I discuss legal hostility directed at radical labor
organizations like the Industrial Workers of the World (IWW)—
as I do in Chapter 5—I do so only insofar as it affected the political considerations of the mainstream labor movement. Such an
omission requires explanation, not only because the IWW was especially active and influential in California and the West, but also
because the line between "mainstream" and "radical" labor unions
in California was especially porous. In California as elsewhere
membership in AFL-affiliated unions and the IWW sometimes
overlapped; workers who belonged to the IWW in one decade
might belong to an AFL affiliate in another, a pattern Howard
Kimeldorf has found in the cities of the East as well. Also, as
Kimeldorf and others have observed, the IWW and the AFL—
despite differences in both organization and rhetoric—shared a
common "syndicalist" suspicion of politics and the state.[34] Constant court and police intervention only confirmed the IWW's
syndicalist conviction that employer-dominated state and political institutions would never serve the needs of workers. Legal
hostility, therefore, shaped the IWW's approach to politics and
the state only to the extent that it underscored its reasons for
eschewing politics and the state in the first place. Most trade
unionists in California, however, retained the hope that political action might, as W. A. Engle informed the federation's annual

convention, "place the power of government in the hands of the governed and . . . sound the death knell of corporation control of court, police, and military."[35] Just how much court and police hostility pushed labor onto the political playing field—and the wins and losses sustained there—is the story I wish to tell.

I

Law and Labor Politics in Progressive-Era California

Chapter 1

POLICING STRIKES AND LOCAL LABOR POLITICS
IN SAN FRANCISCO AND LOS ANGELES,
1901–1911

A Union Mayor can be of little service to unionism, except in the case of a strike, when he can refuse to call out the police to protect non-union labor. Both potentially and actually, this is a very great power.

RAY STANNARD BAKER,
1904[1]

"Police Administration," wrote American Federation of Labor (AFL) president Samuel Gompers in 1914, "is often a determining force in the struggles of workers for social and economic justice." Gompers remarks in this instance concerned the use of police to protect strikebreakers in St. Louis and Indianapolis, but he noted that "grave complaints and protests against brutality, lawlessness, and unjust discrimination" on the part of the police emanated from "many industrial sections of the country." When police intervened in this manner, Gompers complained, they privileged the employer's property rights while denying to workers the "natural and lawful activities necessary to enforce their rights."[2] Gompers's comments echoed the concerns of local labor leaders in cities throughout the United States in the late nineteenth and early twentieth centuries. In San Francisco and Los Angeles police repression of strikes politicized labor disputes in ways that other issues could not. To defend rights of collective action and wrest control of local government from the "employing classes," California's politically minded labor leaders persuaded the more reluctant among their ranks to support third-party politics.

31

THE ANSWER TO THE CRY FOR LIBERTY

Police intervention in the 1910 Los Angeles strikes is compared to British attacks on American colonists in the 1770 Boston Massacre, thereby linking labor's cause to the political ideals of the American Revolution. Illustration by F. Bucks in the *Los Angeles Citizen*, July 1, 1910, p. 1.

The few studies that have considered the role of the police in local labor disputes suggest that labor's political response in San Francisco and Los Angeles was not unprecedented.[3] Employers could not always and everywhere rely upon urban police to break local strikes. In smaller cities, for example, poorly paid police officers sometimes sympathized with strikers, forcing employers to hire "private police" or, on occasion, request the state militia. But as Sidney Harring reminds us in his study of policing industrial disputes in the Great Lakes region, whatever the personal inclinations of individual policemen, the police as an institution more often than not provided effective strikebreaking services.[4] Labor leaders in California would have agreed. Commenting on the "zeal" with which police officers performed their duties, Ed Rosenberg of the San Francisco Labor Council told a reporter in 1901 that the "police are men of our own class. Naturally their sympathies [should] be with us." But, Rosenberg added, "they are human . . . Their hopes of advancement, of reward, of promotion, are in the Police Commission."[5] For organized labor the class background of the individual policemen mattered less than who controlled them.

On at least two occasions concern over who controlled local police prompted California trade unionists and working-class voters into rare instances of independent labor politics. When organized employers wanted to break key strikes, especially those that included demands for the closed shop or union recognition, they sought the services of local police to break up picket lines and protect imported strikebreakers. When local officials complied, even those labor leaders who most distrusted independent labor politics threw their support to third parties—to the Union Labor Party in San Francisco and to the Socialist Party in Los Angeles. In both campaigns labor expressed class grievances by placing them squarely within a familiar and traditional language of rights. Neither of these class-based political challenges produced a permanent labor party, though San Francisco's Union Labor Party controlled city government for nearly ten years and later administrations continued to follow its restrained policing policy.

Labor's response to police hostility in San Francisco and Los Angeles also demonstrates the salience of class in early-twentieth-century labor politics. That the American labor movement failed to sustain independent labor or socialist parties does not mean that American workers lacked class consciousness. Rather, it simply means that a political system that mobilized voters along ethnic, religious, and regional lines rarely appealed to what Richard Oestreicher calls the "untapped class sentiments" that lay just below the political surface. Only under "exceptional circumstances," he concludes, did "class sentiments" find expression in independent labor politics.[6] As I argue below, the blatant use of police to break key strikes or organizational drives—and the conviction that such interventions violated fundamental rights of collective action—provided the "exceptional circumstances" that tapped class sentiments and fueled episodes of class-based politics.

THE 1901 WATERFRONT STRIKE AND LABOR POLITICS IN SAN FRANCISCO

San Francisco's experiment with independent labor politics had its origins in the 1901 waterfront strike, which pitted a powerful citywide Employers' Association against an equally powerful City Front Federation, a single organization that brought together the local teamsters', sailors', and longshoremen's unions. What began as a Teamsters' strike in the summer of 1901 quickly exploded into a sometimes violent conflict that dragged on until the fall of that year. When the strike was only a week old, sailors and longshoremen of the City Front Federation walked out in sympathy with the striking teamsters. With some 16,000 workers on strike or locked out, and nearly as many more idled as a consequence of the strike, economic activity in the city came to a standstill. Beginning as a relatively minor dispute over whether union Teamsters should haul subcontracted work if the original contractor was a nonunion employer, the strike became a prolonged contest over a union's right to demand a closed shop.[7]

The long strike aroused strong feelings from every corner of the city, but Democratic Mayor James Phelan's use of both regular and "special" police sparked the greatest controversy and eventually pushed labor into independent political action. Police not only protected drivers, but gave directions to imported strikebreakers who otherwise did not know their way around the city. When the drivers' inexperience led them into troublesome situations, the police helped them out: pushing wagons from ruts, reloading toppled wagons, and helping "green drivers" navigate San Francisco's notoriously steep hills.[8] In addition, labor complained that police interventions had given "renewed courage" to employers while adversely affecting labor's public support. When police officers became a visible presence in labor disputes, a letter from the San Francisco Labor Council claimed, "ordinary citizens . . . believe that riot and murder are imminent, and that only but for the police no man's life would be safe." Such actions conveyed "to the people of the city that the employers are gentle . . . babes in the woods whom the police must protect from the evil-disposed and malevolent striker."[9]

Even though the first few days of the strike passed without violence, Police Chief William Sullivan offered his department's services to "any business house that asked for protection." On the first day of the strike, even the *San Francisco Chronicle*, a supporter of the Employers' Association and a critic of organized labor, reported that "demonstrations against non-union men were few" and found "nothing to call for police interference." Crowds of strike sympathizers gathered on street corners as police-protected wagons passed, but by all accounts the crowds restricted themselves to "hooting and yelling." Nonetheless, policemen dispersed the crowds with the "free use of [their] clubs." Within a few days, however, incidents became more serious. A *Chronicle* reporter claimed that "the crowd became ugly when clubs were used," and all daily newspapers reported that local hospitals treated scores of strikers and bystanders for injuries inflicted by policemen's riot clubs.[10] Yet the spate of violence that marked the final days of July soon subsided. During the first two weeks of August the daily papers again reported an "unusual calm" and credited this in large part to the work of "union patrols" that maintained order among their own ranks.[11]

Given the consensus that labor was conducting the strike peacefully, San Franciscans must have been surprised when, during the third week of the strike, the major dailies printed a letter sent to Mayor Phelan by George Newhall, who headed both the Police Commission and the Chamber of Commerce. Newhall claimed—contrary to all press reports—that conditions in the city were riotous, and he demanded that Phelan take immediate action. If "the laws and finances do not admit of the immediate augmentation of the police force," Newhall demanded, then Phelan should ask the Governor to send in the state militia.[12] In response to this letter the Labor Council demanded that Phelan remove Newhall from the Police Commission, not only because his letter had been "irresponsible," but because his positions on both the Chamber of Commerce and the Police Commission created a conflict of interest. Phelan agreed that Newhall's letter was "unwise and unnecessary," but he refused to remove him from the Commission, claiming that Newhall had written the letter as head of the Chamber of Commerce, not in his capacity as Police Commissioner.[13]

In the midst of the controversy over Newhall's letter, Mayor Phelan added fuel to the fire by appointing 246 "special police officers" and issuing 117 gun permits to strikebreakers and employers. "Special" or "commissioned" police made up an important but often overlooked part of late-nineteenth- and early-twentieth-century urban policing. Though granted the power and authority of regular police officers, the "specials" were paid by the private citizens or businesses who retained their services. For fiscally conservative urban officials, specials provided a flexible police force without the need for added government expenditure.[14] Individual employers had asked the city for commissioned officers in the past, but now Mayor Phelan appointed specials on a massive scale, paid for by the Employers' Association and in the general service of all struck employers. According to the city charter, the specials were subject to all rules and regulations of the police department; but in practice, once appointed they were under the supervision of their private employers.[15] Although labor's protests prompted the Board of Supervisors to hold hearings and review police policy, the Board concluded that it had no authority to interfere with policies established by the Mayor and the Police Commission[16]

In addition to the use of regular and special police, other acts by local authorities convinced labor of the need to exert greater political pressure. For example, on at least two occasions the Police Commission refused to renew the liquor licenses of saloon owners who allegedly hid strikers from policemen in hot pursuit. The city also permitted nonunion teamsters to violate a city ordinance that barred the heavier teams from well-traveled boulevards, thereby allowing "green drivers" to avoid more treacherous and time-consuming routes. At the behest of the Employers' Association, the San Francisco Grand Jury investigated police court judges who allegedly showed favoritism toward the strikers. At the same time, the Grand Jury failed to indict a number of police officers on charges of police brutality. In explaining the actions of the Grand Jury, labor pointed out that its foreman, Frank Symmes, also served on the Executive Committee of the Employers' Association. Finally, a sweeping injunction issued by a San Francisco Superior Court judge against striking cooks and waiters that same summer offered further evidence to labor that local public officials had conspired with organized employers to deny workers their collective rights.[17]

For the remainder of the strike, clashes between strikers and police generated controversy and violence. Despite Mayor Phelan's later claims that his policing decisions had been a response to strike violence, his statements at the time—and reports by the newspapers, hospitals, and the police department—suggest that outbreaks of violence followed rather than precipitated changes in police policy. The greatest waves of violence came only after 700 specials had been appointed, and Phelan's decision to arrest rather than disperse pickets late in the strike came during a period of declining levels of violence. Phelan's shift to more aggressive policing tactics more likely reflected a growing fear that the state's wheat crop would rot in the harbor. Responding to pressure from business leaders and public officials, Governor Henry Gage came to San Francisco to mediate the dispute on October 2, 1901. While the exact terms of the agreement were never made public, both sides agreed that the employers had won a clear victory: workers who had once enjoyed the closed shop returned to work on an open-shop basis. After three months, five deaths, and hundreds of injuries, the long strike was over.[18]

Although the strike had ended, the San Francisco labor movement's entry into third-party politics had just begun. As in most American cities, advocates of third-party politics in San Francisco faced considerable obstacles. An established two-party system that most often mobilized voters along ethnic, religious, regional, and even neighborhood lines meant that class-based political appeals would have to compete with pre-existing party loyalties. In addition, winner-take-all electoral districts encouraged voters to choose the lesser of two evils rather than "waste" a vote on a third-party candidate who had little chance of winning. For example, in the early twentieth century it was not uncommon for socialist candidates to win 25 percent of the vote in San Francisco's working-class districts. In winner-take-all elections, of course, this level of support did not produce a single socialist officeholder; by contrast, under the British system of representation, 6.4 percent of the national vote in 1910 netted the British Labour Party forty-two seats in Parliament. Third parties in the United States could not establish a foothold unless they displaced a major party.[19]

Yet another obstacle to third-party movements, especially in cities like San Francisco, lay in the ideological and programmatic flexibility of local Democratic and Republican parties. As John Buenker has shown, urban political machines (Republican in some cities, Democratic in others) showed an uncanny ability to incorporate day-to-day working-class and trade union demands without threatening broader, cross-class coalitions.[20] This was certainly the case in San Francisco. For example, in the late 1890s the local Building Trades Council (BTC)—the most powerful

segment of the San Francisco labor movement—formed a fruitful alliance with a Democratic administration, symbolized by the
appointment of BTC president P. H. McCarthy to the Civil Service Commission. In addition, both major parties offered avenues
of upward mobility for politically ambitious workmen and trade
unionists. One study found that of 103 state assemblymen (for
which there is occupational data) elected from San Francisco's
working-class districts between 1892 and 1910, forty-nine were
laborers or skilled or semi-skilled craftsmen, compared to twenty-
three lawyers and thirty-one businessmen. On occasion, trade
union politicians went beyond winning a seat on the board of supervisors or in the state assembly; John I. Nolan, an Iron Molder
and official of the San Francisco Labor Council, represented San
Francisco in Congress as a Republican (and for a time winning
the Progressive Party endorsement as well) for six consecutive
terms.[21] Dislodging established parties required an inflammatory
event that could challenge existing political alignments.

Mayor Phelan's use of the police during the 1901 waterfront
strike provided that inflammatory event. Debates over Phelan's
use of the police dominated the mayoral campaign of 1901, much
to the benefit of the recently formed Union Labor Party (ULP).
The ULP represented the efforts of a minority within the trade
union movement who had always advocated independent labor
politics and now sensed an opportunity. Isadore Less, a Journey-
man barber and a member of the Socialist Labor Party, played the
key role in organizing the new party. Drawing delegates from sixty-
eight unions to its September convention, the ULP represented
a cross-section of the San Francisco labor movement; but most
delegates came from the weaker and more recently established
unions, who were less able to rely solely on collective bargaining
to win better working conditions.

As Mark Voss-Hubbard has recently observed, third-party
movements in American political history, often lacking in political experience, had to rely upon the know-how of experienced
politicians to get started.[22] Thus it was with the help of a former
Republican political operative, Abraham "Boss" Ruef, that the

ULP wrote a platform and nominated candidates for the 1901 municipal elections. Far from radical, the ULP's modest platform called for municipal ownership of public utilities (as did reformers in both parties); municipal support of the union label and restrictions on Asian immigration (as did the Democrats); improved public schools; civil service reform; and such common Progressive-era political reforms as the initiative, referendum, and recall. To head the ticket as mayoral candidate, the ULP nominated Eugene Schmitz, a popular orchestra leader and former president of the Musicians' Union. Despite his former union position, the candidate's credentials as a labor leader were hardly impressive; he was little known in the labor movement and, as a small businessman, was an employer of labor. But his handsome appearance, abilities as a performer, and Irish- and German-Catholic background made him an attractive candidate, one whom Abraham Ruef hoped could appeal to middle-class as well as working-class voters.[23]

Modest policy differences between the ULP and the reform wings of the major parties made the policing issue all the more important. Before the 1901 strike, most San Francisco labor leaders were either lukewarm or strongly opposed to the ULP. Two weeks before the start of the strike, the Coast Seamen's Journal, the city's leading labor weekly, warned workers that "the idea of voting themselves into better economic conditions is a delusion and a snare." As late as August 24, Andrew Furuseth of the Sailors' Union claimed that the ULP was a "sad mistake" that reflected "resentment rather than cool common sense."[24] Through the early stages of the strike most San Francisco labor leaders adhered to the nonpartisan vision of the AFL, advising workers to support friends and punish enemies within the major parties.

Following the appointment of the special police, the ULP made the policing issue the center of its appeal to trade unionists and working-class voters. Repeatedly, the ULP charged that organized employers had used the legal system to pursue class interests. One typical statement claimed that "the employing classes . . . have the full support of the city government and the courts," and they enjoyed this support because they were organized "for political purposes," whereas workers were not. That policemen were "almost driving trucks for non-union men," another statement read, proved that city government in San Francisco was not "of the people, for the people, and by the people." Socialists in San Francisco also took up the issue: they condemned "the capitalist government" for making "constant use of the police and militia to break strikes," and they referred to the San Francisco police as the "armed force of the capitalist class." The strong language of class used by socialists and the ULP was also gradually adopted by the San Francisco Labor Council. In a press statement typical of several issued during the strike and mayoral campaign, the Council claimed that while the "capitalist . . . can buy officials, corrupt legislatures, and purchase courts," the workers had only their votes.[25]

As time passed, more labor leaders wanted those votes to go to a party that would protect labor's right to strike, picket, and boycott. On September 11, the *Coast Seamen's Journal* reiterated its general opposition to trade unions entering politics. But "at the same time," the article added, the individual trade unionist should "take such action politically as is consistent with . . . his aims as a worker and as a citizen." A number of individual unions began endorsing the ULP, but not until late October did the *Coast Seamen's Journal* give its full support to the party. When it did make an endorsement, the paper made no mistake as to why: "Who can forget the policy pursued by the police department . . . the shooting and clubbing of strikers, the wholesale arrests . . . [and] the surrender of the entire police force to the Employers' Association."[26] Meanwhile, Andrew Furuseth, who early on had criticized the ULP, also rethought his position. In an open letter to the press, Furuseth explained his change of heart by reminding readers that during the strike labor had appealed to the Mayor, Chief of Police, Police Commission, the Board of Supervisors, and the Grand Jury, "but to no purpose." To charges that the ULP represented "class government," Furuseth responded, "I realized that the employing class in this city had complete control of

the city's government . . . We had a class government already. . . .
[and] inasmuch as we are to have a class government, I most
emphatically prefer a working class government."[27] Among San
Francisco labor leaders, only P. H. McCarthy and the Building
Trades Council opposed the ULP, a position no doubt fostered
by Mayor Phelan's earlier appointment of McCarthy to the Civil
Service Commission and the mayor's friendly relations with the
well-established building trades unions.[28]

When announcing in favor of the ULP, San Francisco labor
leaders explained their changes of heart by blending a language of
class with a more traditional language of "rights." Not only had the
local police (and local government more generally) come under
the sway of "a small combination of capitalists," as the Iron Trades
Council put it, they had violated the fundamental principles of
representative government and run roughshod over the rights of
workers. A local typographers' union justified its support of the
ULP, and hence its departure from politics as usual, on the grounds
that workers needed to "put men in office who [would] . . . recognize that all American citizens have rights before the law whether
they be 'laborers' or 'employers.'" Similarly, members of San Francisco's small Socialist Labor Party, whose trade union members
would later play a role at the ULP convention, promised a police
commission that would "protect the . . . rights of workingmen."[29]

At times the simultaneous condemnation of "capitalist control"
and appeal to rights was invoked to solicit the support of other
groups. In a statement asking California farm organizations to support labor during the 1901 strike, the San Francisco Labor Council claimed that workers and farmers, as "toilers," faced a common
danger that a "few rich men" could "buy" local judges and public officials. "Farmers of California," the statement asked, "what
would you say to any combination of men that could forbid you
to organize to safeguard your rights?" The "right" to organize and
engage in collective action, the statement added, was foremost
among the "essentials of liberty" for which the American Revolution had been fought. By placing the rights of collective action
at the heart of the nation's revolutionary founding, labor leaders

justified political action and expressed class grievances within a traditional and familiar political discourse.[30]

The ULP realized that Mayor Phelan's use of the police had generated a great deal of public anger—not only among workers and trade unionists, but even among small businessmen, middle-class homeowners, and neighborhood associations who resented Phelan's decision to deploy the entire police force in the strike district while leaving many neighborhoods without adequate police protection.[31] Attempting to make policing the central issue in the 1901 campaign, the ULP received help from its Democratic opponents. Although Phelan decided not to run again, the Democrats nominated his close political associate, Supervisor Joseph Tobin. Both as a member of the Board of Supervisors during the strike, and then later as a mayoral candidate, Tobin's outspoken defense of Phelan and the Police Commission gave Schmitz a clear issue with which to distinguish himself from his Democratic rival. The Republican Party, meanwhile, nominated for mayor a rather bland incumbent auditor, Asa Wells. Wells made a poor candidate; by almost all accounts he was utterly lacking in charisma and had well-known connections to the widely despised Southern Pacific Railroad. For organized labor, the race became a contest between Schmitz and Tobin and their contrasting positions on Mayor Phelan's response to the waterfront strike.[32]

Election results demonstrated just how much the policing issue had polarized the San Francisco electorate. In the final count, Schmitz won with 42 percent of the vote; Wells collected 34 percent and Tobin finished third with less than 25 percent. More telling, however, was the distribution of the vote. Schmitz received a majority of the vote in each of the six most heavily working-class districts south of Market Street, and over 60 percent in three of those districts. In the wealthier residential districts, however, Schmitz received only 25 to 30 percent of the vote. As Jules Tygiel and Steven Erie have shown, these patterns suggested greater polarization along class lines than had existed in previous elections. In the two mayoral races immediately preceding the 1901 election, working-class districts had voted much the same as the rest of the city. Whereas the vote for the winning candidate in 1901 produced a 23 percent voting gap between working-class and non-working-class districts, the gaps in the 1898 and 1899 elections were only 4 and 6 percent, respectively.[33]

After his victory Schmitz assured a worried business community that his program was "conservative and practical." Schmitz disappointed those who thought he might make immediate changes in the Police Commission. Schmitz promised only that the police would maintain strict "impartiality" during any future labor disputes. As we shall see, he faithfully kept that promise during his six years in office. To be sure, a Union Labor administration did not lead to dramatic shifts in power; nor could it be said, as contemporaries sometimes claimed, that organized labor now "ruled" San Francisco. Nonetheless, the policing issues had stirred class sentiments, and organized labor had successfully used this stirring to mobilize trade union and working-class voters around the issue of workers' rights, and the conviction that city government had violated those rights by serving the employing class.

THE UNION LABOR PARTY IN POWER

Mayor Schmitz and the Union Labor Party kept their promise to keep the police out of labor disputes. But in most other ways the ULP proved to be a disappointment, and even an embarrassment, to the San Francisco labor movement. As San Francisco socialist and labor lawyer Austin Lewis noted at the end of the ULP's reign, "the Union Labor Party was an instrument by which labor might have the police and the politicians might have the town."[34] Though the ULP brought a welcome policy of police neutrality to San Francisco, it was eventually driven from office by well-substantiated charges of corruption, an inability to form a distinctive political agenda beyond the policing issue, and a statewide movement for nonpartisan municipal offices. In the aftermath of the ULP experience a chastened labor movement would try to influence public policy through other modes of political action.

As promised, during its six years in office the Schmitz admin-istration consistently refused to assign regular police officers to strike duty, turned a deaf ear to employer requests for special po-lice, and refused to issue gun permits to strikebreakers. In addition, police officers frequently searched strikebreakers for concealed weapons and when necessary made arrests. Police responded to strike violence when it occurred, but they arrested strikebreakers as often as strikers. Employers routinely complained that police-men winked at acts of violence committed by strikers while mov-ing aggressively against those acts committed by strikebreakers. Whether city policemen acted in the biased way that employers claimed is difficult, if not impossible, to determine; but without question employers could no longer count on regular or special police to escort strikebreakers or break up picket lines.[35] Union Labor candidates and the labor press took every opportunity to remind trade unionists of the city's changed policing practices and advised them to vote accordingly. When Schmitz came up for re-election in 1903, the president of the San Francisco La-bor Council advised union members to vote for Schmitz so that "armed guards [do not] ride on the heads of workers." Schmitz won a three-way race with a 44 percent plurality. The polarized voting patterns first seen in 1901 continued in 1903, with Schmitz collecting 55 percent of the vote south of Market Street, while winning only 34 percent in the rest of the city.[36]

In 1905, despite increasing reports of ULP corruption (espe-cially its links to the city's brothels), San Francisco voters not only re-elected Schmitz and other Union Labor incumbents but gave the party a sweep of all contested municipal offices. Once again, the policing issue figured prominently in the campaign, thanks in part to the efforts of the Citizen's Alliance, a nation-wide network of open-shop organizations formed in 1903.[37] The San Francisco chapter of the Citizen's Alliance, formed in 1904, condemned the Schmitz administration for its biased handling of labor disputes. Alliance literature charged that the police ig-nored strikers' assaults on nonunion workers, and that even on those few occasions when strikers were arrested for blatant acts of violence, vote-conscious police court judges gave them only light fines. Anticipating an argument that San Francisco businessmen would repeat many times over the next three decades, the Alliance claimed the city's reputation for tolerating labor lawlessness created a climate that drove away new businesses and accounted for the rapid growth of Los Angeles and Seattle as challengers to San Francisco's dominant position on the Pacific Coast.[38]

In the two previous three-way elections, Schmitz had failed to win 50 percent of the vote; thus, in 1905 his opponents hoped that a Republican-Democratic "fusion" ticket, headed by local businessman John Partridge for mayor, would unseat Schmitz. Although Partridge tried to distance himself from the Citizen's Alliance, the ULP successfully painted Partridge as a tool of open-shop employers. Even as many labor leaders started to suspect that charges of ULP corruption were true, they still feared the prospect that the police might once again be placed at the service of organized employers. Edward Livernash, labor reporter for the *San Francisco Examiner*, expressed this same ambivalence: "While I detest Eugene Schmitz and Abe Ruef," Livernash wrote, "whenever the shadow of policemen killing union men arises, then Schmitz looms large."[39]

As the Citizen's Alliance pressed its open-shop campaign into the political arena, even Patrick McCarthy and the Building Trades Council (BTC) were moved to endorse the ULP. McCarthy and the BTC had doubted the wisdom of the 1901 waterfront strike and adamantly opposed the Union Labor Party in previous elections.[40] By 1905, however, McCarthy stressed the need for a united front against the Citizen's Alliance, claiming that a victory by Partridge would place the police at the service of employers and recreate the conditions of 1901.[41] With a united base of union support, the ULP won its most impressive victory. Not only did Schmitz solidly defeat Partridge with 59 percent of the vote (and taking almost 70 percent of the vote south of Market Street), ULP candidates won all eighteen seats on the Board of Supervisors.[42] At least through 1905, therefore, the ULP successfully used the policing issue to win elections and expand its hold on power.

Beyond the policing issue, however, the ULP could point to little in either its platform promises or its record of achievement that distinguished it from the major parties. The ULP agenda looked very much like the platforms put forward by the reform wings of both the Democratic and the Republican parties. Moreover, once in power the ULP failed to follow through on many of its campaign pledges. For example, the ULP officially supported municipal ownership of public utilities, as did most trade unionists and working-class voters. But, as Michael Kazin has shown, when given the opportunity the ULP either bungled or at times deliberately delayed the city's efforts to purchase private utility companies—even though San Francisco voters had approved municipal bonds to finance such purchases. Nor did Kazin find much to applaud in the ULP's record on labor issues: "The neutrality of the police during labor disputes remained the ULP's only pro-labor achievement."[43]

Perhaps nothing better exemplified the extent to which the ULP practiced politics as usual than the charges of vice and corruption that, once confirmed, ended the party's charmed success. Although ULP members were mostly indicted for bribes taken from the city's brothels, San Francisco's infamous "graft trials" revealed that they had also taken money from the city's public utility corporations as "kickbacks" for the continuation of lucrative franchises.[44] Most telling, the trials revealed the ULP's furtive relationship with the United Railroads. With its near monopoly on streetcar lines, the United Railroads not surprisingly opposed efforts to create a municipal streetcar system—a reform that organized labor supported. During the street car strikes of 1902–1903, Mayor Schmitz won labor's enthusiastic praise for his refusal to provide regular or special police protection to the United Railroad Company. Yet the graft trials revealed that, at the same time, the ULP took $200,000 in bribes in exchange for maintaining the United Railroad's streetcar franchise. By the time the graft trials had ended, Mayor Schmitz and sixteen of the eighteen ULP Supervisors had been forced to resign; Boss Abe Ruef (who as the ULP attorney had orchestrated the bribes) was convicted and sent to San Quentin prison.[45]

The graft trials did not immediately destroy the Union Labor Party, but they did sour many labor leaders on independent politics and erode the united base of trade union support that had once supported the party. In the November 1907 elections Patrick McCarthy stood as the ULP candidate for mayor, but most labor leaders outside of the Building Trades refused to support him. Compared to Schmitz's 59 percent of the vote in 1905, McCarthy polled only 36 percent in 1907.[46] McCarthy and the ULP made a brief comeback in 1909, but it was to be the party's last stint at the helm of city government. McCarthy won with 50 percent of the vote in 1909, but the party he headed bore little resemblance to that which had come to power in 1901. McCarthy campaigned not on labor issues but on the need to end the graft trials. In so doing, McCarthy appealed to popular sentiment that the trials, dragging on without resolution, only further tarnished the city's already sullied reputation. Though McCarthy had won a final victory for himself, the ULP had lost the united trade union base of support that had allowed its earlier successes. Disillusioned by the ULP experience, organized labor once again divided on the merits of independent labor politics.[47]

By 1911, with the graft trials over, P. H. McCarthy and the ULP made their final bid for public office, but they had little to offer the San Francisco electorate. McCarthy failed once again to win the united support of the labor movement; the divorce between the ULP and organized labor was now complete. Further diminishing the long-term prospects of the ULP, the graft trials had helped fuel a 1910 charter revision that made all city offices nonpartisan. Although McCarthy was still seen as the ULP candidate, his nonpartisan opponent in 1911, James "Sunny Jim" Rolph, enjoyed a record that was both pro-business and pro-labor. A wealthy shipowner and banker, in 1902 Rolph was the first member of the Shipowners' Association to sign an agreement with the Sailor's Union. He rejected the belligerent tone of the open-shop movement and favored working with unions; when the Shipowners' Association came under the sway of the open shop Citizen's Alliance in 1906, Rolph withdrew his membership.[48]

Rolph's campaign, with its slogan "a mayor for all the people," appealed to "industrial harmony" and an end to "class agitation." Even trade union leaders who had once supported the ULP now called for a "government that is above class" and supported Rolph instead of McCarthy and the remnants of the ULP. Careful not to arouse the class sentiment that had brought the ULP to power, Rolph's platform called for recognition of labor's rights and strict police neutrality in labor disputes. In all ways, Rolph's tone was conciliatory. McCarthy, on the other hand, attacked his opponent as a tool of the Citizen's Alliance and the open shop. But this tactic failed, for Rolph's style and personal history made the open-shop label implausible. When voters finally went to the polls in 1911, they gave Rolph more than 60 percent of the vote, while McCarthy earned just 37 percent, failing to win a majority in even the most heavily working-class districts.[49] Though subsequent administrations would continue to use the police reluctantly, if at all, San Francisco labor's decade-long experiment in third-party politics had ended.

POLICING STRIKES IN LOS ANGELES, 1900–1907

Ten years after the policing of the 1901 strike had prompted labor in San Francisco to embrace independent political action, local repression of a major strike wave in Los Angeles produced similar results. In stark contrast to San Francisco after 1901, Los Angeles police routinely intervened in labor disputes. Felix Zeehandelaar, head of the city's vehemently anti-union Merchants' and Manufacturers' Association, informed a federal commission investigating industrial relations in California that, unlike the situation in San Francisco, requests for police protection in Los Angeles were "always granted."[50] Zeehandelaar complained only that the Los Angeles police department was too small, which sometimes meant that employers had to rely on private guards, pay for special police, or turn to the Los Angeles County Sheriff for special deputies.

Zeehandelaar might have exaggerated when he claimed that police requests were *always* granted, but not by much. With the help of local police, organized employers thwarted an emerging labor movement in Los Angeles. That Los Angeles would become synonymous with anti-union sentiment and the open shop should not obscure the fact that unions grew considerably in Los Angeles in the first few years of the twentieth century. Between 1900 and 1902 the number of unions in Los Angeles increased from twenty-six to sixty-eight, making the Los Angeles labor movement the fastest growing movement in the state for a brief period.[51] But this union growth spurred an equally impressive rise in open-shop employer associations. Between 1901 and 1903 alone, at least a dozen trade-based employer associations formed in Los Angeles, each of which committed itself to maintaining the open shop.[52] As importantly, in 1903 the Merchants and Manufacturers Association (M&M), which had formed in 1894 to lure people, business, and capital to the Los Angeles basin, took up the open-shop crusade. Working closely with smaller trade-based associations, the M&M imported strikebreakers and arranged police protection.[53] During the same years that the San Francisco labor movement grew without fear of police intervention, organized employers in Los Angeles used police-protected, imported strikebreakers to defeat dozens of Los Angeles strikes. The 1903 streetcar strikes, the 1906 pressmen and printers' strike, and the 1907 teamsters' strike in particular illustrated just how employers used police as part of their larger open-shop strategy.[54]

Nothing better demonstrated open-shop tactics in Los Angeles than the 1903 streetcar strikes. Like many Los Angeles employers, streetcar magnate Henry Huntington championed the open shop and gave both his time and his money (which was considerable) to the anti-union efforts of the M&M.[55] Huntington presented himself as a friend of the worker—so long as he or she did not join a union. According to one historian of Huntington's business and labor practices, he paid his workers above-average wages and pioneered in offering the fringe benefits usually associated with the "welfare capitalism" of the 1920s. But Huntington steadfastly refused to deal with unions and summarily dismissed union members.[56] In 1903, however, Huntington faced two simultaneous strikes: one by the carmen who operated his streetcars, and another by the Mexican-born laborers who built the tracks. With Los Angeles police protecting his imported strikebreakers, Huntington beat back both challenges and strengthened the resolve of his fellow open-shop employers.

The streetcar strikes began in early 1903 when two San Francisco labor organizers—William Shafer and Harry Knox—arrived in Los Angeles to help form the Amalgamated Association of Street Railway Employees (AASRE), Local 203.[57] In late March Shafer, Knox, and a group of about twenty workers discharged for union activity congregated at the ends of the streetcar lines, where they distributed union "coupons" and tried to convince the men who remained on the job to join the union. If the men feared retribution from Huntington, they could join secretly by mailing the coupon and a one-dollar membership fee to union headquarters. Even though all of the papers noted that the men used "peaceful methods,"[58] Huntington's general manager, J. A. Muir, convinced Los Angeles Police Chief Charles Elton to dispatch city policemen to the scene.

But the police actions only temporarily halted Shafer and Knox. In late April the union announced its intention to strike for union recognition, reinstatement of discharged workers, and negotiations to establish a "reasonable" wage scale.[59] The strike started well enough from labor's perspective. At the designated hour strike leaders gathered at the carbarns; the first few cars to emerge came to a halt, as the first seven conductors and five motormen walked off the job. Yet as soon as the first strikers left their posts, groups of strikebreakers, company officials, and city policemen took over the abandoned cars. At least one police officer rode each car that proceeded down the line. Other groups of policemen dispersed crowds of strike sympathizers or kept them away from the carbarns and moving streetcars. "Once a group [of strike sympathizers] started to yell 'scab,'" the *Los Angeles Times* reported, "but they were quickly silenced by the police."[60]

For many labor leaders, however, the response of Huntington's employees was more surprising and regrettable than the actions of the police. After the first abandoned cars moved under police protection, the remainder of the carmen refused to leave their posts. According to Los Angeles labor organizer Fred Wheeler, at the last moment workers who had wanted to strike "got cold feet" when they saw how promptly and easily policemen and strikebreakers commandeered the streetcars and beat back the crowds of strike sympathizers.[61] William Shafer tried to put the best possible face on a bad situation. "The strike looks like a fizzle, but it is not," he told a newspaper reporter. The goal of the strike "was to test local conditions, to see just what officials were arrayed against us." If there were any doubts as to who those officials had served, the pro-labor *Los Angeles Record* eliminated them by printing an exchange of letters between J. A. Muir, General Manger of the Los Angeles Railway, and Chief of Police Elton. Muir thanked Elton for his cooperation during the strikes and added that if events had created any added costs for the police the company would gladly reimburse the department. Elton responded that reimbursement was neither necessary nor proper, but he added that "we are pleased that in performing a public duty, we also had the opportunity of serving you and your company."[62]

In the meantime Huntington faced trouble from another group of employees: the Chicano laborers engaged in the back-breaking construction of "*el traque.*" With help from Lemuel Biddle—a Socialist labor organizer and the Secretary of the Los Angeles Council of Labor—two Mexican-American labor organizers, Alefo Fernandez and A. M. Nieto, organized the *Union Federal Mexicanos* (Mexican Federal Union). Eventually recognized by the Council of Labor and the California Federation of Labor, and given tacit recognition by the AFL, the Mexican Federal Union (MFU) had already organized between 700 and 900 Chicano streetcar workers by the time Biddle announced its formation in April of 1903.[63] Acting as the union spokesmen, Biddle demanded that Huntington raise the laborers' wages to twenty cents per hour, with time-and-one-half for night work and double time for Sundays. When

Huntington, who was in San Francisco at the time, heard that his managers had conceded to the demands, he angrily rescinded the offer and forbade any further negotiations with the union.[64] When the MFU called its men out on strike, 700 workers on the Pacific Electric's Main Street line walked off the job. Virtually all of the Chicano workers quit, leaving only about sixty men (mostly Irish- and African-American) on the job. A day later several hundred more Chicano workers walked off construction sites on Hunting- ton's Los Angeles Railway lines. In all as many as 1,400 workers joined the strike.[65]

Despite frequent charges by mainstream labor leaders that Mex- ican workers were "docile," and therefore not good union material, the Chicano track workers displayed a degree of labor solidarity rarely seen in Los Angeles. As such, their actions drew a swift and certain response from the Police Department and harsh crit- icism from the city's daily press. "Anticipating [the strike]," the *Times* proclaimed, "the police were prepared."[66] Placing its entire night force on strike duty, the police prevented striking workers from even talking to their replacements. Management kept small, police-protected construction crews working through most of the night, and over the next few days they replaced strikers with about ninety Japanese and African-American laborers from Los Ange- les and about 200 Mexican workmen transferred from company construction sites in nearby cities and towns. With police able to keep strikers at bay, and Huntington able to tap a broad network of nonunion laborers, track construction continued with very lit- tle interruption. Within four days, crews operated at almost full strength.[67]

Within a week the Mexican Federal Union, like the carmen's union, had all but conceded defeat in its strike. The *Record* re- ported that the strikers either drifted into other lines of work, left the city for other parts of California and the Southwest, or re- turned to Mexico.[68] In the wake of the two failed strikes, the situ- ation for organized labor in Los Angeles went from bad to worse. A strike by electrical linemen one week later also saw constant po- lice protection of nonunion crews.[69] A group of the city's businessmen created a "Safety Committee," while the M&M called upon Chief of Police Elton to order San Francisco "agitators" to leave the city. The *Los Angeles Times* praised Huntington and his managers for their "manly" stand against unionism, and both the *Times* and the M&M called for "counter-organization" and greater vigilance on the part of employers to resist union demands.[70]

In the years following the streetcar strikes organized employers in Los Angeles, with the help of city police, intervened repeatedly in strikes both small and large. But the larger strikes—especially those that demanded the closed shop—drew larger and more serious responses, as the printers' and pressmen's strike of 1906 and the Teamsters' strike of 1907 demonstrated. Although the *Times* had run on an entirely nonunion basis since 1890, union printers, pressmen, and press feeders managed to win contracts with other daily papers and a number of smaller printing shops.[71] Recognizing the *Times* as one of the strongest anti-union papers in the country, the International Typographic Union (ITU) spent $25,000 on the local printers' union in 1903 and 1904 and provided complete strike benefits when the printers, with the support of the pressmen and feeders, announced a walk-out on January 2, 1906.[72] Immediately, the union demanded the eight-hour day, but it also announced that it would demand the closed shop at an unspecified point in the future. Although printers at the *Times* would not likely have walked out, Los Angeles Times publisher Harrison Gray Otis nonetheless rallied the fifty-five firms of the Employing Printers' Association to resist union demands. The strike came amid great concern among trade unionists over the hostile tactics of the Citizen's Alliance and the M&M, especially the importation of strikebreakers and the near-constant stream of anti-union propaganda. That the local unionists received financial support from the ITU and several other California and Pacific coast labor organizations only intensified the employers' determination to defeat the strike.[73]

Both the M&M and the Citizen's Alliance played key roles in the dispute, importing printing tradesmen from the East and securing special police from the city. Although the exact number of specials provided cannot be determined, press reports suggested that one to three officers guarded any printing shop that made a request.[74] In early April, 1906, the Central Labor Council's Lemuel Biddle and James Roche—both prominent labor organizers and socialists—appeared before the Police Commission as representatives of labor's so-called "Anti-Citizen's Alliance," a group of labor leaders who advocated countering the actions of the Citizen's Alliance, and other groups of organized employers, with greater political action. Biddle and Roche asked the Commission to remove the hated specials, who they claimed had harassed or assaulted peaceful strikers or shouted "foul language" at women.[75] But labor's protest accomplished little. By October the ITU stopped sending strike benefits to Los Angeles and the local called off the strike. Union workers eventually went back to work on an open-shop basis and without winning the eight-hour day.[76]

An even more serious setback occurred in the teamsters' strike of 1907. Since 1901 the local teamsters' union—one of the strongest unions in Los Angeles—had signed annual union shop agreements with the employing Draymen's Association, which counted among its members the six largest trucking firms in the city. The 1907 Los Angeles dispute started in much the same way as the 1901 Teamsters' strike in San Francisco, in that a large, city-wide employers' organization disrupted a working relationship between a union and a smaller trade-based employers' association. When the union asked for a fifty-cent per day raise as the only modification of the existing union shop contract, they expected the Draymen to grant or at least negotiate the wage demand. On the day the contract expired, however, the Draymen's Association notified the union that henceforth it members would operate on an open-shop basis and refuse to negotiate with unions. They offered a twenty-five cent pay raise to those who accepted their terms. The Draymen's Association enjoyed the backing of the M&M, which had imported strikebreakers and paid for special police protection.[77] In addition, the M&M hired private guards and paid the salaries of special sheriff's deputies to supplement the regular and special police force.[78] After only ten days, the strike ended with teamsters going back to work on the employers' terms: at a twenty-five cent per day increase but on an open-shop basis.[79]

According to interviews conducted by Grace Stimson several years later, labor leaders remembered the 1907 teamsters' strike as one of the worst defeats in Los Angeles labor history. A union claiming 500 members at the start of the strike had only thirty-five one year later.[80] Both labor and employers recognized that teamsters could halt economic activity, and that this gave them substantial power to support other unions through sympathetic actions. Adding to the import of labor's loss, the strike came at the culmination of a concerted effort by organized employers to maintain the open shop where it existed and to impose it where it did not. As Stimson concluded, with its quick victory over one of the strongest unions in the city, "the open shop had within a short space of ten days won a victory which clinched its hold over the city of Los Angeles."[81] Both the Los Angeles police department and the County Sheriff had made critical contributions to that open-shop victory.

TOWARD INDEPENDENT LABOR POLITICS IN LOS ANGELES, 1902–1911

As in San Francisco, police hostility shaped labor's approach to politics in Los Angeles. Yet even before the 1903 streetcar strikes, Los Angeles labor leaders—a significant minority of whom were socialists—showed a penchant for independent labor politics. In 1902, shortly after the ULP victory in San Francisco, the Los Angeles Council of Labor convened a conference to consider approaches to political action and appointed an advisory committee to study alternatives. After two months a divided committee issued two reports. The majority report recommended the AFL policy of endorsing major party candidates who supported labor's agenda; the minority report claimed that both major parties supported the "employing class" and recommended that labor endorse the local Socialist Party. Much to the dismay of more conservative labor leaders, the conference adopted the minority report. When Samuel Gompers threatened to revoke the Council of Labor's AFL charter if they supported the Socialists, the Council instead sponsored a convention to organize a "Union Labor party." Bowing further to AFL pressure, the Council agreed to have no official relationship with the new party. The Los Angeles Union Labor Party—effectively if not officially the creation of the Council of Labor—adopted a platform calling for municipal ownership of public utilities, civil service reform, direct legislation, and several other standard progressive and labor reforms. The party nominated a full slate of nominees, with George McGahan of the Retail Clerk's Union as mayoral candidate.[82]

Hopes for the Union Labor Party in Los Angeles ran higher than conditions warranted. The Los Angeles Socialist Party, contrary to the wishes of the national party, agreed not to run candidates at the municipal level and endorsed the Union Labor Party in exchange for the latter's support for Socialist candidates at the state level. Throughout the first half of 1902, the *Los Angeles Socialist*, the local party weekly, observed that "a spirit of revolution" generated by events in San Francisco had spread to Los Angeles. In its appeal to trade unionists, Los Angeles socialists and other backers of the new party drew comparisons between the actions of police, organized employers, and local officials during a recent Los Angeles planning mill strike and the repressive police actions that had preceded the ULP victory in San Francisco. Just as employer and government hostility led to the victory of the Union Labor Party in the northern city, the *Socialist* claimed, "the same result will undoubtedly be accomplished here."[83]

But the same result was not accomplished, as Union Labor candidates finished a distant third in all races. Grace Stimson has noted that the defeat of the Union Labor Party in Los Angeles owed a great deal to demographics: in 1902 trade unionists and working-class voters did not constitute the same proportion of the electorate that they did in San Francisco. Moreover, because those fewer working-class voters were more widely dispersed throughout the city, Los Angeles lacked the concentrated working-class neighborhoods found in San Francisco's South of Market district.[84] Perhaps most importantly, Los Angeles in 1902 still lacked San Francisco's large and galvanizing 1901 waterfront strike. As we shall see, when in 1910 a strike of similar proportions elicited a similarly massive police response in Los Angeles, trade unionists and working-class voters would mount a more serious political challenge. In the meantime, however, labor in Los Angeles needed political allies if it expected to mitigate local government hostility.

For a time labor hoped that such allies might be found among urban political reformers in Los Angeles. As Dan Johnson has recently argued, the Los Angeles working class, relative to most Eastern cities (and, indeed, relative to San Francisco), was highly skilled and ethnically homogeneous. Mostly native-born and Protestant, the Los Angeles working class had scant interest in political machines that built constituencies elsewhere by providing services to the urban, immigrant working class. Ethnically and religiously, Los Angeles workers had more in common with the home-owning, middle-class voters who sought to break the power of political "machines" through a variety of nonpartisan political reforms (e.g., direct primaries, civil service, the initiative, referendum, and recall, nonpartisan offices, at-large elections, and municipal ownership of utilities). Middle-class reformers especially targeted a linchpin of urban political corruption—the police.[85] In San Francisco, where after 1901 both the political machine and the police protected labor's rights, trade unionists developed an antagonistic relationship with urban reformers. In Los Angeles, on the other hand, where the police and the political machine consistently took the employers' side against unions, labor joined the reformers' effort to clean up both politics and the police.[86]

Despite these areas of cooperation, the labor movement in Los Angeles always remained somewhat suspicious of the urban reformers who organized the city's Good Government League in 1908. Likewise, the Good Government League, while not as belligerently anti-union as the *Times* or M&M, was hardly enthusiastic about organized labor. Still, when the Good Government

League finally had its candidate, George Alexander, elected to the mayor's seat in December, 1909, Los Angeles labor leaders, though not supporting Alexander, assumed that Good Government reformers would show more sympathy for labor than had past administrations. This assumption seemed justified when Mayor Alexander appointed the head of the local printers' union to the Fire Commission. The Los Angeles Labor Council praised the new mayor for placing the first labor leader in an important position in city government. Though still wary, labor leaders expressed hope that Alexander might display more tolerance of the union cause than had his predecessors.[87] Events soon demonstrated, however, that this hope had been misplaced. In Los Angeles, as in San Francisco in 1901, authorities used local police to defeat a major strike, and organized labor turned to third-party politics in defense of workers' rights.

In the summer of 1910 Mayor Alexander's administration revealed its approach to policing strikes when brewery workers and metal tradesmen, with the financial and organizational support of San Francisco unions, went out on strike. The administration at first acted with some ambivalence. On the one hand, Alexander allowed employers to hire special police, paid for from a fund of $350,000 raised by the M&M to maintain the open shop in Los Angeles. On the other hand, Chief of Police Galloway refused the requests of saloon owners (who sold "unfair" beer) to have regular police disperse the pickets who gathered in front of their establishments. By mid-June the city's labor weekly, the *Citizen*, noted cautiously that "Mayor Alexander is not the stamp of a man to be manipulated" by employers. But the *Citizen* had too quickly read these incidents as signals of Alexander's support. Only days later, Mayor Alexander warned that police would henceforth arrest any pickets blocking the streets.[88] Just as menacing, in late June lawyers for the Founders' Association and the M&M won injunctions against the Metal Trades Council in Los Angeles Superior Court.[89]

But apparently the police actions and the injunctions did not have the desired effect.[90] On July 1, 1910, Earl Rogers and

Wheaton Gray—attorneys for the M&M and the Founders' Association, respectively—presented a proposed "anti-picketing ordinance" to the Los Angeles City Council. The proposed ordinance made it unlawful for any person "to picket in front of, or in the vicinity of" any business engaged in a labor dispute, and it outlawed "loitering . . . carrying or displaying banners, signs, or transparencies, or speaking in public streets in a loud or unusual tone" for the purpose of discouraging employees or customers from entering a place of business. In short, the proposed ordinance made even peaceful picketing unlawful. Violating the ordinance netted a fine of up to $100 or fifty days in jail.[91]

The City Council did not act on the proposed measure immediately, but instead called a public hearing. At a hearing "packed to suffocation," Earl Rogers and Fred Baker of the Founders' Association and a number of other employers spoke on the need for the ordinance, claiming that the pickets gravely interfered with their right to run a business. Socialist labor lawyer Job Harriman and several members from the Central Labor Council responded that the ordinance infringed upon the strikers' constitutional right to freedom of speech and assembly. Furthermore, both press and police reports suggested that pickets had conducted themselves peacefully. Despite these pleas, the nine-member Council voted unanimously for the ordinance, and Mayor Alexander signed it. Because "this ordinance [was] urgently needed for the immediate preservation of the public peace," the City Council invoked emergency powers to put it into effect immediately.[92]

Police arrested fifty-seven pickets in the first two weeks and hundreds more over the next few months. By early November nearly 300 of those arrested still awaited trial. Jails and court dockets became so crowded that more than 200 cases were dismissed in November and December of 1910. By the time the metal trades' strike officially ended in defeat in early 1912, at least 470 pickets had been arrested under the ordinance. According to Harriman's estimates, only fifty to sixty of these cases went to trial, as crowded court calendars, difficulty in assembling juries, and lack of evidence led to large-scale dismissals. Though many strikers spent considerable time in jail before the judges dismissed their cases, fewer than a dozen were convicted. Both picketing and arrests decreased from January to March 1911, but when picketing resumed in the spring of 1911 police charged pickets not with violating the ordinance, but with a "conspiracy" to violate the ordinance. Conspiracy, a more serious crime, warranted a more substantial fine: $300 or 150 days in jail. Thereafter, picketing virtually ceased.[93]

Like a replay of the 1901 San Francisco strike, the repressive actions by local authorities caused the Los Angeles labor movement to embrace third-party politics. Exploiting these episodes of legal hostility, Fred Wheeler and a number of other socialists within the Los Angeles labor movement pushed the Central Labor Council and local trade unionists toward independent politics. As socialists, they had always encouraged labor to take this path, but the recent actions of the police, courts, and City Council made their arguments all the more persuasive. At about the same time, Stanley Wilson, editor of the Central Labor Council's weekly newspaper, *The Citizen*, expressed his support for independent labor politics.[94]

At a packed meeting of the revived Union Labor Political Club on June 26, labor denounced local government with a strong language of class, while at the same time rooting their cause in the United States Constitution and the American political tradition. Wheeler and the others waved copies of judicial restraining orders as they implored workers to put an end to "class government." Wheeler argued that the M&M controlled both major political parties and all three branches of government. Another speaker pointed out that voters could knock the judges off the bench just as they had elevated them to the bench. Reflecting upon this meeting in its next issue, the *Citizen* proclaimed that "the injunctions did one good thing. It [sic] showed conclusively that if the workers want anything resembling a square deal they must put men in office who have more respect for the constitution of the United States."[95]

As arrests increased, calls for political action and condemnations of the mayor and City Council intensified. Although the

Union Labor Political Club had still not decided whether to support the Socialists or create a new party modeled after San Francisco's Union Labor Party, it did issue a "platform" calling for statutory recognition of the right to strike, picket, and boycott, and a prohibition on injunctions in labor disputes. In addition, the platform included a number of planks long endorsed by labor, socialists, and even many progressive reformers: public ownership of utilities, better schools, parks, and playgrounds, a public library and public hospital, and promises to abolish municipal "graft," among others.[96] But mostly the platform condemned the actions of local courts and police as a gross violation of labor's rights. Of course, employers and the *Times* also invoked a language of rights. From their perspective, the injunctions and the anti-picketing ordinance preserved public peace, protected the rights of those workers who chose not to join a union, and, most of all, protected the employers' right to run their businesses without union interference.[97]

Labor leaders responded to the employers' arrogation of the mantle of "law and order" with an alternative version of law and its usurpation. First, labor maintained, and the press for the most part agreed, that the pickets had conducted themselves peacefully, and that "armed thugs" hired by the employers caused the few incidents that had occurred. Moreover, labor maintained that the "shameful subservience" of local officials to the will of the employers violated much higher principles of law. "When a court usurps power that does not constitutionally belong to it," one *Citizen* editorial put it, "when it exalts property above mankind, then the court is no longer deserving of the respect of men." In support of this labor spokesmen invoked the English Puritans, who had argued that a King who broke his "covenant" with the people no longer warranted respect. Labor repeatedly cited the Declaration of Independence and the "spirit of '76" or compared labor's cause to that of abolitionists who deliberately violated the Fugitive Slave Act. An editorial cartoon depicting British troops beating American colonists at the Boston Massacre, followed by a frame showing the Los Angeles police beating strikers in a similar fashion, linked labor's collective actions to the nation's revolutionary founding.[98]

In the midst of this intensified political debate, on October 1, 1910, an explosion destroyed the *Los Angeles Times* building, killing twenty people. The story of the *Times* bombing; the indictment of the McNamara brothers, officials in the Bridge and Structural Iron Workers' Union; the McNamaras' extradition from Indiana to California; the long and well-publicized trial featuring Clarence Darrow as the defense lawyer; the eventual confessions of the McNamara brothers; and the subsequent trial of Darrow for witness tampering rank among the most fascinating tales in American history.[99] A photograph of the smoking rubble of the *Times* building, which appeared in newspapers and periodicals around the country, has become one of the most graphic symbols of Progressive-era labor violence. But more immediately, as C. B. Wiseman of the Los Angeles Waiters' Union correctly predicted at the time, open-shop employers used the incident to discredit the local labor movement, making little distinction between bombs and picket lines. In the wake of the bombing, newspaper editorials lumped "boycotting, picketing . . . and dynamiting" within a single category of labor "lawlessness," forcing organized labor to defensively profess its commitment to lawful and peaceful methods.[100]

Debates about the bombing, the injunctions, the anti-picketing ordinance, the policing of the on-going strikes, and labor's right to strike, picket, and boycott dominated the 1911 mayoral campaign in Los Angeles. In April 1911 the Union Labor Political Club and the local Socialist Party jointly endorsed a common slate for the Fall elections. When labor lawyer Job Harriman accepted the labor-Socialist nomination for mayor, he promised to repeal the anti-picketing ordinance as his first official act. In the October election Harriman shocked many political observers in Los Angeles. Mayor Alexander and his supporters assumed that they would easily win a majority in the three-way race and avoid the need for a December run-off election. Instead, of some 45,000 votes cast, Harriman won 44 percent, Alexander 37 percent, and the

Times-backed Republican, Mushet, only 17 percent. The failure of any candidate to win a majority necessitated a run-off between Harriman and Alexander on December 5, 1911.[101]

Despite placing first in the October election, Harriman received only 37 percent of the vote in the December run-off election. Harriman's chances were no doubt hurt by the confession of the McNamaras just four days before the election, but that was not the only reason for his defeat.[102] First, Harriman had received only 44 percent of the vote in the three-way race in October, but the December election featured only two candidates, Harriman and Alexander. Stalwart Republicans who supported Mushet in October most likely voted for Alexander in December. Second, the run-off election brought out more than three times as many voters as the October election. In particular, California's women voted for the first time in the December election. In its post-election issue, the *Citizen* claimed that women's votes played a key role in Harriman's defeat, largely because middle-class women registered and voted in greater numbers than working-class women.[103] Whatever the cause, Harriman's defeat signaled the end of organized labor's venture into third-party politics. The Los Angeles police department continued to respond favorably to employer requests for protection, and Harriman's defeat demonstrated that a weak Los Angeles labor movement could do nothing about it.

CONCLUSION

Despite the different outcomes of labor's political challenges in San Francisco and Los Angeles, the patterns of collective and political action had much in common. Labor organized and struck at an unprecedented pace, and employers organized to combat this rising tide of activism. As organized employers turned to local authorities to protect imported strikebreakers, organized labor at the local level turned to politics with greater urgency. Thus the same legal hostility that pushed the AFL's national leaders in a more conservative and apolitical direction at times had the opposite impact on local labor leaders. In both cities labor leaders appealed to workers as a class and denounced "capitalist" control of local government. By blending a language of class with an equally clear language of rights, politically minded labor leaders convinced more reluctant trade unionists and working-class voters to support independent labor parties.

Such a conclusion suggests not only the need to reconsider the impact of legal hostility on labor politics, but also the need to rethink the nature, meaning, and consequences of labor's "language of rights." A number of scholars, especially those who write from the perspective of Critical Legal Studies, have stressed the negative consequences of legal liberalism and "rights talk" for workers and other oppressed groups. Though the appeal to rights may bring occasional victories, in the long run it locks the oppressed within the linguistic and ideological confines of bourgeois liberalism. Such interpretations portray the law and legal discourse much as Alan Dawley once portrayed political democracy in the United States: as a "nail in the coffin of class consciousness."[104] Yet the California case suggests the potential for "rights consciousness" to sharpen rather than blunt working-class political consciousness.[105] In San Francisco in 1901 and in Los Angeles in 1911 the need to defend labor's collective rights from local courts and police tapped, to borrow Richard Oestreicher's useful phrase, those usually "untapped class sentiments." A language of rights co-existed with a language of class; rights consciousness reinforced class consciousness.

Yet it is also true that even when such class-conscious political challenges proved successful in restraining the power of the police, as was the case in San Francisco, local labor politics still proved frustrating. Not only did scandal, incompetence, and nonpartisan political reforms eventually drive the ULP from power, but trade unionists in San Francisco soon learned that control over the police did not eliminate all of the employers' legal resources. Denied adequate or effective police protection, employers turned to more politically insulated Superior Courts for labor injunctions. In so doing, California employers and their judicial allies frustrated San Francisco's successful bid to control the local police. Yet, as we shall see in the following two chapters, such frustration did not cause a political retreat so much as it required a political readjustment.

Chapter 2

"A Use of Psychology": California Courts and the Labor Injunction, 1890–1909

What makes the labor problem so perplexing is that it involves primarily the question of the employer's authority. The assured right of the employer to manage his business as he pleases is challenged by the union insisting upon the right to be consulted as to the conditions of work.

Henry White,
Labor Clarion, 1904

[The labor injunction] was a use of psychology [on] the strikers' minds. It was an intimation in high falutin' judicial languages, that they were against the law, doing something that was bad, wicked, and evil.

Paul Scharrenberg,
Secretary-Treasurer, California Federation of Labor, 1910–34

The effort to defend labor's collective rights from local police intervention had prompted both the San Francisco and the Los Angeles labor movements to take the unusual step of supporting third-party politics. But even where these efforts succeeded, as they did in San Francisco, employers could usurp labor's local political power by turning to the more politically insulated courts for help. By the turn of the century the injunction had emerged as the most common form of judicial intervention in American labor disputes, providing employers with a quick and efficient means of intervention. Issued as *ex parte* restraining orders solely on the basis of an employer's affidavit, injunctions could defeat a strike or boycott even before organized labor had an opportunity to defend itself or counter an employer's allegations. Workers who violated injunctions faced possible prison sentences without the benefit of a jury trial. By the early 1900s, therefore, trade unionists throughout the United States had come to see "government by injunction" as one of the gravest threats to the labor movement.[1]

This chapter departs temporarily from a consideration of the law's impact on labor's approach to politics to examine the incidence of injunctions in California, judicial reasoning that justified their use, and why labor found the injunction so threatening. Judges in California accepted labor unions as a legitimate expression of workers' collective self-interests and recognized a formal right to strike. But this formal right to strike meant very little when the courts severely restricted the means by which workers might exercise that right. While the vast majority of strikes never prompted a judicial response, the injunction nevertheless allowed organized employers to target key strikes and organizational drives. In addition to the injunction's immediate impact on any given strike, California labor leaders worried even more about its harmful ideological consequences. The language of the injunction portrayed labor's methods as inherent forms of "lawlessness," distorted labor's public image, and justified other forms of repression.[2] By defining the employer's "property rights" broadly enough to include a "right to do business" free from union "dictation" or "interference," the injunction also reinforced the employer's authority and the hierarchy of the workplace. As we shall see in Chapter 3, the need to combat the practical and ideological consequences of the injunction propelled the California labor movement into the political arena once again and forced it to reevaluate its relationship to the state.

HOW MANY INJUNCTIONS? NUMBERS AND PATTERNS IN CALIFORNIA

On November 19, 1890, Judge Armstrong of Sacramento Superior Court, in what was probably California's first labor injunction, ordered the local printers' union to cease distributing leaflets calling for a boycott of the *Sacramento Bee*. The printers demanded the reinstatement of a fellow union member whom, they claimed, the *Bee* had discharged for engaging in union activities. When the printers continued to distribute leaflets in violation of the injunction, Judge Armstrong levied $20 fines against the union's president and the labor editor who had printed the leaflets. More than a year later the *Bee* had yet to reinstate the discharged worker and the California Supreme Court had refused the union's request to review Judge Armstrong's ruling.[3] While this novel use of the injunction in California received little attention beyond the labor press, it nonetheless anticipated circumstances surrounding later labor injunctions: it involved highly visible appeals to public sympathy and included demands other than those involving wages and work hours. It would be another decade before the injunction became a significant factor in California labor disputes. But once it did, as a University of California labor economist observed in 1908, the "use of the injunction . . . rapidly developed, until at the present time there remains but a narrow range of trade-union activity which the courts recognize as lawful."[4]

In California, as elsewhere, employers recognized the injunction's advantages. Unlike charges of criminal conspiracy or suits to recover damages, the labor injunction could be issued before the damage had been done, and it did not depend upon a costly trial with an unpredictable jury.[5] Even where a judge was not entirely sympathetic to an employer's concerns, the injunction procedure allowed employers to receive a "temporary" or "preliminary" restraining order in advance of a hearing or trial. Counsel for the employers invoked a number of delaying tactics, so that by the time that the hearing took place—and labor was given a chance to present its side of the story—the preliminary injunction might already have served its purpose. These delayed hearings represented one of labor's greatest concerns. As a 1906 resolution of the California Federation of Labor (CFL) put it, "our first grievance relates to the manner in which restraining orders and injunctions have been issued without an opportunity for a hearing on the part of the defendants . . . [W]e protest not only against the substance of the restraining orders, but more especially against the procedure employed."[6]

While the injunction had clearly become a problem for organized labor by the first decade of the twentieth century, determining the actual numbers issued is probably impossible. Even labor leaders at the time were uncertain as to the exact numbers. At its annual convention in January of 1906, the Executive Committee of the CFL, claiming that judges within the state had issued "more than fifty" injunctions in the previous year, initiated its own survey. A CFL resolution asked that local labor councils send to the Executive Committee information on recent injunctions issued within their jurisdictions. By mid-April the Executive Committee had received reports from "many" of the local councils—enough, they hoped, to estimate the scope of the injunction problem in California. But in the early morning hours of April 18, 1906, movement along the San Andreas Fault initiated one of the most tragic days in San Francisco's history. The earthquake and ensuing fire destroyed much of the city, including the CFL offices and the unanalyzed data on injunctions in the state.[7]

Like the information collected by the CFL, much of the documentary evidence on labor injunctions has disappeared. First, records of the county-level Superior courts—where all state court injunctions originated—are fragmentary at best; some court records were lost to earthquake and fire, but most, no doubt, vanished with less drama. Second, because injunctions started as temporary restraining orders and rarely reached the hearing or trial stage, they often never generated a case file.[8] Finally, even where files still exist in California, county court cases are indexed, not by type of proceeding, but by the name of the plaintiff. To locate even those injunctions that left a trace in the court records, one would need to go through all files by hand in all of California's fifty-eight county courthouses. Such a task would be daunting and, at any rate, of dubious value. We will never know how many labor injunctions were issued in California during these years, but by using selected court records in combination with other sources, one can at least offer estimates and discern general trends.

Edwin Witte, an economist at the University of Wisconsin and an early-twentieth-century pioneer in the field in industrial relations, made one of the first attempts to estimate the number of injunctions issued in the United States. Witte had first studied the injunction issue for the United States Commission on Industrial Relations (USCIR) between 1913 and 1915, and in later years he undertook the massive project of estimating the total number of injunctions issued between 1880 and 1930. Starting with 509 injunctions reported in state and federal reporters and a list of 531 additional injunctions he had compiled while working for the USCIR, Witte and his assistants then researched newspapers, labor periodicals, and local labor histories from throughout the nation and added substantially to the list. In all, Witte found references to 1,845 separate injunctions issued between 1880 and 1930, fifty-one of which were in California.[9] While one must marvel at Witte's ambition, a more thorough reading of the same sources (as well as the district reports at the annual convention of the California Federation of Labor, which Witte did not consult) suggest that Witte greatly undercounted injunctions in California. Union proceedings, local union histories, and even the publications of open-shop employer organizations demonstrate that scores of injunctions escaped Witte's attention.

Other studies have confirmed that Witte overlooked many injunctions. William Forbath, who has offered the most recent reevaluation, more than doubles Witte's estimate. Rather than survey the width and breadth of the United States—which inevitably leads to errors of omission—Forbath concentrated on selected areas to determine the ratio of unreported to reported cases, and he then used this ratio to estimate the total number of injunctions in the United States. Forbath relied upon three studies of selected areas: data collected by the Massachusetts Bureau of Labor Statistics; Paul Brissenden's study of injunctions in New York; and Forbath's own analysis of injunctions in Chicago. More restricted in time and place, these studies found injunctions that Witte had understandably missed. Whereas Witte found a ratio of unreported to reported cases of less than four-to-one, Forbath's analysis suggested a ratio of more than eight-to-one. Using this ratio, Forbath estimated that some 4,300 injunctions were issued between 1880 and 1930, noting that even this figure was conservative, for it assumed that unreported cases found their way into nonlegal sources and that researchers did not miss any of those so recorded. Applying Forbath's analysis to California, we could conservatively increase Witte's estimate to about 119 injunctions between 1890 and 1926, or just over three per year. Given that the California Bureau of Labor Statistics (CBLS) reported anywhere from twenty to more than 100 strikes per year during this period, one could estimate that the percentage of strikes enjoined ranged from 3 to 15 percent in a given year.[10]

But such aggregate statistics are at best inadequate and at worst misleading, for injunctions were not spread evenly over the entire period. Instead, injunctions came in waves that, in the short run, did not always correspond to levels of strike activity. For example, while the CBLS reported a record-high 104 strikes for 1903, Witte found that only two of these strikes (or just under 2 percent) were enjoined. By contrast, while the CBLS reported only twenty-nine strikes in 1905, Witte found nine injunctions enjoining seven different strikes (or 24 percent enjoined). Furthermore, within any given year, the likelihood that a strike would draw an injunction varied regionally. San Francisco accounted for six of the seven enjoined strikes in 1905, even though the city accounted for only twelve of the state's twenty-nine recorded strikes for that year. Thus, while an astonishing 50 percent of all San Francisco strikes were enjoined in 1905, only one in seventeen (less than 6 percent) was enjoined in the remainder of the state.[11]

When and where courts issued injunctions appears to have depended largely upon both the kinds of strikes that labor engaged in and the degree to which organized employers perceived such strikes as a threat. Whether relying upon Witte's data or upon the reports (and complaints) of local labor leaders, it is clear that most of the California injunctions came in three waves: from 1904 to 1907 in Northern California; from 1910 to 1911 in Los Angeles; and from 1916 to 1921 throughout the state. Each of these periods corresponds with cycles of union growth and organization and, as important, employer counter-organization. The first wave of injunctions came after a period of unprecedented union growth in Northern California had prompted the formation of several Northern California branches of the Citizen's Alliance, a nationwide network of employers' associations dedicated to maintaining the open shop, checking union growth, and outlawing labor's preferred forms of collective action. The second wave of injunctions, more narrowly focused in time and place, coincided with the efforts of San Francisco trade unionists to organize Los Angeles. The third wave of injunctions coincided with the rise in labor activism and the revived employer's open-shop movement that accompanied World War I and its aftermath. Each of these periods saw not only increased union activism, but an increasing number of "organizational strikes," which demanded union recognition and were called in tandem with well-publicized organizational drives. These patterns support Forbath's claim that the strikes most likely to draw injunctions were those that went beyond wage and hour demands. Employers most often turned to the courts when they wanted to check union expansion or protect open-shop enclaves. [12]

In addition to timing, the waves of injunctions reveal another telling pattern. Most of the injunctions were issued in Northern California, with the greatest wave coming in San Francisco during the Union Labor Party period. Denied police protection, organized employers in San Francisco turned to local courts to prevent picketing and boycotts. Such injunctions were, on the other hand, relatively rare in Los Angeles before 1910. Indeed, during a period of marked union activity and labor conflict—from the post-depression revival of labor activism in 1897 to the 1907 economic downturn that brought a decrease in union activity—only two labor injunctions were issued against unions in Los Angeles. And one of these injunctions, which was dismissed after a preliminary hearing, had been sought by an employer who only wanted his name removed from the Labor Council's "fair" list, so as not to be known as a pro-union employer in open-shop Los Angeles. By contrast, San Francisco judges issued one or more injunctions on at least thirty separate occasions over the same period. To be sure, given that San Francisco saw a greater number of strikes than did Los Angeles, one would expect more injunctions. But this does not begin to account for the vast difference in the number of injunctions. San Francisco had slightly more than two times as many strikes as Los Angeles, but at least fifteen times as many injunctions.[13]

Why were injunctions so rare in open-shop Los Angeles, where labor faced hostility from the local press, employers, and public officials, and so frequent in pro-labor San Francisco? Employers in Los Angeles simply did not need injunctions. Seeking an injunction involved time and money. An employer, or employer organization, seeking an injunction had to post a bond, usually between 500 and 1,000 dollars.[14] In addition, a lawyer was needed to file the complaint and, if necessary, defend the injunction at any subsequent hearing or trial. Employers sought injunctions, therefore, only if a labor victory seemed imminent and they enjoyed no other means of squelching strikes. In Los Angeles, where labor won only about 8 percent of its strikes—as opposed to the 45 percent success rate in San Francisco—labor rarely posed a threat.[15] More importantly, when labor did threaten, Los Angeles employers found it easier to obtain police protection than seek an injunction. Only in 1910, when the involvement of the San Francisco labor movement threatened to upset open-shop conditions, did Los Angeles employers turn to the courts for injunctions.[16] In San Francisco, conversely, a stronger labor movement posed stronger threats, and employers could not rely on police intervention. Injunctions were most likely, therefore, where labor had enough political clout to restrain local police.

Despite turning to different institutions, employers in both cities called upon local authorities for the same reasons and used the same justifications for doing so. Both police intervention in Los Angeles and injunctions in San Francisco most often restrained strikes for union recognition or the closed shop, for, unlike strikes for wages and hours, such issues were not as readily compromised.[17] Second, employer demands for court and police intervention usually occurred in conjunction with well-orchestrated efforts by organized employers to import strikebreakers from outside the community. Finally, whether turning to courts or police to protect these strikebreakers, employers drew from the language of the injunction to condemn labor's methods as inherent forms of "coercion" and "intimidation" that threatened the nonunion worker's right to sell his labor and the employer's right to use his property in the manner that he chose.[18]

That employers used judicial language to justify police as well as court interventions points to yet another problem that the injunction created for the labor movement. In addition to allowing organized employers to usurp labor's political control over the police and target key organizational strikes, the injunction had less direct, but no less important, ideological consequences. As the CFL's Executive Secretary Paul Scharrenberg recalled years later, the injunction "was a use of psychology . . . It was an intimation, in high falutin' judicial languages, that [strikers] were against the law, doing something that was bad, wicked, and evil."[19] As William Forbath has put it more recently, the language of the injunction depicted labor's methods as "semi-outlawry."[20] Injunctions, and the "high falutin'" language that justified them, colored the public's perception of labor disputes and frustrated labor's efforts to win both public and legal approval of its methods. To fully appreciate the ideological implications of the labor injunction, it is necessary to look at the leading cases of the California appellate courts, which not only confirmed or overturned lower court injunctions, but issued general statements on the legitimacy of labor's most important economic weapons and defined the respective rights of workers and employers.

PURPOSE AND METHOD: LAW AND LABOR DISPUTES AT THE TURN-OF-THE-CENTURY

California judges inherited a body of legal discourse that considered the right to strike in terms of "purpose" and "method."[21] As to which strike objectives constituted a lawful purpose, the several state courts failed to establish a consensus. Nonetheless, in making their determinations, all relied on similar versions of the "just cause" and "malice" doctrines.[22] In matters of trade and commerce, as both the American and British courts had ruled, economic competition involved seeking advantages in a market-place to the disadvantage of one's competitors; in the world of business, that is, the successful pursuit of self-interest not infre-quently caused a certain amount of economic harm to someone else. One had "just cause" to inflict such harm on another so long as one's actions were motivated by the natural "instinct of self-advancement and self protection," and not by a "malicious" de-sire to harm someone else. Malicious acts, that is, were done not in pursuit of one's legitimate interests, but for the sole purpose of injuring another.[23] Labor lawyers in Britain and the United States hoped that such doctrines might also justify labor's collective ef-forts, even when such efforts caused a certain amount of economic harm to employers.

But labor's hopes proved unwarranted, for the same doctrines gave judges the rather extraordinary power to define the "legit-imate interests" of striking workers. In 1911 the Massachusetts Supreme Court reiterated a position that most courts had adhered to since the 1890s, clearly stating that judges alone would define a legal "purpose": "To justify interference with the rights of oth-ers the strikers must in good faith strike for a purpose which the court decides to be a legal justification for such interference . . . the purpose of the strike must be one which the court, as a matter of law, decides is a legal purpose."[24]

While judges arrogated the power to define "a legal purpose," they did not always offer the same definitions. By the mid-1890s most state and federal judges considered strikes restricted to wage and hour demands as legal in purpose.[25] But when strikers went beyond wage and hour demands, the judicial consensus crumbled. For example, state courts divided on the lawfulness of demands for the "closed shop" (where an employer hires only union members). Massachusetts considered such strikes illegal, while neighboring

New York did not. In *Plant v. Wood* (1900) the Massachusetts court held that a demand for the closed shop was unlawful because it did not "directly and immediately" affect the legitimate economic interests of the individual worker. To be sure, a closed-shop agreement might indirectly benefit workers by strengthening the union, the court ruled, but such a benefit was too "remote" to justify interference with the employer's right to hire without regard to union status.[26] In a dissenting opinion, Oliver Wendell Holmes, Jr., objected to the majority's arbitrary distinction between "immediate" or "direct" interests, which the court deemed just, and "remote" interests, which it considered malicious. Holmes agreed that the "purpose [of a closed-shop strike] was not directly concerned with wages. It was one degree more remote." But if workers could, with legal justification, form unions to strike for higher wages, Holmes reasoned, it followed that they must also be permitted to make the union "effectual" by preparing "the means which they might use in the final contest."[27]

Holmes never persuaded his fellow justices in Massachusetts, but his arguments found a more receptive audience on New York's high court. In *National Protective Association v. Cumming* (1902), the New York Supreme Court defined workers' interests broadly enough to include demands for the closed shop.[28] In his majority opinion Chief Justice Parker reasoned that a striker had the right to "refuse to work for another on any ground that he may regard as sufficient." Parker did not reject a consideration of a strike's "purpose" altogether, acknowledging that a strike motivated by "malice" could still be illegal. Yet according to Parker, only if the "sole purpose" of an act was to inflict injury, with no other benefit whatsoever in mind, should the malice doctrine be applied. Workers had the right to organize and strike for "purposes deemed beneficial to themselves," Parker concluded, and their "right to stop work is not cut off because the reason seems inadequate or selfish to the employer or to organized society."[29] Thus, while Massachusetts and New York both inquired into the purpose of a strike, they differed as to what constituted a lawful purpose.

According to Progressive-era labor economist John Commons, other state courts were "about evenly divided as between the Massachusetts and New York decisions."[30]

Questions of purpose did not exhaust judicial considerations. Even a strike with limited and lawful objectives could face legal repression as a consequence of its "methods." Like the distinction between "just cause" and "malice" on questions of purpose, the test for determining lawful methods was deceptively simple: so long as strikers limited themselves to peaceful "persuasion" the courts approved; but as soon as persuasion became "coercion" or "intimidation," courts withdrew the blessings of legitimacy.[31] For the more restrictive courts, picketing inevitably led to intimidation if not outright violence. In *Vegelahn v. Guntner* (1896), the Massachusetts court held picketing unlawful even in the absence of violence or threats of violence. "Intimidation is not limited to threats of violence or of physical injury," the majority wrote, "it has a broader signification, and there may also be a moral intimidation which is illegal."[32] In 1905 a federal district court took this logic one step further, ruling that picketing, by definition, violated the law: "There is and can be no such thing as peaceful picketing, any more than there can be chaste vulgarity, or peaceful mobbing, or lawful lynching."[33]

Not all courts took the drastic stand that picketing by definition entailed unlawful intimidation; but even for those that did not, the terms "coercion" and "intimidation" left much room for interpretation. Everyone agreed, including virtually all spokesmen for organized labor, that violence and physical force should not be tolerated. For some courts, however, nearly any form of intimidation made picketing an unacceptable method. For example, the threat of financial loss implicit in a boycott equaled "economic intimidation," or the ill feeling directed toward those who crossed a picket line amounted to "moral intimidation." Yet most courts left terms deliberately vague, leaving a large gray area that encompassed anything from physical assaults to dirty looks. The very ambiguity of the law gave local judges considerable leeway to either condemn or confer legitimacy upon labor's methods.[34]

That judges assumed the power to define legal purposes and methods still does not explain why, by the 1890s, the injunction had replaced the criminal conspiracy trial as the primary method of judicial intervention in labor disputes. Legal precedent did not require that courts acquiesce to employer demands for labor injunctions. In fact, precedent should have pushed courts in the opposite direction. According to William Forbath, the "courts had to cast aside customary limits on the purpose and scope of injunctions to accommodate [their] new role" in labor disputes.[35] Traditionally, courts of equity issued injunctions only when two conditions had been met: first, when failure to act quickly would result in "irreparable damage" to person or property; and second, when there existed no other "remedy at law." In theory, the principle of equity allowed the court to prevent an obvious and irreparable injury from occurring in cases where a strict adherence to statute or common law would result in an obvious injustice. Equity powers, that is, gave judges the flexibility to intervene on those occasions when the formal rules ran contrary to common sense notions of fairness and justice.[36]

Traditional usage presented certain obstacles to using the injunction in labor disputes. First, critics of the labor injunction claimed that employers did, in fact, have other "remedies at law." If a strike or boycott resulted in severe economic loss, for example, the employer could file a suit for damages on the basis of either the Sherman Act or the common law. If workers destroyed property or committed acts of violence, as complaints for injunctions often charged, then the police could arrest the guilty parties but an injunction need not be issued. In response to these objections judges noted that in a strike or boycott the employer enjoyed no "adequate" remedy at law. For example, an employer could not expect to recover full damages from workers with few or no assets; and because strikes often involved large numbers of workers, the police could not easily arrest all of them. In short, from the employer's (and judge's) point of view, no practical legal remedies existed.

A second obstacle to the labor injunction concerned the definition of "property," which according to traditional equity usage referred to concrete, tangible objects. An injunction might be proper if strikers broke windows or destroyed machinery, or if they threatened to do so. But when an employer claimed that a strike or boycott destroyed his "property," he merely meant that profits would suffer if a strike brought operations to a halt or if a picket line drove customers away. In the area of constitutional law late-nineteenth-century courts had already begun to define the "right to do business" as a property right protected by the Fourteenth Amendment.[37] However, it did not necessarily follow that this broader definition should apply to equity law, for the "property" that equity traditionally protected from immediate and irreparable damage applied only to "things." According to Forbath, judges transformed equity law and procedure by redefining property to include anything that had "pecuniary" or "exchangeable" value, "including a man's business or labor."[38]

By the early twentieth century, therefore, state and federal judges had made the injunction a powerful defense of the employer's expansively defined property rights. Although the courts failed to reach a consensus as to the exact parameters of lawful purpose and method—as the differences between the New York and Massachusetts courts demonstrate—they nonetheless provided ample precedent for employers to seek, and most often receive, judicial assistance in case of a strike. Armed with a powerful legal weapon, judges defined the "legitimate interests" of workers and set the legal boundaries of working-class collective action.

"MEN OF ENERGY AND ENTERPRISE": THE EMPLOYER'S RIGHTS IN CALIFORNIA

When the first labor cases came before them, California judges looked to federal and other state courts for guidance: they considered the means and ends of labor's collective action and relied upon the injunction to prohibit behavior they deemed unlawful or otherwise threatening to an employer's property. Yet as legal scholar James Atleson has argued, judicial rulings never follow entirely from legal logic or precedent; they are also "based upon other, often unarticulated, values and assumptions." These values and assumptions, in turn, were shaped at least in part by a judge's daily associations and social background.[39] California's appellate court judges came mostly from the middle to upper-middle classes. By the early twentieth century most appellate judges in California had graduated from college, but very few had attended law school, most receiving their legal training in a law firm. As the official biographies and obituaries of California's appellate judges reveal, they were representative of neither large corporate wealth nor of society at large. Instead they came to the appellate courts following careers as lower court judges or lawyers; their fathers before them had been educated professionals, clergymen, or moderate-sized but prosperous businessmen.[40]

Judges, therefore, tended to come from the same social backgrounds as the small- to moderate-sized employers most likely to seek injunctions. As Edward Johnson pointed out in his two-volume collection of biographies, the men who sat on the California appellate courts were seen by their contemporaries as "men of energy and enterprise" who had been actively involved in the civic and business affairs of their communities.[41] Almost all of the state's Superior Court and appellate judges belonged to one or more organizations—Masons, Native Sons of the Golden West, Chambers of Commerce, or private professional and businessmen's clubs—where they associated with members of the business community. This is not to suggest that judges reflexively did the employers' bidding, but that they shared a common set of values and assumptions. Most California judges embraced the entrepreneurial world view so vividly described in Daniel Ernst's study of the businessmen and lawyers associated with the American Anti-Boycott Association, men who feared the rise of the corporation as much as they feared labor unions.[42] As we shall see, judicial rulings in California were not simply anti-labor; indeed, in many ways California went farther than any other state in recognizing labor's formal right to strike and boycott. Still, California judges often vitiated this formal right due to their stronger

conviction that the employer, as a proprietor, enjoyed a fundamental right to run his business as he pleased, without union interference.

Although California judges were elected to the bench, at least
four factors insulated them from electoral politics. First, superior
court judges—unlike the municipal "police court" judges who
were sometimes accused of pandering to the labor vote—were
nominated by conservative local bar associations, not by the political parties. Second, superior and appellate court judges ran for
longer terms, either six or twelve years instead of the two- or four-
year terms of municipal and other state offices. Throughout the
Progressive era, labor fought a losing battle to prevent the extension of judicial terms. Third, incumbent superior and appellate
court judges often ran unopposed. Finally, as a number of historians of legal thought and education suggest, judges took seriously
the notion that they stood above the political fray. One of the
central tenets of the prevailing "legal formalism" was the separation of law and legal reasoning on the one hand, and politics
and public policy choices on the other. This does not mean that
judges in fact accomplished this separation, but at least rhetori-
cally the autonomy of the law stood as a central proposition by
which judges understood their work. To a considerable extent,
the larger political culture accepted this proposition and, in ways
both structural and informal, devised ways to cushion judges from
electoral pressures so that the law would not be "politicized."[43]

Before these politically insulated "men of energy and enterprise" deliberated on the rights of unions and the proper scope of
the labor injunction, they followed a national trend by establishing the employer's right to run a business as a full property right.
The initial decisions establishing this right did not involve union
efforts to strike, picket, or boycott, but they were to have great
consequences in each of those areas in later decisions. Two decisions discussed below—*Ex Parte Kubak* and *Ex Parte Jentzsch*—
were issued before the court took up the rights of organized labor,
but they reveal the justices' fundamental assumptions about the
nature of work and the right of individuals to "pursue a lawful call-

ing." Originally the concept of a "calling" had suggested not only a right but a religious duty to ply a trade; but as a legal concept it evolved into an employer's right to run his business without undue interference and an individual worker's right to sell his labor under terms of his own choosing. Both "rights," as we shall see, imposed considerable restraints on trade union activity.

The California Supreme Court first expressed a commitment to "liberty of avocation" in *Ex Parte Kubak* (1890), which struck down a Los Angeles ordinance making it a crime for any city contractor to hire Chinese labor or to employ any person for more than eight hours per day.[44] The ordinance embodied two political objectives of the late-nineteenth-century California labor movement: the eight-hour movement and labor's ongoing crusade against Asian immigrants.[45] Finding that the ordinance went beyond the "police power" of the state, the court declared the law unconstitutional. Legislated restrictions on who could be hired and how many hours they could work unreasonably infringed upon "the rights of . . . persons to make and enforce their contracts" and the "liberty to pursue a lawful calling." Like judges elsewhere, California's appellate court justices construed the state's "police power" narrowly and struck down legislation that interfered with the employment relationship.[46]

A second case, *Ex Parte Jentzsch* (1896), considered an 1895 amendment to the state Penal Code that made it unlawful for a barber to conduct his shop on Sundays or holidays past noon.[47] When San Francisco barber Leo Jentzsch kept his shop open one Sunday afternoon, he was arrested and jailed by the local sheriff; he then requested a writ of habeas corpus to win his release from the San Francisco county jail. A brief filed on Jentzsch's behalf argued that the Sunday closing law violated his constitutional right "to use one's faculties in all innocent and lawful ways [and] to earn his livelihood in any lawful calling." In support of this argument the brief cited Article I, Section I of the California Constitution, which stated, "All men are by nature free and independent, and have certain inalienable rights, among which are those of enjoying and defending life and liberty, acquiring, possessing and protecting property, and pursuing and obtaining safety and happiness."

Taken together, the *Kubak* and *Jentzsch* rulings established the "right to do business" free from outside interference as a property right. While these rulings protected this right from state interference, the California courts would soon demonstrate that the same principle also protected businesses from interference by private parties, especially labor unions. By the turn of the century the individual's right to pursue a calling had become an assertion of the employer's right to run his business as he saw fit without outside interference—whether from the state or from a labor union.

CALIFORNIA COURTS AND THE LABOR INJUNCTION, 1896–1909

If the employer enjoyed the right to run his enterprise without undue interference, what corresponding rights did labor possess? How far did the liberty to strike, picket, and boycott extend before it encroached upon the employer's "right to do business"? At what point did legitimate economic pressure become unlawful or destructive interference subject to the equity powers of the courts? California's position on the labor injunction, and on the respective rights of workers and employers, developed in three phases that I outline below. The first phase, from about 1896 through the passage of a 1903 anti-injunction law, appeared to set limits on the court's power to enjoin trade union activity. During the second phase, from about 1904 to 1906, organized employers—especially the open-shop Citizen's Alliance—encouraged and even pressured fellow employers to resist labor's demands and persuaded the courts to nullify the 1903 anti-injunction law. The third phase, from 1908 to 1909, saw the California courts make definitive statements on the questions of lawful "purpose" and "method" in the *Parkinson* and *Pierce* cases, respectively. Taken together, these decisions granted organized labor a formal right to strike while at the same time limiting the means by which labor might realize that right. Not only did these rulings give employers an important weapon, they depicted labor's methods as lawless efforts to subvert the employer's fundamental right to control his business.

Early Limits on the Injunction in California, 1896–1903

The first case concerning the rights of organized labor reached the California Supreme Court in 1899. *Davitt v. American Bakers Union* stemmed from an 1896 dispute between the American Baker's Union and one John B. Davitt, the owner of three nonunion bakeries in San Francisco. Davitt charged that the union had "maliciously conspired and combined to cripple and destroy [his] business," drove off employees and customers by means of "force, menaces, and threats and intimidat[ion];" and distributed "false, vicious, and offensive circulars" against the employer. If these actions were not stopped, the complaint charged, Davitt's business would "become subject to the dictation of [the] Union."[48] On the basis of this complaint, Judge D. J. Murphy of the San Francisco Superior Court issued a "temporary" injunction restraining any union interference with Davitt's business.

Judge Murphy's "temporary" restraining order remained in effect for over six months, until George Montieth, a lawyer for the Baker's Union, moved to dissolve the injunction before San Francisco Superior Court Judge George Bahrs. Montieth argued that Davitt's complaint was insufficient to sustain an injunction, for its wording was "ambiguous" and did not show the specific "manner and means employed by the defendants." Davitt's attorneys had made bold claims of "malice," "conspiracy," and "intimidation," Montieth noted, without specifying any overt acts. Judge Bahrs deliberated on Montieth's motion for nearly two months, and in June of 1897 granted the union's request to dissolve the temporary injunction.[49] While Judge Bahrs' order pleased organized labor in San Francisco, it had come too late to help the Bakers' Union, which had temporarily abandoned its effort to organize Davitt's employees.

The legal battle resumed one year later when the union re-newed its boycott effort, prompting Davitt to ask the California Supreme Court to either overturn Judge Bahr's order dissolving the original injunction or issue a permanent injunction against the Bakers' Union. When the Supreme Court finally heard the case in early 1899, it ruled that California's lower courts must demand hard evidence of violence, or specific threats thereof, before issuing an injunction. Writing for a unanimous court, Jus-tice Garroute noted that the original complaint "deals in gener-alities throughout and does not state any specific overt acts." A complaint for an injunction needed to specify the exact nature of the "threats," "force," "intimidation," or "menace" charged; if the complaint charged that pickets carried "false and malicious" signs or circulars, it had to specify how they were false or malicious. Because the original complaint offered none of this, the Supreme Court ruled, the lower court had erred in issuing the injunction.[50]

Organized labor welcomed the *Davitt* decision, for by their reck-oning it called for strict evidential standards in showing cause for an injunction. But the *Davitt* ruling was by no means a clear-cut victory for organized labor. First, labor's victory on appeal did not change the fact that, for eight months, the original injunction had frustrated the Bakers' Union efforts to organize Davitt's workers. Second, while the Supreme Court ruled in this particular case that the employer had failed to show specific unlawful acts on the part of the union, it did not deny that an employer's property rights in-cluded the right to run his business as he pleased. The court still had not asserted any corresponding rights on the part of organized labor. Finally, as counsel for employers would argue in later cases, the justices had simply thrown out a poorly written and clearly defective complaint. As such, employers' counsel reasoned, the decision was inadequate as precedent.[51]

Whatever the meaning of the *Davitt* ruling, the newly formed California Federation of Labor (CFL)—which would dedicate it-self primarily to serving organized labor's interests in the state legislature—made curbing the power of the courts one of its first

legislative goals. Using a model bill proposed by the American
Federation of Labor (AFL), the CFL included an anti-injunction
bill as one of several legislative proposals submitted to the state
Assembly and Senate in 1901. But labor's anti-injunction bill
failed to get out of the Judiciary Committee of either house. Judiciary Committee members claimed that the small numbers of
injunctions issued in California did not warrant legislative interference with the courts' equity powers.[52] The Committee's failure to act was not without reason, for evidence suggests that the
courts enjoined only three strikes or boycotts in California between 1896 and 1900. If there were others they did not create
much of a stir. Of the three that left traces, one was dropped after
the employer reached a settlement with his workers; one was dis-
solved at a second hearing; and the third, the *Davitt* injunction,
had been overturned by the California Supreme Court in 1899.[53]
The CFL's initial effort, therefore, seems to have had more to do
with following the lead of the national federation than with local
conditions in California.[54]

But conditions in California soon changed. Almost constant
labor unrest in San Francisco from the spring to the fall of 1901—
climaxing in the violent waterfront strike—brought injunctions,
police interventions, and calls for the state militia. The following year a long and sometimes violent strike by tannery workers
in Benicia, California, brought sweeping injunctions against all
picketing. When the CFL delegates met during the first week of
January 1903, less than a month after the Benicia strike, they
resolved to reintroduce the anti-injunction bill in the upcoming
legislative session. Noting the failure of the 1901 bill, the *Labor Clarion* reported that the San Francisco Labor Council—who
co-sponsored the CFL bill—had "secured all available data" on
injunctions in the state and were now "better fortified" than they
had been in the previous session.[55] Labor's 1903 anti-injunction
bill aimed to create a blanket restriction that would ban injunctions in labor disputes. The key portion of the bill stated that
"no act in the contemplation or furtherance of any trade dispute

between employers and employees . . . shall be deemed criminal . . . nor shall any restraining order or injunction be issued in relations thereto."[56]

Legislative agents for both the CFL and the San Francisco Labor Council presented the bill to Grove Johnson, a member of the Assembly Judiciary Committee. Johnson—whose more famous son, Hiram, would later serve as Progressive Governor of California—was, at first glance, an odd choice. Unlike his reform-minded son, who took the Governor's chair in 1910 with a promise to kick the corrupt Southern Pacific Railroad out of politics, Grove Johnson was an attorney for the Southern Pacific. In addition to serving corporate capital, however, the elder Johnson had gained some favor with labor by defending Sacramento printers in their 1890 legal dispute with the *Sacramento Bee*. Johnson agreed to present labor's bill to the Judiciary Committee and to make every effort to send it out with a favorable report. But he took the bill only on condition that he be free to amend it if necessary.[57]

Before the bill was reported out of committee, Johnson had added a simple, single clause: "Provided, that nothing in this act shall be construed to authorize the use of force, violence or intimidation." When CFL labor lobbyists and their supporters saw the amendment, they immediately opposed the word "intimidation," arguing that it was simply too vague a word. Labor leaders in California, as elsewhere, knew all too well that judges had already used the term "intimidation" to justify enjoining acts that labor considered only forms of "peaceful persuasion." Adding the word "intimidation," labor feared, would effectively nullify the bill. Since Superior Court judges almost always justified their injunctions on the grounds that labor's methods amounted to "intimidation," the bill as amended simply recast the hated "judge-made law" into the form of a statute.[58]

With labor's representatives opposed to the amendment, the Assembly returned the bill to the Judiciary Committee. The bill stayed in committee for nearly two more weeks before Johnson and labor's legislative agents reached a compromise. The proviso that nothing in the bill should be construed to permit "force, violence, or intimidation" was changed to read "force, violence, or threats thereof." The change seemed minor and, perhaps in retrospect, insignificant; yet the debate demonstrated how closely attuned labor leaders had already become to the finer points of judicial language and reasoning. The revised bill passed in the Assembly and Senate with little debate and became law on March 21, 1903, with Governor Pardee's signature.[59]

Expanding the Scope of the Injunction, 1904–1906

The Governor's signature, however, provided no guarantees on how judges would interpret the 1903 anti-injunction law. Superior court judges continued to issue injunctions, and the law languished in uncertainty until unceremoniously declared "void and unconstitutional" in 1906 by the very branch of government that its authors had hoped to restrain. Because of the ultimate fate of the act, those few California labor historians who mention the bill write it off as a meaningless gesture or poorly worded legislation;[60] but the early history of the act suggests that its death was not inevitable. Lucile Eaves, a Berkeley labor economist who began her study of California labor legislation before the earthquake and fire destroyed the relevant court records, claimed that at least three injunctions then pending in San Francisco Superior Court were dismissed as a result of the legislation.[61] Moreover, the 104 strikes recorded by the California Bureau of Labor Statistics for 1903 (most of which came after the 1903 act passed) more than doubled the number of strikes of any year that came before it. Yet according to extant records, only two strikes faced injunctions that year and both of those came from federal courts not beholden to state laws.[62]

The 1903 Act was rendered meaningless not by its own words or inherent flaws but through the deliberate efforts of Northern California businessmen organized in local chapters of the Citizens' Alliance. Organized in 1904, the Citizen's Alliance pressured employers to reject closed-shop agreements and provided struck employers with loans, strikebreakers, and legal aid and advice.[63] By the end of 1904 the San Francisco Citizen's Alliance boasted that it had already initiated nineteen injunctions against picketing and, in the following year, continued to take credit for the increasing number of labor injunctions in the state. Indeed, the name of Bush Finnell, head of the Citizen's Alliance "Legal Department," appeared as the attorney of record on several injunction requests, and he later argued two of the most important cases to come before the California Supreme Court. Finnell and the Citizen's Alliance also challenged the 1903 anti-injunction act. In a 1904 dispute with the San Francisco Stablemen's Union, Finnell convinced Superior Court Judge John Hunt to declare the law unconstitutional on the grounds that it jeopardized the employer's right to use, enjoy, and protect his property. Labor lawyers spent the next five years appealing Hunt's decision; in the meantime, trade unionists faced a barrage of hostile court rulings.[64]

While Judge Hunt's ruling slowly worked its way toward a hearing before the California Supreme Court, two appellate court rulings eroded whatever protections labor supposed it had won in the 1899 *Davitt* ruling and under the 1903 anti-injunction law. In *Jordahl v. Hayda* (1905), the Third District Court of Appeals upheld a Humboldt County injunction in a dispute between the local Cooks' and Waiters' Union and a Eureka restaurant owner. Union lawyers contended that both the original complaint and the injunction made charges of "violence" and "intimidation" without identifying specific acts. They also claimed that the injunction violated constitutional rights of free speech by banning even peaceful picketing and carrying placards. The Court of Appeals rejected both arguments. To the charge that the injunction failed to specify acts, the court ruled that it was not "practicable" for the court "to enumerate the particular acts which in its opinion would be regarded as acts of intimidation." Thus, while the Davitt opinion had appeared to establish strict standards as to what constituted "intimidation," the majority in *Jordahl* ruled that the plaintiffs need not show actual violence or force, for "conduct falling short of actual violence" might still result in "the [wrongful] injury of the plaintiff." As to the union's claim that the injunction violated the right to free speech, the court responded that, "while the right of free speech" was guaranteed, the California constitution also guaranteed the "right of 'acquiring, possessing and protecting property.'" Since the employer's "business" was his property, any interference with his access to customers or employees infringed upon his property rights (which presumably trumped the workers' right to free speech).[65]

The state supreme court addressed very similar issues the following year in *Goldberg, Bowen, Co. v. Stablemen's Union* (1906), and in the process unequivocally asserted the employer's right to run a business without union interference, defined labor's methods as inherent forms of "intimidation" and "coercion," and all but nullified the 1903 anti-injunction law. Writing for a unanimous court, Justice McFarland ruled that a court of equity would enjoin any strike or boycott that had "the purpose or effect" of intimidating customers or employees. Intimidation, that is, need not involve physically threatening or coercive acts; the mere intent or effect of intimidation—including "moral intimidation"—was sufficient cause for the courts to intervene. Assuming inherent intimidation in any form of picketing, McFarland placed the burden of proof upon the defendants to show that the acts had *not* been intimidating: "It cannot be successfully contended that [the defendants' acts] could not, in the nature of things, have had the effect of intimidating . . . patrons."[66]

McFarland devoted just one short paragraph to the defendants' claim that the injunction violated the 1903 anti-injunction law. Though the legislation in question was "difficult of construction," McFarland contended, lawmakers most certainly had not intended to prohibit a court from preventing irreparable damage to property. If that were the law's intent, McFarland opined, then it must be considered "void," for it denied the employer the legal means by which he might ensure his "constitutional right to acquire, possess, enjoy, and protect property." The court did not strike down the law entirely, but it was difficult to see under what circumstances it could be invoked.[67]

Taken together, the *Jordahl* and *Goldberg* decisions effectively reversed what labor thought it had won in the *Davitt* ruling and in the 1903 anti-injunction act. The decisions made it clear that the Supreme Court and the Courts of Appeal would allow lower court judges to define "intimidation" broadly enough to include "economic" or "moral" intimidation and to enjoin any actions that had the "intent" or "effect" of keeping employees or customers away from the employer's business. Two critical assumptions embedded within these rulings deserve reiteration. First, by assuming that patrons and replacement workers stayed away because they were intimidated, the justices refused to distinguish between successfully "convincing" or "persuading" customers or employees on the one hand, and "morally intimidating" them on the other. They therefore dismissed the possibility that employees or customers who stayed away did so out of sympathy with the strikers. Second, the judges held sacrosanct the employer's right to control his enterprise. They believed that any demands or actions that interfered with the employer's right to set the terms of employment or hire whomever he chose amounted to nothing less than an effort to "subject the control" of the business to the "dictation" of a union. Control of the workplace was not merely an employer's prerogative but a "property right" that the state would protect. In addition to mediating conflicting rights between employer and employee, the law reinforced traditional workplace hierarchies.[68]

"A Barren and Impotent Right": Parkinson and Pierce, 1908–1909

Although *Jordahl* and *Goldberg* greatly restricted labor's methods of collective action, the California courts had yet to rule definitively on the questions of "purpose" and "method." According to both contemporaries and the first generation of labor law historians, state courts adopted either the "liberal" approach of New York, or the more "conservative" approach of Massachusetts.[69] The former, as we have seen, defined the legitimate "purposes" of strikers broadly and allowed for the possibility of peaceful picketing. The latter restricted a strike's legitimate interests to wage and hour disputes between an employer and his immediate employees and prohibited picketing as an inherently unlawful method. When the California courts finally addressed these matters, they opted for neither alternative entirely. In *Parkinson v. Building Trades Council of Santa Clara County* (1908) the California Supreme Court ruled that the purpose of a strike was immaterial as a determinant of its legality. Only California went so far as to disregard questions of purpose altogether, seemingly placing itself somewhere to the left of liberal New York. But the following year, in *Pierce v. Stablemen's Union* (1909), the same justices adopted the conservative reasoning of the Massachusetts courts that picketing was invariably a form of unlawful intimidation. Pierce allowed lower court judges to define the range of legal "methods" so narrowly as to make the unlimited right to strike recognized in *Parkinson* virtually meaningless.[70] In this way the California courts remained consistent with federal and other state courts: judges continued to set the boundaries of labor conflict, recognizing a formal right while restricting the means necessary to realize that right.

From the beginning *Parkinson* had the makings of an important case. Not only did lumber and tinning mill owner J. F. Parkinson head the Santa Clara County Citizen's Alliance, but the Building Trades Council secured a team of San Francisco lawyers headed by the well-known socialist and labor lawyer, Austin Lewis. Moreover, due to the absence of picketing on the part of the union, questions of "method"—which hinged on the meaning of such uncertain terms as "intimidation"—were eliminated. Instead, the case turned on a more narrow issue: in the absence of unlawful means, what constituted a lawful purpose?[71]

Despite his position as head of the local Citizen's Alliance and his open-shop sympathies, J. F. Parkinson had signed an agreement with the Santa Clara Building Trades Council to the effect that he would maintain a closed shop in his lumber mill.[72] When Parkinson hired a nonunion worker, the Building Trades Council reminded him that this violated the standing agreement. Parkinson, however, contended that the employee in question had purchased five shares of the company's stock (out of a total of 12,500 shares) and therefore was not an employee at all, but an employer. Such a small amount of stock, according to the union, did not make one an employer in any meaningful sense. As a result, union workers in Parkinson's mill went out on strike. In addition, the Building Trades Council notified the contractors who usually purchased materials from Parkinson that union members would not handle Parkinson's nonunion materials. Most of the contractors that had been put on notice by the Council terminated business with Parkinson until he adhered to the union contract. The union relied solely on the strike against Parkinson and the threatened labor boycott of the building contractors. At no time did the union maintain pickets near Parkinson's mill.[73]

In response, Parkinson requested an injunction on the grounds that the Building Trades Council had interfered with his constitutional right to run his business and unlawfully coerced the building contractors to violate existing purchasing agreements. Santa Clara Superior Court Judge Tuttle responded favorably to Parkinson's request, granting a temporary injunction against the boycott of the contractors. Tuttle then made the injunction permanent at a later hearing. When Judge Tuttle denied a request for a new trial, the Building Trades Council appealed to the California Supreme Court.

The *Parkinson* decision was the first California Supreme Court labor case not to end with a unanimous judgment. The Court voted six to one in favor of the union, but it did not offer a single majority opinion. Instead, the seven justices issued four separate opinions: three concurring, one dissenting. Chief Justice Beatty's leading decision affirmed the legality of the boycott and the closed-shop demand. In all, Beatty ruled on no less than fifteen points of law, all of which went in favor of the union.[74] Most importantly, however, Beatty ruled that where striking workers do not employ unlawful methods, "a bad motive" could not make their acts unlawful: "Without violence, threats, or intimidation . . . their motives must be held immaterial." Beatty then considered a number of British and American cases that had ruled on the "closed-shop" strike, giving particular attention to New York's *National Protective Association v. Cumming.* In upholding the closed-shop strike the New York court had held that "the right to strike is absolute, and no one may demand a reason for it." Yet in the same decision New York qualified this right with the phrase, "provided the object [of the strike] is not to gratify malice." But if "no one may demand a reason for it," Beatty wondered, how could the court know if the "object" of the strike was to "gratify malice?" If one could not demand a reason for a strike then one could not possibly know its motive or purpose. Beatty concluded, therefore, that California courts "would not inquire into the motives of the strikers."[75] Contrary to all other state courts, California rejected a consideration of purpose altogether.

Five of the other justices concurred with Beatty's judgment in favor of the union, with Justice Shaw filing the lone dissent. Shaw's dissent conceded that workers had an absolute right to strike, but he argued that a boycott, by its very nature, constituted unlawful means. According to Shaw, no matter how "peaceful" its explicit means to "induce" or "persuade," a boycott implicitly threatened economic injury to those who did not comply. Shaw noted that numbers alone (the Building Trades Council consisted of twenty-two member unions covering all of the building trades) made even the most polite request a form of coercion, for the contractor who did not comply "would be unable to carry on his business without substantial loss." According to Shaw, the Council sought to "control . . . another's conduct against his will" through means calculated to induce "fear." It made no difference, Shaw concluded, whether their actions produced fear of "pecuniary loss" or fear of "bodily injury." Yet Shaw believed that physical threats often lay close at hand, quoting a British decision to the effect that, in trade union disputes, what begins as "peaceable persuasion . . . generally does become peremptory ordering, with threats . . . of very unpleasant consequences to those who are not persuaded."[76]

Though only Shaw dissented, the concurring opinions showed that the other judges shared Shaw's concern that labor's methods of persuasion too often became coercion and intimidation. Justice Sloss, for example, agreed with Beatty's judgment in favor of the union, but he filed a concurring opinion to stress that the case at hand did not present "any of the features of violence . . . to be found in so many" labor disputes. Even though *Parkinson* did not involve questions of method, Sloss took the opportunity to give a broad definition of "intimidation" and to express his opinion that, unlike the case before them, most labor disputes led to violence or intimidation of some sort:

> There was here no effort to threaten or interfere by physical force . . . nor any intimidation—using the term "intimidation" as meaning an act tending to inspire fear or violence to person or property. One may . . . be put in fear of violence without the use of any word indicating an intent to resort to force. "Picketing," as practiced in labor disputes, may, and perhaps usually does, constitute an intimidation of the employees and patrons of [the employer]. So too words which . . . purport to express merely a request may be uttered in such a manner . . . as to convey to the hearer a plain threat that refusal to comply . . . will result in physical harm.[77]

Despite such caveats, California labor leaders viewed the *Parkinson* decision as an important victory. In its final issue of 1908 the *Labor Clarion* noted that the decision, coming as it did in late December, heralded good things for the New Year.[78] The article showed less concern for the legal content of the decision than for the fact that it marked a defeat of J. F. Parkinson and the Citizen's Alliance. Yet a number of factors should have tempered the author's optimism. First, each of the justices, whether concurring or in dissent, pointed out that the case did not consider methods and therefore in no way reversed the hostile *Goldberg* decision, with its broad and highly restrictive understanding of "intimidation." Second, while the court ruled six to one in favor of the

Building Trades Council, it did not speak with a single voice, offering no "majority" opinion. Finally, while Justice Shaw's dissent
suggested that he alone viewed the boycott as an unlawfully coercive method, the other members of the court agreed more than
disagreed with his views on "intimidation" and his conviction
that, in labor disputes, the most innocent persuasion often mush-
roomed into threats, coercion, and even outright violence.[79] The
author of the *Labor Clarion* article may have rightly predicted that
Parkinson hinted at what the New Year would bring, but he or she
would have been surprised by the way that it did so.

The following year, the high court's ruling in *Pierce v Stablemen's
Union* (1909) demonstrated that *Parkinson* fell far short of labor's
expectations.[80] In his majority opinion Justice Frederick Henshaw acknowledged labor's formal right to strike regardless of purpose.[81] He then, however, turned to the issue of "picketing" and
the questions of method that *Parkinson* had not addressed. Henshaw reaffirmed that strikers could advertise their boycott through
"fair publication and fair oral or written persuasion." They may,
he continued, in seeming contradiction to *Goldberg,* engage in
"moral intimidation." However, according to Henshaw, picketing inevitably went beyond "fair publication" and oral persuasion.
Even where the pickets "do not engage in any express words or acts
of threats and intimidation," Henshaw reasoned, equity courts
may properly intervene. For no matter "how artful the means," the
intent and effect of a picket line was always to injure an employer's
business through "physical molestation and physical fear to the
employer, to those . . . who may seek employment from him, and
to the general public." In other words, there was no such thing as
peaceful picketing.[82]

Henshaw concluded that the right to strike must be balanced
against the employer's "right to do business" and the nonunion
worker's right to pursue a calling free from the "molestation" of
pickets. Drawing a link between picketing and unwanted social
disorder, Henshaw claimed that the picket line also violated the
"public's rights," for picketing "naturally" incited "crowds, riots,
and disturbances of the peace," which were "always imminent and

of frequent occurrence." As to the 1903 anti-injunction law, Henshaw made explicit what had only been strongly implied in the *Goldberg* ruling: the 1903 law was "void and unconstitutional."[83]

While the court unanimously agreed with Henshaw's judgment in favor of the employer, Justices Angelotti, Sloss, and Shaw wrote concurring opinions. Angelotti and Sloss agreed that, in the case before the court, the pickets had engaged in threats and intimidation. But they did not want to go as far as Henshaw: "So far as 'picketing' is concerned . . . we are not prepared to hold that there may not be acts within that term . . . that are entirely lawful and should not be enjoined."[84] Justice Shaw, who had filed the lone dissent in *Parkinson*, believed that Henshaw had not gone far enough. Shaw agreed, of course, that the injunction should be upheld. But as he had in the earlier case, Shaw argued that a boycott always coerced and intimidated, and it should be enjoined even if not accompanied by picketing.[85] While the court's majority did not go this far, they had effectively outlawed, or at least drastically undermined, the few economic weapons that organized workers possessed.

Lucile Eaves, a Berkeley labor economist who authored a 1908 study of California labor law, clearly understood the legal dilemmas faced by organized labor in her time. Though Eaves completed her study before the California Supreme Court issued its major opinions in *Parkinson* and *Pierce*, she anticipated the direction that the court would take. According to Eaves, "[labor] actions enjoined are not generally those of the small group . . . but those which enlist the sympathy of the public, or of a large group of organized workers."[86] Thus, while the high court found nothing objectionable in the tactics of the Building Trades Council in the *Parkinson* case (which did not involve picketing or a public appeal for a boycott), they found the more publicly visible picketing and boycott in *Pierce* beyond the bounds of legal persuasion. Thus the well-established building tradesmen, who could forgo picketing and rely on their unique skills and organizational solidarity to bring employers into line, were less likely to face injunctions. Less skilled workers, on the other hand, found that the highly visible collective actions that were their only source of power did not muster judicial approval.

Eaves also understood that formal rights meant little when the courts restricted the means necessary to realize those rights. "The right of peaceful persuasion is allowed," Eaves wrote the year before the *Pierce* ruling denied even this right, "though the value of this concession is not great, since the means and opportunities for persuasion are held subject to injunction." Eaves concluded that court restrictions had been so great that it was "easier to state the few remaining forms of trade union activity . . . still [permitted], than attempt a summary of prohibited actions."[87] California labor leaders agreed that the formal right to strike meant little if judges were still free to prohibit the actions that necessarily accompanied a strike. As an editorial in the *Labor Clarion* noted, "Without the right to picket . . . the right of the modern workingman to organize with his fellows is . . . a barren and impotent right."[88]

In short, the California courts recognized a formal right to strike regardless of purpose while at the same time restricting the means by which trade unionists might realize that right. The California experience, therefore, raises questions about Daniel Ernst's recent claim that the first two decades of the twentieth century witnessed "a remarkable change . . . in the law of strikes and boycotts in the United States." By the time America had entered World War I, Ernst contends, "organized labor had acquired a much surer footing in the law." While Ernst convincingly demonstrates that "the leading edge of American legal thought" accepted labor combinations as a legitimate expression of group solidarity, his own evidence suggests that most judges lagged far behind that leading edge.[89] Moreover, even when judges did recognize that unions were legitimate institutions with *formal* rights, as they did in the *Parkinson* case, they placed severe restrictions on the "methods" that labor could employ during a strike or boycott. Any claim that labor's legal status had greatly improved during the Progressive era would have surprised most California labor leaders.

CONCLUSION: IDEOLOGICAL IMPLICATIONS
OF THE LABOR INJUNCTION

From labor's perspective, the full impact of the injunction could not be measured by the number or percentage of strikes enjoined. To begin with, waves of injunctions came during key strikes and at those times when the California labor movement had made, or were threatening to make, organizational advances. Injunctions were not arbitrarily sought by individual employers concerned with a single strike, but by *organized* employers who used the injunction as a weapon in a larger campaign against unionism.[90] But there is still more. Injunctions reinforced the employer's authority while simultaneously denying legitimacy to labor's only source of power, collective action. As E. P. Thompson has noted, the law is both a set of coercive institutions and, as importantly, an ideology—that is, a more or less coherent set of values and assumptions that seek to explain (and usually justify) social relations and the distribution of power that goes along with those relations. Though it most often reinforced existing power relations, Thompson noted, the language of the law was still malleable enough to permit the less powerful to assert alternative values and assumptions.[91]

Henry White, a labor organizer and later a federal labor mediator, was a keen observer of the values and assumptions that lay beneath the contests between workers and employers. In 1904 White observed that the much-discussed "labor problem" of his day centered on "the question of the employer's authority." In direct opposition to the employer's "right . . . to manage his business as he pleases," his organized employees demanded "the right to be consulted as to the conditions of work."[92] White recognized that labor's demands reflected not only a desire for higher wages, but also for a degree of "workers' control." For a labor movement confronting large-scale industrialization and the introduction of mass production techniques, salvaging a degree of workers' control was paramount. In the modern workplace, however, control of the production process increasingly shifted to employers or "manage-

ment."[93] As the "labor problem" became a question of competing rights, the struggle for workers' control moved from the shop
floor to the courtroom—before judges much more accustomed to,
and comfortable with, employers' control. In large measure, the
employer's control and authority were rooted in his ownership of
property and its accompanying rights.[94] But the employer's authority had still more ancient roots in the law of master and servant. As
Karen Orren, Christopher Tomlins, and Amy Dru Stanley have
shown, even "liberal" labor law at times treated the employment
relationship as one of master and servant. According to Orren,
the two key principles of master and servant law were *hierarchy* and
protection—that is, not only was the employment relationship one
of domination and subordination, but that relationship was protected from "outside" interference. Remnants of master and servant law—a "belated feudalism," as Orren calls it—informed judicial reasoning on labor matters well into the twentieth century.
Treatise writers may have construed the employment relation in
terms of a liberal theory of contract, but judges employed doctrines
rooted in much older, indeed medieval, structures of thought.[95]

So it was in California that the legal order of master and servant
saturated the debate over the injunction. Employers turned to the
courts not only to protect property—though they certainly did
do that—but to protect the authority that they saw as a natural
extension of ownership. Whenever they petitioned the court for
restraining orders, employers assumed as a matter of course that
they enjoyed an absolute right to run their workplaces as they
saw fit. When organized workers attempted to shape workplace
conditions—especially to have a say in who was hired—they were
at best "arrogant" and at worst attempting to "subject control
of the business to the dictation of a union," a phrase which, in
some form or another, appeared in almost every complaint for
a restraining order. After the *Parkinson* ruling the injunction in
California no longer turned on the object of labor's demands;
according to the *Goldberg* and *Pierce* rulings, the employer's "right
to do business" included a right to "control" that business free from
outside "interference."[96]

Judicial opposition to "interference" with the employment relationship at times rested quite explicitly upon the doctrines of
master and servant law. Nowhere were the remnants of judicial
feudalism more apparent than in a 1901 injunction issued by San
Francisco Superior Court Judge Max Sloss (who later went on to
the California Supreme Court). In support of a sweeping injunction that banned all picketing by striking culinary workers, Judge
Sloss invoked the feudal "enticement" doctrine, which made ac-
tionable "the enticement of a wife from her husband, a child from
its parent [or guardian], or of a servant from his master." According to Sloss, asking employees not to cross a picket line was the
equivalent of "enticing" a servant away from his master. In the
eyes of the law, Sloss made clear, the "plaintiff and his employees
bear the relation known to the law as that of master and servant,
and one who . . . induces his servants to leave him violates one
of the plaintiff's legal rights." Even when injunctions did not explicitly invoke the enticement doctrine, they sometimes implied
a feudal relationship. As the Sailors' Union's Andrew Furuseth
argued, whenever the courts treated picketing as an interference
with "property rights," they assumed that the employer had a property interest in the employment relationship. As William Forbath has put it more recently, the broad definition of property
rights amounted to a "re-feudalization" of the employment relationship.[97]

The ideological consequences of the injunction did not stop
at the legitimacy it lent to the employer's assertion of authority
or the implication that the employer/master had a property interest in his employee/servant. Of equal damage were the ubiquitous
portrayals of labor's methods as inherent forms of "coercion" and
"intimidation" that often, if not always, led to violence and social
disorder. As Dianne Avery has shown in a study of federal injunctions, judges evoked "images of violence" by equating the *economic*
coercion and intimidation of boycotts and picketing with images
of *physical* coercion and intimidation. These images of coercion,
intimidation, and violence found their way into newspapers and
other public forums, prompting Samuel Gompers to complain that

ONE ARM FREE!

Labor turned to political action in order to free itself from the restraints of the injuction. Illustration by Baer from *Labor Age*, October 1922, p. 10.

the language of the injunction "disfigured" labor in the court of public opinion. So too did California labor leaders bemoan the "psychological" impact of legal interventions that portrayed labor as "bad, wicked, and evil," while portraying employers as "gentle babes" whom the law must protect from "malevolent" strikers.[98]

In order to combat both the instrumental and the ideological effects of the labor injunction, the California labor movement turned once again to politics. This turn might seem surprising, for in some ways the California experience supports the claims of William Forbath and Victoria Hattam that court hostility could dampen labor's political enthusiasm by demonstrating the futility of politics. Injunctions, after all, nullified the political control that San Francisco labor had won over the police, and the courts

Y. American.
Robbing the Eagle's Nest

Labor expressed its objection to the labor injunction in a traditional language of rights—in this case, the First Amendment rights of free speech, press, and assembly. Illustration from *Labor Age*, January 1923, p. 25.

easily struck down the 1903 anti-injunction act that the CFL had considered one of its earliest and most important political victories. Why would they still have any faith in politics? Yet for state and local labor leaders in California, court hostility caused not a retreat from politics, but a political readjustment. At the 1909 CFL convention, Paul Scharrenberg implored delegates to resist the injunction. One way they could do so, he said, was by simply "ignoring . . . injunctions, holding themselves ready to take such consequences as may befall."[99] Another way, Scharrenberg advised the following year, was to place a new, and more judicially

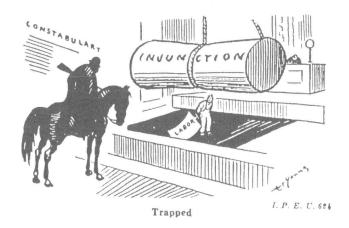

Trapped

I. P. E. U. 62

Labor, apparently in a court of law, is trapped between the injunction and the police. Illustration by Art Young in *Labor Age*, February 1922, p. 13.

resistant, anti-injunction bill at the top of the CFL's list of legislative demands. As the newly elected Executive Secretary of the CFL, Scharrenberg would oversee that lobbying effort. We now turn to labor's political struggle to defeat the pernicious implications of "judge-made law."

Chapter 3

LABOR'S ANTI-INJUNCTION BILLS IN A PROGRESSIVE LEGISLATURE, 1910–1916

That organized labor has been the leader in this country in progressive thought cannot be denied, and that organized labor is still in advance of other economic organizations in its advocacy of legislation which will one day redound to the benefit of all those who are today victims of unfair and unjust conditions, there can be no room for doubt.

EDITORIAL,
Labor Clarion, 1913

During the first decade of the twentieth century the courts had frustrated labor's political efforts. When the San Francisco labor movement gained political control over local police, employers turned to the courts for injunctions; when the CFL won an anti-injunction bill in 1903, the California Supreme Court struck it down. But these setbacks did not cause labor in California to give up on political action. Indeed, both the practical and the ideological burdens of the injunction made political action all the more necessary. Foregoing any third-party challenge at the state level, organized labor instead took advantage of Progressive-era political changes and adopted the techniques of interest-group politics. This approach may have been nonpartisan, but it was neither apolitical nor antistatist, as labor sought to curb the power of courts while at the same time pursuing positive state reforms that defy the usual definitions of "voluntarism." Efforts to limit the state's role in labor disputes, as we shall see, did not dictate that labor oppose state intervention more generally.

This chapter examines how both legal hostility and progressive political changes shaped labor's political strategy; how the anti-injunction campaign revealed the political and ideological limits of labor's alliance with the California Progressives; and how labor sought to limit the state's role in labor disputes while at the same time expanding its role in other areas. In so doing, labor constructed an alternative understanding of law and the state that challenged progressive allies and judicial adversaries alike. In California a politically active and pro-statist labor movement rejected the "court-minted ideology" of injunction judges for its own more "modern" and "progressive"—albeit racially exclusive—understanding of law and the proper role of the state.

LABOR'S "PROGRESSIVE" APPROACH TO POLITICS

The more historians study the Progressive era, it seems, the less certain they become as to what distinguishes it as an *era* and what the central concept of *progressivism* means. While Peter Filene's call for "an obituary for the Progressive movement" did not lay the topic to rest, it nevertheless forced historians to confront the fact that there was no unified Progressive movement, outlook, or profile.[1] Since Filene's 1970 essay, the problem he identified has only become worse: the term "progressive" has been applied to so many varied groups and movements of the early twentieth century that one can no longer state with certainty who the progressives were, what motivated them, or what they accomplished. All we can say is that the Progressive era—roughly the first two decades of the twentieth century—witnessed a proliferation of political, economic, social, and moral reform movements: to combat urban political corruption; to regulate an emerging corporate industrial economy; to improve the living and working conditions of the masses; to assimilate "new immigrants"; and to eradicate the evils of urban vice. In short, in the Progressive era many Americans, armed with a faith in progress and human reason, organized themselves into groups and called upon government (to varying degrees) to address the matrix of social problems associated with industrialization, urbanization, and immigration.[2]

How and where does organized labor fit into the history and historiography of the Progressive era? Even while recognizing the diversity of progressivism, many historians have identified the era's reform efforts with the white, native-born, and Protestant middle- to upper-classes. According to Richard Hofstadter's classic account, the progressives were members of an older, upper-middle-class (lawyers, doctors, newspapermen, middling-sized businessmen) who feared that they were losing status to emerging forms of organized power—whether it be the new urban "political machine," huge corporate enterprises, or organized labor.[3] While Hofstadter's "status anxiety" thesis has fallen out of fashion, a recent synthesis nonetheless finds that "the spirit and methods of Progressivism unquestionably emanated from the native-born, urban middle to upper-middle classes" and that "the Progressive ethos" was "rooted in evangelical Protestantism."[4] Of course one has always found dissenters from this view. New Left historians, for example, attributed progressive reforms not to a status-anxious middle class, but to enlightened capitalists who furtively sought to save capitalism by removing its worst abuses.[5] The highly influential "organizational synthesis" understood progressivism as a process of Weberian "rationalization" and "modernization," as America evolved from an agrarian nation of "island communities" into a centralized, bureaucratic, industrial society.[6] In all of these versions labor appears not as an actor, but as something acted upon. While the "labor question" loomed large in the Progressive era, labor and the working classes most often appear as the object of reform in Progressive-era historiography.[7]

Though the historiography of California progressivism has in many ways mirrored scholarly debates on progressivism more generally, California historians have devoted much more attention to the relationship between organized labor and progressivism. George Mowry's seminal study—which greatly influenced Hofstadter's view of progressivism—found an antagonistic relationship between a California labor movement that sought to increase its political and economic power on the one hand, and middle-class reformers who feared that modern industrial society threatened traditional standards of morality on the other. Reformers looked to a past—either real or imagined—in which men of good standing governed wisely for the common good. They viewed organized labor much as they viewed corporate titans like the Southern Pacific Railroad; that is, as "monopolists" who pursued "class interest" at the expense of the "public interest." Progressives especially feared labor leaders who spoke a language of class conflict at odds with the progressive dream of class harmony.[8]

Later historians claimed that Mowry overlooked the high degree of cooperation between organized labor and progressives in California. They pointed, in particular, to California's 1911 and 1913 state legislative sessions, which passed a flurry of progressive labor laws endorsed by organized labor and reformers alike.[9] In addition, voting studies show that the California working class supported many (but certainly not all) reform candidates and measures.[10] Both the older and newer interpretations contain important truths. It is clear, for example, that many progressive reformers distrusted and opposed the power of organized labor (though these reformers included both large and small businessmen as well as the "middle class"). Yet it is equally true that labor frequently received support and cooperation from progressive reformers, and because of this many progressive politicians won labor's official endorsements and working-class votes at election time.[11]

As important as the nature of the relationship between labor and progressivism, however, were the institutional changes wrought by progressivism. In California as elsewhere, Progressive-era political reforms created what Walter Dean Burnham has called "new rules of the game."[12] Progressive political reforms weakened political parties and strengthened the hand of organized interest groups in the policy-making process. Through various forms of "direct democracy" (the direct primary; the initiative, referendum, and recall; and the direct election of U.S. Senators) reformers diminished the power of party bosses to select candidates and set the legislative agenda. Especially in California and the West, the creation of "nonpartisan" offices and "cross-filing" (a system that allowed candidates to file with more than one party) either eliminated or greatly reduced the significance of party labels at election time.[13] Finally, an array of appointed government commissions created a policy-making arena one step removed from partisan and electoral pressures. While it is possible to overstate the decline of the political party, Progressive-era political reforms created channels through which well-organized interest groups circumvented the parties and lobbied directly for policies that suited their interests.[14] The new rules of the game rewarded interest group politics, while making partisan and electoral politics—whether through alliances with major parties or the creation of third parties—more difficult and less fruitful.

Adapting to the new rules of the game, California labor leaders hoped to use the power of organization to effect a legal environment more conducive to trade unionism. Formed in 1901, the California Federation of Labor (CFL) quickly emerged as the central lobbying group for organized labor in the state, and lobbying became its primary function. As a clearinghouse for labor's political demands, the CFL posed questions to all candidates and published their responses, published the voting records of state legislators, and, most important, sent lobbyists to the state legislature in Sacramento.[15] During the Progressive era such methods produced results, and the 1911 and 1913 state legislative sessions became the most fruitful in labor's history. Although CFL lobbyists mainly focused on defending the rights and interests of trade unions, the organization's most important legislative victories benefitted both organized and unorganized workers: it won employer liability and workmen's compensation laws; an eight-hour law for women; the creation of various state commissions to investigate, regulate, and report on workplace conditions; a Labor Camp Sanitation Act; restrictions on child labor; laws regulating private employment agencies; state-funded employment bureaus; and the creation of county "public defender" offices to provide legal counsel for the poor. In addition to this quite "statist" legislative bonanza, Progressive Governor Hiram Johnson appointed several former trade unionists to positions on the new state regulatory and policy-making commissions.[16] In this more favorable political climate, and having learned the new rules of the political game, the CFL drafted an anti-injunction bill that it hoped would withstand judicial scrutiny and curb the power of the courts.

TWO VIEWS OF THE STATE:
ANTI-INJUNCTION VS. ARBITRATION

Introduced by Senator Anthony Caminetti of Jackson, California, a mining district in Amador County with a significant working-class constituency, labor's 1911 anti-injunction bill responded directly to one of the most objectionable aspects of injunction law: the broad definition of "property" that allowed judges to intervene almost at will. Caminetti's bill prohibited injunctions in disputes between employer and employee "unless necessary to prevent irreparable damage to property." Since courts already issued injunctions only to prevent irreparable damage to property, this last clause would have made the bill little more than a restatement of existing law. To prevent this possibility, the Caminetti bill provided a more limited definition of "property": "[S]uch property right must be particularly described . . . and for the purposes of this act no right to continue the relation of employer and employee, or to assume or create such relation . . . or to carry on business of any particular kind shall be construed, held, considered, or treated as property or constituting a property right."[17] In short, "property" would refer only to existing or tangible assets, not to the employer's relationship with his employees or customers. The "right to do business" and to have access to customers or replacement workers did not constitute a property right within the meaning of the act. By restricting the definition of property, Caminetti's bill also challenged the most objectionable assumption of judge-made law: that the employer had a property interest in the employment relation and, by extension, in his employees.[18]

A slim majority on the Senate Judiciary Committee reported the bill out of committee with a favorable recommendation. Six committee members, however, signed a minority report holding that the bill's redefinition of "property" went beyond the proper powers of the legislature. They claimed that the "right to carry on business" had been recognized since "time immemorial" and was "as dear to all Anglo-Saxon people as the right of life and liberty itself."[19] Only a broad definition of property, the bill's opponents believed, could ensure the employer's control of his business. When the bill finally reached the floor of the Senate, it passed by four votes. But Senator Lee Gates of Los Angeles, one of the bill's leading opponents, invoked an arcane Senate procedure that mandated attendance of all forty members to vote on reconsideration. Although Gates's delaying tactics kept the senators locked in chambers all through the night, the full Senate passed the bill by a narrow margin the next day and sent it on to the Assembly.[20]

Labor's bill met a less favorable fate in the Assembly, where the Judiciary Committee delayed its consideration until the last day of the session. According to a report in the *Los Angeles Times*, Governor Johnson opposed the bill and asked Assemblyman Bohnett of Santa Clara, who looked after the administration's interests in the Assembly, to keep the bill buried until the last day. After a vote to give the measure emergency consideration failed, labor's anti-injunction bill died with the end of the legislative session.[21] Labor leaders thought it a "mystery" that the bill did not pass in the Assembly, since that body was generally more friendly to labor than the Senate. The labor press did not comment on the reports that Governor Johnson had stalled the bill, and instead praised Johnson for his overall support of labor's measures and concluded that the bill failed only because it had reached the Assembly too late. Organized labor remained hopeful and vowed to begin the process much earlier at the next session.[22]

When the legislature next convened in 1913, CFL agents quickly introduced three separate bills to restrain the courts. In addition to the anti-injunction bill, they submitted one bill that made peaceful picketing lawful and another demanding that those charged with contempt of court for violating a labor injunction be granted a jury trial.[23] Labor lobbyists hoped that if the anti-injunction bill failed, legalizing peaceful picketing might serve

the same effect, since virtually all injunctions in California targeted even peaceful picketing.[24] On other fronts labor lobbyists
enjoyed yet another successful legislative session in 1913, but all
of the efforts to curb the power of the courts failed once again.[25]
C. H. McConaughy, a lobbyist for the San Francisco Labor Council, reported that the anti-injunction bill died in the Assembly
committee because certain "progressive members" wanted a substitute bill that expunged the restrictive definition of property.
McConaughy feared that any law that did not redefine property
would leave both picketing and boycotts subject to restraining
orders, and the substitute bill died in Committee as well. In his
final report to the San Francisco Labor Council, McConaughy
could only express perplexity as to why labor's usual allies opposed
labor's anti-injunction measure.[26]

Although not as successful as the previous two rounds, the 1915
legislative session once again witnessed important labor victories, and once again the anti-injunction bill did duty as labor's
most conspicuous failure.[27] CFL Secretary Paul Scharrenberg had
hoped that the 1914 Clayton Act, passed by Congress to exempt
labor from anti-trust laws, would set a precedent for the CFL bill
and sweep "aside the fine spun web carefully woven by corporation lawyers and given legal sanction by our injunction judges."[28]
Instead, the Senate Judiciary Committee proposed amending the
anti-injunction bill so that strikes and picketing would be free
from the threat of an injunction only if it could be shown that
labor had exhausted "all peaceful means" to resolve the dispute.
Andrew Furuseth of the Sailor's Union expressed labor's opposition to any amendment that allowed judges to define "all peaceful
means"; moreover, the amendment implied that strikes and picketing were not themselves "peaceful means." It hardly mattered,
however, as the 1915 bill never left committee. After placing the
anti-injunction bill at the top of its agenda for three consecutive
legislative sessions, labor had encountered the limits of the labor-
Progressive alliance.

Why did the anti-injunction bills fail when labor had managed
to win so many other pro-labor measures from California's pro-

gressive legislature? Labor attributed this failure to the "double-headed actions of some Progressives." A CFL report claimed that the defeats threw "a powerful light on the heterogeneous elements composing the leadership of the state Progressive Party" and wondered about the "Assemblymen who were with us on every other labor bill [but] failed us when this one was brought before them." Paul Scharrenberg noted that, as usual, much of the opposition came from Southern California, but he cautioned workers to beware of any politician who took the label "progressive" in an attempt to win working-class votes. The true test of a progressive, the *Labor Clarion* later contended, was where he or she stood on labor issues.[29]

A quick look at the Senate votes for the 1911 and 1913 legislative sessions bears out many of labor's assumptions. In both sessions all but one member of the San Francisco delegation voted for the anti-injunction bill, while all but one of the senators from Santa Barbara southward voted against the bill. Many labor bills followed this pattern. But the San Francisco and Southern California delegations together made up less than half of the Senate, so the success of the bill depended on the ability of the San Francisco and Southern California legislators to bring members from the rest of the state to their respective positions. As such, Southern California votes alone did not defeat the anti-injunction bill. Given the narrow margins in the votes on the anti-injunction and related bills, had lawmakers from South of the Tehachapi mountain range given their support, the bills would have passed. But this does not explain why the anti-injunction bills alone failed to pass, for labor's other important measures passed despite consistent opposition from Southern California.[30]

A closer look at the voting records suggests that the anti-injunction bill failed because it lost the support of those senators with impeccable records as "progressives" and better than average records as "friends of labor" on all labor issues other than the anti-injunction bill. For example, in his reports on the legislative sessions the progressive political journalist Franklin Hichborn listed the votes of all legislators on a number of "progressive" test votes. An analysis of Hichborn's data shows that those who voted against the anti-injunction bill in both 1911 and 1913 voted in favor of "progressive" reforms more often than did senators as a whole. More interesting are the votes of seven senators who sided with labor leaders more than 50 percent of the time (including four who voted with labor 70 to 75 percent of the time), but who voted against them on the anti-injunction bill in 1913. Each of these senators voted overwhelmingly in favor of progressive issues, and five had perfect records. In all, Hichborn's tables show that the progressive Senate of 1913 voted at a ratio of approximately 4:1 in favor of progressive measures. But those who voted against the labor injunction voted 7:1 in favor of progressive measures, and the seven "friends of labor" who went against labor on the anti-injunction bill voted at a ratio of 27:1 in favor of progressive issues.[31] In short, the anti-injunction bills failed because they did not receive the support of those progressives who supported labor most of the time.

Outside of the state capital the bill drew similar patterns of support and opposition. Harrison Gray Otis's Los Angeles Times, with the usual hyperbole it displayed on labor matters, predicted that "the proposed anarchical anti-injunction law" would lead to the "legal destruction of industrial freedom by inviting picketing, boycotting, and other forms of disorder."[32] Yet it was not only militant open-shop advocates like Otis who feared the anti-injunction bill. As Paul Scharrenberg noted, while progressive reformers from Southern California supported most "political" reforms, they "voted against the most meritorious economic reform measures, so long as the same originated from labor." As with the lawmakers, Southern California progressives outside of government, even some of those who supported labor on other issues, very much opposed the anti-injunction bill. E. T. Earl and Edward Dickson, publisher and editor, respectively, for the progressive Los Angeles Express, opposed the bill as "class legislation." Meyer Lissner, a leading Los Angeles progressive, informed Hiram Johnson that he would rather give up the whole progressive program than pass the anti-injunction bill and allow Los Angeles to become another labor stronghold like San Francisco.[33]

Given that most injunctions were issued in Northern California up to this point, the especially strong opposition to the anti-injunction bill from Southern California might seem odd. In part Southern California's opposition must be understood in the context of its overall opposition to organized labor. But even those few Angeleno lawmakers who voted with labor most of the time opposed the anti-injunction bill. Some Southern Californians—while clearly mistaken in their assessment that the anti-injunction bill was aimed at them—feared that the anti-injunction legislation might cast doubt on the legality of anti-picketing ordinances that had passed in Los Angeles and San Diego. Moreover, at the time of the first anti-injunction bill, Los Angeles was still in the midst of a disruptive metal trades strike and only a few months removed from the explosion of the *Times* building. Angelenos were determined to allow no act that might subject their city to the same union "dictation" that plagued San Francisco.[34]

Yet it would be unfair to lay blame, as labor leaders frequently did, entirely at the door of Southern Californians. Just as the bill failed to win the support of progressives inside the legislature, it also failed to earn the backing of progressive spokesmen outside of the legislature, North or South. Chester Rowell, progressive editor of both the *Fresno Republican* and the weekly *California Outlook*, publicly opposed the bill and privately asked Hiram Johnson to veto the measure if it passed. The bill also failed to receive support from such leading progressive voices as C. K. McClatchy's *Sacramento Bee*. Nor did Sacramento's Harris Weinstock, the quintessential "businessman-reformer" and one of the state's most progressive voices on a variety of reforms advocated by organized labor, support the bill. Fremont Older's *San Francisco Bulletin*, alone among the state's progressive newspapers, endorsed the anti-injunction bill.[35]

Finally, the anti-injunction bill never won the support of that most important of pro-labor progressives, Governor Hiram Johnson. The labor press praised Johnson for his tireless support and gave him much of the credit for their legislative success on other issues. Urban working-class voters, who had been cool to Johnson

in 1910, apparently approved of the governor's first term and provided a key base of support for his re-election in 1914.[36] C. W. Mc-
Conaughy, the labor lobbyist for the San Francisco Labor Council,
even suggested that Johnson was the key to winning the support
of other progressives. If Johnson ever left, McConaughy claimed,
"Labor will learn that the Progressive Party . . . is no more favorable to labor than the old standpat Republicans." But apparently
even Johnson's pro-labor sympathies had limits, for the governor
remained silent on the injunction issue. Paul Scharrenberg, who
had been more exuberant in his praise for Johnson than anyone,
in later years corroborated reports made at the time in the *Los Angeles Times* that Johnson had worked behind the scenes to defeat
the bill. In an interview in 1954—long after Johnson's death and
Scharrenberg's retirement from public life—Scharrenberg admitted that Johnson supported everything labor wanted "except that
anti-injunction bill." Johnson did not "make a public utterance,"
Scharrenberg recalled, "but he told me 'That's going too far . . .
I can't see that.'" Just as the *Times* had reported in 1911, Scharrenberg revealed that Johnson and Al McCabe, the governor's
key liaison with the legislature, "lined up enough votes in the Assembly (which was supposed to be ours) to kill our bill . . . It was
killed from the office of the Governor . . ."[37] The governor, like
so many other progressive friends of labor, consistently opposed
the anti-injunction bill.

Why did usually pro-labor progressives—be they legislators,
editors, or the governor—oppose the anti-injunction bill? Despite wide areas of agreement, organized labor and most of California's progressive reformers had opposing views on how the
state should respond to industrial conflict. Nowhere were these
opposing views more apparent than in the debates over the
Weinstock Arbitration Bill, the progressive alternative to labor's
anti-injunction bills. Harris Weinstock, owner of a Sacramento
department store, was a leading California reformer and served
on several Progressive-era commissions at the state and national
level. As a "Special Labor Commissioner" for the governor, Weinstock had studied labor relations in other countries, and he

strongly advocated the systems of government arbitration that he had encountered on his fact-finding journey.

In 1911 Weinstock drafted a bill based on the Canadian Lemieux Act, which called for arbitration in all public utility strikes on the grounds that such strikes upset normal business routines and directly affected the "public interest." The Weinstock bill made strikes and lockouts illegal during the arbitration process. In the event of a strike, the governor would assemble a three-person arbitration board with one member selected by labor, another by the employer, and a third "public" member selected jointly. If the two sides could not agree on a third party within three days, the governor would appoint one. The board could not issue binding decisions, but Weinstock hoped that fear of negative public opinion would prevent either side from rejecting a fair and "neutral" settlement. While the bill applied only to public utilities and municipal railroads, both supporters and opponents saw the bill as a first step toward some system of government arbitration of all labor disputes, public or private. The Weinstock Arbitration Bill first went down to defeat in the same Senate session that the 1911 anti-injunction bill passed its first hurdle (only to die later in the Assembly). With only two exceptions, all senators who voted in favor of one opposed the other.[38]

The anti-injunction and arbitration bills reflected contrasting views on the proper role of the state in labor disputes and, as such, revealed the ideological limits of labor's alliance with the California progressives. Harris Weinstock and his fellow progressive reformers and publicists accepted that both labor and capital enjoyed the right to organize; indeed, they believed that the organization of both had helped to facilitate material progress. But they also held that labor and capital must exercise their rights "with moderation and regard for the common welfare."[39] Because prolonged strikes and lockouts inconvenienced "the public"—whom Weinstock believed also had rights—the state had a responsibility to intervene. Government, progressives assumed, could broker a neutral settlement that respected the rights and interests of all three parties to the dispute: labor, capital, and the public.

In this sense, the arbitration board would act much like the various Progressive-era government commissions that, in theory, transcended "class interests" to serve the broader "public interest."

Like organized labor, Weinstock opposed reliance upon local courts and police to manage labor disputes, but for different reasons. Whenever courts and police intervened they always took one side over another, Weinstock claimed, convincing the losing side that the legal system was stacked against it: "Labor is likely to contend, when decisions are rendered against it, that the court has been . . . bought up by the power of capital; and capital is likely to feel, when decisions are rendered against it, that the court has been intimidated by labor, or to get votes, has toadied to labor." This, according to Weinstock, dangerously undermined the authority of the courts and of government more generally.[40]

Weinstock's arbitration bill enjoyed the backing of many of the state's leading businessmen and corporations. John Britton, Vice-President and General Manager of Pacific Gas and Electric (PG&E), supported an even stronger system of arbitration and called for an absolute ban on strikes by public utility workers. As he testified before the United States Commission on Industrial Relations in 1914, Britton believed that local courts and police had failed to adequately manage labor disputes. Denied police protection in San Francisco, Britton complained that his company had to rely on often incompetent private guards, and he thought that injunctions "were not very often effective" since striking workers frequently found ways of circumventing them. Britton, like Los Angeles foundry owner Fred Baker, supported "compulsory arbitration" with binding decisions, whereas Weinstock's bill called only for "compulsory investigation," relying upon the board ruling in combination with the pressure of public opinion. Although some employers were dubious about state arbitration, within a few years the driving force behind an arbitration law would shift from moderately pro-labor progressives like Weinstock to the state's anti-labor, open-shop Chambers of Commerce.[41]

Organized labor opposed arbitration bills with as much energy as it demanded anti-injunction bills.[42] In presenting labor's position, Walter Macarthur of the San Francisco Labor Council put forward both specific and general objections to Weinstock's arbitration bill. Labor suspected—correctly, it seems—that Weinstock saw the bill as a first step toward arbitration of private as well as public strikes. In addition, labor opposed the provision that allowed the governor to appoint the third board member. So long as Hiram Johnson served as governor, labor could expect a fair appointment. But some future, less sympathetic governor might appoint an enemy of labor to that all-important third position.[43] Finally, labor contended that mandatory arbitration was simply unnecessary. Many trade unions and employer associations had already established mechanisms for voluntary mediation and arbitration. Moreover, as the SFLC's Andrew Gallagher noted, "the public"—whom the bill allegedly protected—only took notice of industrial relations when there was a strike or lockout, not realizing that the vast majority of the time employers and unions reached agreements without recourse to strikes or lockouts. Trade unionism and collective bargaining was itself a form of private mediation and arbitration.[44]

Macarthur also attacked the arbitration bill on the progressives' own terms, stressing the harm that might come to the state itself. If Weinstock had supported arbitration out of fear that biased court and police intervention discredited state authority, MaCarthur predicted that biased arbitration would produce the same result. The arbitration bill was "dangerous," Macarthur argued, because it would "create discontent and distrust on the part of the workingmen toward the State, and if enforced would lead to revolt inspired by a sense of injustice." Playing to the worst fears of the progressives, Macarthur warned that in the end "the system would break down . . . and thus bring the State into contempt and ridicule."[45]

Labor's insistence upon calling Weinstock's measure a "compulsory" arbitration bill, even though the board's rulings would not have been binding, highlighted one of labor's more general objections. Weinstock objected to this frequent characterization of his bill, pointing out repeatedly that, like the Canadian system, it called only for "compulsory investigation." But to labor it *was* compulsory in the sense that striking workers had no choice but to submit to arbitration. An even greater problem, from labor's perspective, was that the bill banned strikes during the period of arbitration. Labor feared that temporarily suspending strike actions would have the same effect as the "temporary" injunction, allowing employers to prepare the means (especially by recruiting strikebreakers) for a prolonged strike should the board's ruling prove unsatisfactory to the employer.

But even had the board succeeded as a practical matter, Macarthur insisted, the state could never justly deny labor's absolute and fundamental right to strike. To compel strikers to return to work violated the Thirteenth Amendment's prohibition against "involuntary servitude," and it struck at the workingman's only source of power: the ability to withhold his labor in unison with fellow workers. To protect this sole source of power, labor wanted to create a sphere of working-class collective action into which the state could not intrude. "The power of labor," Macarthur contended, "being a gift of Nature, cannot rightfully be made a matter of state interference or regulation." Such a principle, *Labor Clarion* editor James Mullen added, was deeply rooted in the nation's political tradition: "American thought is opposed to the imposition of any compulsory authority in relations that can be adjusted through voluntary collective action."[46]

Fremont Older, editor of the progressive *San Francisco Bulletin,* stood nearly alone among middle-class reformers in supporting labor's anti-injunction bills and opposing arbitration. Older and his *Bulletin* enjoyed a complex relationship with the California labor movement. While some within the labor movement still resented Older's role in the prosecution of San Francisco's Union Labor Party, the *Bulletin* was the most pro-labor daily newspaper in the state and the only progressive paper to back the anti-injunction bill. A public exchange between Weinstock and Older went to the heart of the disagreement between labor and the progressives. As a member of the United States Commission on Industrial Relations, Weinstock asked Older—as he asked nearly all who testified before the Commission—about his stand on arbitration. When Older appeared less than enthusiastic, Weinstock suggested that arbitration was the only way to bring about "peaceful settlements." Older responded that arbitration might bring about "peace and harmony," but he did not know if "it would bring about justice." State mediation or arbitration "might quiet the workers, get them back to work . . . [But] the injustice might still be there."[47] The best way to limit industrial unrest, according to Older, was to promote the organization of labor, for "as organized labor gains in power there is less likelihood of conflict."[48] Older had identified a central tension in the labor-progressive alliance: most progressives sought to foster "peace and harmony" by increasing the regulatory power of the state; organized labor, and a few progressives like Older, sought to secure "justice" by increasing labor's collective power.[49]

Differences between labor and the progressives, and among progressives like Weinstock and Older, reflected variations on what has since become known as "industrial pluralism." Although often associated with New Deal labor relations, industrial pluralism had its origins in Progressive-era labor conflicts and in the emerging field of "industrial relations."[50] The pluralist model rejected classical political economy's emphasis on "individualism" and "liberty of contract." While such concepts may have accurately described the economy and polity of the past, they had less relevance in a modern industrial society. In place of the classical economy of freely contracting individuals, the industrial pluralist saw a new political and economic order marked by a plurality of interest groups, the most significant of which in the early twentieth century were organized capital and organized labor. Pluralists saw conflicts between organized labor and organized capital as inevitable but not irreconcilable. The problem of industrial relations, therefore, was to construct a mechanism by which the competing interests of workers and employers might be reconciled.[51]

In California both labor and the progressives accepted these tenets of industrial pluralism, but they disagreed as to the best mechanism for settling disputes between competing collective interests. Their disagreement centered upon two issues: the proper role of the state and the nature and relevance of the "public interest." Unlike the progressives, organized labor had seen too many injunctions and policemen's clubs to assume that the state would always be "neutral" or "disinterested" during labor disputes. It was not that the state was invariably hostile to labor, or that the state could not take positive steps to serve labor's interest; rather, it was that labor's right to pursue its collective interests through its chosen forms of collective action was so fundamental that it could not be surrendered to the state, whether in the form of courts or of progressive commissions. Labor would limit the state's role to creating a more or less level playing field. Since the employer invariably enjoyed greater power in bargaining position, resources, and the ability to sway media and public opinion, labor reasoned, fairness demanded that the state lift restraints on labor's only source of power: collective action. If the progressives wanted a broker state that would mediate labor conflicts in the "public interest," trade unionists wanted the state to protect labor's collective rights and then step aside.

Closely related to labor's doubts about the neutrality of the state was its suspicion of the progressives' concept of a "public interest" that transcended "class interests." In support of Weinstock's arbitration bill, both progressives and employers stressed the "inconvenience" that strikes caused to the public. This was especially true, of course, in the public utility strikes to which the bill applied, but all strikes caused disruptions of some sort. But if "the argument of public convenience [were] carried to its logical conclusion," Walter Macarthur contended, it "would lead to the virtual enslavement of certain classes for the benefit of *other classes*."[52] In other words, "the public" did not represent a group apart from the "class interest" of the contending parties, but simply another constellation of class interests. Of course the public had interests too, but they were no more pure than those of labor and capital. Moreover, the public's interests were too remote to justify a place at the bargaining table. As *Labor Clarion* editor James Mullen argued, the state's obligation was to recognize and protect "voluntary collective action *by those immediately concerned.*"[53] For labor, if not for the progressives, the "public" was not among the "immediately concerned."

NOT QUITE LAISSEZ-FAIRE: LABOR'S POSITIVE USES OF THE STATE

It might be tempting to interpret labor's insistence on defending its collective rights, and its opposition to government arbitration, as an example of what recent studies refer to as "antistatist voluntarism" or "collective laissez-faire." But to suggest that labor's suspicion of state intervention in labor disputes produced a more general "anti-statist" cast of mind oversimplifies labor's position and ignores the totality of its political agenda. In California, at least, it was not anti-statism, but *ambivalence* about state power, that characterized labor's political philosophy. Labor was by no means alone in this regard. Many Progressive-era reformers expressed a similar ambivalence toward the state even while their reforms expanded the power and capacity of the state. Progressives accepted the need for state intervention in a modern industrial society, however much they debated the parameters and proper arenas of state intervention.[54]

So too with organized labor. During the same legislative sessions in which it pursued anti-injunction legislation and opposed arbitration, the CFL endorsed, and won, the following measures: a compulsory workmen's compensation law; county public defender offices; free textbooks for schoolchildren; municipal ownership of public utilities; stricter regulation of private detective agencies; the establishment of state-owned employment bureaus; and extending the power of the State Labor Commissioner and other Progressive-era agencies to investigate and regulate an array of safety and sanitary regulations. Some of the labor-backed measures that failed even better demonstrate labor's support for a more active state: state-financed public works during periods of high unemployment; unemployment insurance; and government-financed health insurance. Such measures can hardly be called "anti-statist" and instead resemble what would later be called "social unionism," or the use of the state to promote broad social and economic reforms that went beyond the immediate interests of trade unionists to serve the needs of the working class more generally.[55]

To be sure, California labor leaders shared with their national counterparts the voluntarist assumption that workers should not seek from the state that which they could better secure from their unions. At the state level, however, voluntarism manifested itself not as absolute antipathy to political action or state-sponsored reforms, but as a robust confidence in the power of organization and unfettered collective action. In a report praising labor's legislative achievements, Paul Scharrenberg could still declare his "most emphatic belief in the superior value of economic power," noting that "the free exercise of our economic power has and will continue to bring greater returns and benefits than the promised results of any political effort."[56] Yet Scharrenberg's comments came at a convention devoted primarily to developing a legislative agenda, evaluating the voting records of state legislators, drafting bills, and devising lobbying strategies.[57] This theoretical preference for organization over legislation ran through the California labor movement's rather wide political spectrum, from the likes of the very mainstream Paul Scharrenberg to the labor lawyer Austin Lewis, usually associated with the left-wing of the California Socialist Party. In their appearances before the United States Commission on Industrial Relations, both Scharrenberg and Lewis testified that while they supported labor legislation, they believed that it was even more important to organize workers into unions. The two goals were not mutually exclusive, they insisted; indeed, as Scharrenberg testified, only a strong and politically influential labor movement could successfully lobby for the enactment and enforcement of labor laws.[58]

Ironically, in responding to questions on how California should resolve its unemployment problem, it was the socialist Lewis

who showed the most distrust of the state. Scharrenberg and
the CFL had consistently placed the creation of state-run and
state-financed employment bureaus near the top of its legislative
agenda, an objective that was finally realized in 1915. Lewis, on
the other hand, arguing that the state should "utilize . . . trade
unions" as instruments of social reform, advocated only state sub-
sidies for a system of union-controlled labor exchanges.[59] Scharrenberg and the CFL hoped that state-owned bureaus would
replace the private employment agencies that exploited mostly
unskilled, unorganized, and unemployed workers with excessive
job-finding fees. Worse still, during strikes, these private agencies often provided strikebreakers without notifying their clients
that a strike was in progress. As such, the CFL also lobbied for,
and eventually won, a law requiring private agencies to inform
prospective workers when a strike was in progress.[60]

Many of labor's legislative initiatives assumed that reform could
benefit both organized and unorganized workers—that is, the unorganized received benefits, but in ways that did not undermine
trade unionism. This was especially evident in the CFL's support
for measures affecting two other mostly unorganized groups in California: agricultural laborers and women. During the Progressive
era, regulation of the working and living conditions of California's
migrant farm laborers fell largely to the Commission on Immigration and Housing (CIH), in part on the assumption that most
farm workers were immigrants. In order to allay labor's mistaken
fear that the Commission's purpose was to encourage immigration
to the state, Governor Johnson appointed Paul Scharrenberg as
one of the original commissioners (a position he held until 1922).
While the CFL's half-hearted efforts to organize farm workers invariably failed, it worked jointly with the CIH to pass labor camp
sanitation laws and, into the 1920s, introduced amendments that
increased the Commission's investigative, regulatory, and enforcement powers. Both labor and reformers argued that this would
not only improve the lives of farm workers, but would indirectly
help organized labor. Removing abysmal farm labor conditions,

the reasoning went, would make migrant farm laborers less likely to drift into the cities where they might work as strikebreakers or drive down wages.[61]

A similar logic shaped labor's support of protective labor laws for women. Although women's organization most often led the drive for protective labor laws for women and children, the male leadership of the AFL and other labor organizations supported many, but not all, of these measures. Most male trade unionists shared the prevailing cultural norms that urged women to stay at home and made men the primary "breadwinners," but they also saw women as low-wage competitors who undermined male wages. Protective labor laws limited women's employment opportunities (for example, by barring night work or limiting women's hours) and made them less attractive to employers by requiring additional workplace standards or regulations.[62] Yet, as was often the case, the CFL's approach to these matters differed somewhat from the AFL's. While the AFL supported maximum hour laws only for women, the CFL sponsored a universal eight-hour law that applied to all workers and opposed minimum wage laws for both men and women. As Rebecca Mead has argued, labor in California viewed hours and wage legislation quite differently. While the hours law would have fixed eight hours as a maximum across the board, the minimum wage law empowered the newly created Industrial Welfare Commission (IWC) to play a permanent role in administering wage rates for different categories of workers. Hence the state intruded upon the power of unions to set wage rates.[63]

Yet the history of California's minimum wage law for women, and the IWC that was created at the same time to monitor and enforce the law, demonstrates how the California labor movement's quite flexible understanding of "voluntarism" could lead it to embrace more, not less, state intervention. Although many CFL leaders initially opposed the minimum wage law for women—on the voluntarist assumption that wage rates should be set by collective bargaining between employers and unions—it nevertheless came to support the IWC as its domain expanded to include the investigation of many facets of the wages, hours, and workplace conditions of women and children. Throughout the Progressive era and into the 1920s, the CFL supported expanded powers and increased appropriations for the IWC, even while opposing minimum wage laws in principle.[64] As with its support for laws regulating the state's migrant farm workers, the CFL accepted state intervention on behalf of workers who did not have a union to protect them. While California labor leaders usually argued that such workers *should* be organized so that they need not rely upon state "paternalism," they apparently found it easier to hand over responsibility for protecting farm laborers and women to Progressive-era commissions than to make more concerted efforts to organize those workers.[65] Thus, while historians often treat "exclusiveness" and "antistatism" as two pillars of trade union "conservatism," such a conflation ignores the extent to which exclusiveness could lead to greater acceptance of statist solutions.[66]

Even if one sees labor's measures on behalf of the unemployed, farm workers, and women as still within the voluntarist framework—insofar as they limited state intervention to those measures that would make trade unionism more effective—other labor-backed and labor-sponsored reforms cannot be so construed. For example, labor in California either initiated or strongly supported laws regulating the payment of wages, municipal ownership of public utilities, a universal eight-hour day (which the AFL strenuously opposed), free school textbooks, University of California Extension courses for workers, women's suffrage, elimination of property qualifications for jurors, and the creation public defender offices. These laws benefitted the working class more generally with or little or no direct benefit for trade unionism.[67]

The public defender movement in particular illustrates the point. Although not the only force behind the public defender movement, in California labor emerged as a leading advocate. Public defenders, who in California took criminal cases and civil cases up to $100, would have been of no use to trade unionists; they could not have defended unions or union officials who could afford counsel. At any rate, labor preferred that its own lawyers handle these cases. Indeed, there is no indication that

CFL leaders, or anyone else, believed that public defenders would defend trade unionists. According to California's first public defender, Walton Wood, the main beneficiary of the law were those attempting to recover unpaid wages and those charged with violation of state and local vagrancy laws. Neither category would have likely applied to trade unionists. Disputed claims over wages were most common among unskilled day laborers who worked without formal contracts. Trade unionists working under collective bargaining agreements would rarely find themselves in this situation, and if they it did it would be handled through union grievance procedures. Nor would trade unionists have likely faced vagrancy charges; in fact, given labor's concern that "a reserve army" of unemployed constituted a fund of low-wage competition and potential strikebreakers, institutional self-interest should have dictated more aggressive prosecution, not legal protection, for vagrants. But the CFL's support for public defenders was simply one of a number of instances in which organized labor in California supported measures that served the interests of the working class more generally.[68]

Other measures that labor supported, but which failed to pass, even further demonstrate how labor supported positive state action and anticipated the "social unionism" that emerged on the national political stage in the 1930s. During an economic recession that began in 1913, the CFL proposed a system of public works projects to provide relief for the unemployed. The CFL proposed that during periods of unemployment, especially during the winter months, the state should finance road construction and other public works projects. Although Progressive-era labor leaders looked to the state houses rather than to Congress, such measures anticipated New Deal public works programs as well as labor's version of the post-World War II Full Employment bill. Indeed, as California economic historian Gerald Nash astutely observed several years ago, labor's later role in creating and supporting the New Deal welfare state "represented not so much a new departure as a reflection of the shifting administrative burden from the states to the federal government."[69]

But perhaps the issue that most expressed the CFL's social unionism—and its departure from the national political program of the AFL—was its support for government health insurance. Overcoming the concerted opposition of the California Medical Association and the private life insurance industry, the California legislature created a Social Insurance Commission in 1915 to study the issue of health insurance. For the next three years the Commission promoted health insurance legislation and issued a formal report recommending a state system based on joint contributions by employers, employees, and the state.[70] Between 1915 and 1918 (when the plan went down to defeat in a statewide referendum), the CFL consistently endorsed, and lobbied for, government health insurance. A minority of CFL delegates echoed the arguments of AFL leaders, opposing the "compulsory" features of the recommendation. But both Scharrenberg and CFL President Daniel Murphy dismissed these objections, pointing out that labor already supported compulsory workmen's compensation insurance. "The objection to the compulsory idea can be met," President Murphy contended, "by showing its necessity." Murphy then cited reports of state commissions and private charity organizations identifying sickness as a major cause of unemployment and destitution. While the CFL might have preferred to secure health insurance through unions, Murphy pointed out that of 501 unions filing reports with the Social Insurance Commission, 351 gave no benefits at all and 150 gave only sick benefits that partially covered a worker's time away from work. None paid for medical costs. While a few unions and fraternal orders were "doing all they [could] do," Murphy concluded, "the cost of full protection" was more than the average wage earner, or trade union, could bear.[71]

"INDUSTRIAL LIBERTY": LABOR'S PROGRESSIVE LIBERALISM

By proposing social reforms that benefitted all workers, organized labor in California self-consciously presented itself as progressivism's cutting edge. No one could deny, Walter Macarthur wrote in 1913, that "organized labor has been the leader in this country in progressive thought." Well "in advance" of other organizations, he claimed, organized labor advocated legislation on behalf of all "victims of unfair and unjust conditions."[72] But it was in its attack on the courts that labor most forcefully presented itself as an agent of progress and modernity. While Samuel Gompers and the AFL hierarchy may have adopted the "court minted ideology" of their judicial adversaries, the Progressive-era CFL most certainly did not.[73] Instead, the CFL ridiculed the "ancient" reasoning of judge-made law, always presenting its own view of law and the state as a "modern" and "progressive" alternative.

Labor found the court's reasoning hopelessly backward-looking, first for its reliance on pre-liberal vestiges rooted in master and servant law and the procedures of equity, and second for its inconsistent and outmoded Lockean liberalism. Rejecting the archaic doctrines of the courts, CFL spokesmen demanded an updated liberalism more conducive to industrial society, one that would ensure "industrial liberty." Human history, Paul Scharrenberg claimed, would witness "three great struggles" for liberty. Two of these great struggles had already brought "political and religious liberty," Scharrenberg contended, "but industrial liberty . . . remains more a shadow than a reality for a large portion of the world's workers." It would be labor's historic mission to extend the principles of liberalism to the modern workplace and economy, to create a broader conception of "liberty" and "human rights."[74] On the one hand, expanding liberalism required limiting state power so as to protect labor's rights of collective action; on the other hand, it required positive state action to address the inequalities of condition and opportunity that trade unionism alone could not ameliorate.

Advancing the cause of industrial liberty first required stripping the law of its "feudal" remnants. No one developed this line of reasoning more forcefully than Andrew Furuseth of the Sailor's Union. One of California's best-known labor leaders, Furuseth earned national recognition for his role in drafting the 1915

LaFollette Seaman's Act, a federal law that extended to merchant seaman some of the most basic legal rights. As with the ancient maritime law that treated merchant sailors as virtual slaves while they were at sea, Furuseth found the labor injunction a product of an earlier time. In numerous articles and testimony before state and federal legislative committees, Furuseth repeatedly traced the equity functions of the court to the chancery courts of pre-liberal England. Just as the chancery courts dispensed arbitrary rulings that allowed the king to ignore the "rule of law," so too judges sitting in equity were allowed to make law, to ban actions that were otherwise lawful such as picketing, and to invent legal remedies where none existed in statute or common law. "As government by equity . . . advances," Furuseth argued, "government by law, republican government, recedes." Even when judges did not expressly invoke a feudal doctrine, such as enticement, the restrictions placed upon workers' collective self-assertion assumed an essentially feudal relationship. Furuseth especially objected when judges enjoined picketing on the grounds that it interfered with the employer's property rights, for this implied that the employer had a "property right" in the employment relation. Such injunctions, Furuseth and many other labor spokesmen noted, at best made human labor a commodity, and at worst reduced the worker to the status of a "serf" or "slave" by "assuming that one may have property rights in the labor . . . of another."[75]

It was not only the law's feudal lags and remnants that provoked the wrath of labor's self-taught legal scholars, but also its outmoded emphasis on "individualism." The plea for "individual rights," a Los Angeles labor weekly declared, "is a pet with the judicial mind." In an industrial society, however, individual rights were "impossible without combination." Similarly, Paul Scharrenberg condemned injunction judges and open-shop advocates for promoting a "cynical doctrine" of " 'Every man for himself' " and exploiting the "defenselessness of the individualized worker." Open-shop advocates and their judicial allies presupposed "an individualistic state of industry," even though that presupposition fell "to the ground immediately" once one reflected upon the "actual conditions under which the world's work is carried on." While injunction judges and open-shop employers attempted to "revive eighteenth century conditions of labor," labor's insistence upon a right of collective action was "a twentieth century idea applied to twentieth century conditions of industry."[76]

California labor leaders did not reject the notion of individual rights, but, as Walter Macarthur argued, "Individual rights are effective only as they are exercised collectively and by concert."[77] *Labor Clarion* editor James Mullen developed this point in a series of essays on labor's right to picket as a necessary adjunct of its right to strike. For Mullen, modern conditions required an evolutionary understanding of rights. The "right to strike" and the "right to picket," he admitted, were new rights. Such rights were implied in the First and Fourteenth Amendments, but even if they were not, Mullen reasoned, the Constitution could not have enumerated all modern rights. For some rights "have not yet been discovered, just like some of the great laws of nature still remain a secret . . . to become known [when] . . . the human mind requires them to be applied and enforced for the welfare of humanity."[78] Mullen's evolutionary view of law mirrored that of Progressive-era legal scholars in many ways, but he did not fully embrace the "legal realism" emerging among some intellectuals. For example, he did not go so far as the Berkeley labor economist Ira Cross, who claimed that "the time has come when all should realize that there are no such thing as natural inalienable rights." For Cross rights were socially constructed, "given to the individual by the society in which he lives." But for Mullen the right to strike and picket were both "natural" and "inalienable"; if they were not written in the United States Constitution, then they were written in the "constitution of nature and humanity."[79]

Most California labor leaders who spoke or wrote on the subject accepted a liberal understanding of rights as natural and inalienable, and they believed along with John Locke and the authors of the Declaration of Independence that governments had been instituted among men in order to protect such rights. They also accepted, with some modifications, the "possessive individualism" that C. B. Macpherson finds at the core of liberal political theory. The "power of labor" was not a commodity but a "gift of Nature" and therefore an inalienable possession of the individual worker.[80] Where labor parted company with classical liberalism was in holding that the individual worker could only protect his or her labor power by joining together with fellow workers and engaging in voluntary collective action. Labor's vision also demanded a considerable rethinking of the hierarchy of liberal rights. While classical liberalism privileged "individual rights," labor stressed "collective rights." In addition, labor's law would have dislodged "property" from the privileged position that it had assumed in nineteenth-century America. Labor did this first by "restoring" a definition of property as physical objects or tangible assets, as opposed to the intangible "right to do business" that judges had come to treat as "property" by the late nineteenth century. But more importantly, they claimed that in a modern world the "right to collective action" was equal to, if not greater than, the right to property. The right of collective action—to free speech, free assembly, and free association—were "human rights" that could never be surrendered to "property rights."[81]

RACE AND THE LIMITS OF LABOR'S PROGRESSIVE LIBERALISM

However eloquently labor spokesmen condemned backward-looking judges, trumpeted their own "modern" and "progressive" liberalism, or called upon the state to "promote human rights rather than exalt property rights," in one crucial area their actions exposed the limits of their liberal commitments. For the same labor leaders who defended the "rights and liberties of toilers" sought to restrict the rights of those without white skin. While the California labor movement most often ignored African-American and Latino workers, it led an often vicious campaign against persons of Asian descent. Organized labor in California led the campaign to extend the 1882 Chinese Exclusion Act to all Asians;

it joined state farm organizations and many middle-class reformers in supporting the 1913 Alien Land Law, which denied Asian
immigrants—as "aliens ineligible to citizenship"—the right to
own or permanently rent land in the state. Organized labor fought
for local ordinances to mandate segregation in the public schools;
to subject all Asian-Americans, whether citizens or not, to strict
"alien" registration requirements; and to keep Asians out of many
occupations.[82] In 1917 the CFL joined with the state's farm organizations to form the California Union of Producers and Consumers. In addition to advocating a number of progressive social
reforms, the organization's political platform called upon state
government "to preserve California as a heritage of the white
race."[83] Here again labor demonstrated its willingness to form
coalitions and expand the power of the state; but in this case
labor sought to protect the rights and interests of only *some* workers, thereby belying the alleged universality of its rights platform.
Labor's commitment to human rights and liberal progress stopped
abruptly at the color line.

   In many ways labor's Progressive-era campaign to exclude
Asian immigration, and to impose restrictions on the rights of
those already here, was a legacy of labor's anti-Chinese movements of the nineteenth century. According to Alex Saxton, Chinese immigrants provided the California labor movement with an
"indispensable enemy." Not only did trade union agitation convince Congress to ban Chinese immigration in 1882, it unified the
California labor movement organizationally and politically. Although facing very little competition from Chinese immigrants,
California's skilled white trade unionists exploited working-class
racism in order to solidify their control over the labor movement
and to present themselves in the political arena as the representatives of all California workers. Moreover, the anti-Chinese movement provided a common cause for a labor movement otherwise
divided by skill, religion, and ethnicity. With Chinese immigration banned after 1882, the movement died down until about
1900, when increasing immigration from Japan (and to a lesser
extent Korea and India) created fears of a new "yellow peril." In

1905, under the leadership of the San Francisco Building Trades
Council, California trade unionists formed the Japanese and Korean Exclusion League (renamed the Asiatic Exclusion League in
1907) to pursue three political and economic goals: to extend the
Chinese Exclusion Act to all Asians, to organize boycotts against
Japanese merchants and goods, and to compel segregation in the
schools. Although Californians from all classes supported these
causes, organized labor welcomed the mantle of leadership.

Labor frequently, if unconvincingly, made economic arguments
on behalf of exclusion. "Whether in the mining camps of the early
fifties, in the factories or the workshops of the later periods of industrialization, or as tillers of soil," wrote Paul Scharrenberg, "we
find the same bitter complaints of the evils of [job] competition."
White Californians, he concluded, "cannot compete with them
[Japanese immigrants] and maintain an American standard of living."[84] Despite these claims, Japanese immigrants rarely offered
direct competition to white workers, and least of all to the skilled,
urban trade unionists who spearheaded the anti-Japanese movement. About two-thirds of Japanese immigrants who entered California in these years moved into rural areas, where they worked
as farm laborers and tenant farmers before eventually acquiring
land of their own. Those who remained in the cities worked as
merchants, or the employees of merchants, serving a segregated
Japanese community.[85] While labor leaders sometimes acknowledged this fact, they still expressed the fear that, if left unchecked,
"hordes" of cheap Asian workers would flock to the Golden State
and, eventually, undermine the "American standard of life." Only
a few trade unionists, and only in rare instances, argued that the
best way to prevent Asian immigrants from undermining wages
was to organize them into unions. But these voices were over-
whelmed by the majority of trade unionists who opposed organizing Asian workers as forcefully as they favored exclusion.[86]

Few California labor leaders rested the case for exclusion
on economics alone. "Fundamentally," Walter Macarthur stated
bluntly, "the question is a matter of race." Even his fellow seaman Paul Scharrenberg, who usually stressed labor's economic

motivations, openly spoke of preserving California for "our kind of people" and defending the "heritage of the white race."[87] Labor's leading exclusionists—most of whom were immigrants—also expressed anxiety about newcomers from Southern and Eastern Europe. But labor's demands to restrict immigration from Southern and Eastern Europe lacked the explicitly racist arguments in favor of total exclusion of Asian immigrants. Southern and Eastern Europeans, especially if exposed to trade unionism, would eventually embrace an "American standard of living" and American ideals, but Asian immigrants were deemed "unassimilable" by virtue of race. Going far beyond recitations of cultural differences— from religion and language to clothing styles and dietary habits— an endless stream of racist literature and speeches attacked the "character" of the Japanese. "It is not alone the displacement of white labor . . . that has developed this resentment [against the Japanese]," wrote Abraham Yoell of the Electricians' Union. "It is their general characteristics, dishonesty, drunkenness, trickiness, proneness to quarrel, and insolence that has brought upon them the detestation of the people of California."[88]

At times labor leaders linked their support of exclusion to concerns about "citizenship." Federal naturalization laws dating to the 1790s classified Asian immigrants as "aliens ineligible for citizenship." Though the American-born children of Asian immigrants automatically became citizens, their parents were excluded from a naturalization process open to European and (after 1870) African immigrants. But organized labor opposed the "unassimilable element from Asia" not only because they were legally ineligible for citizenship, but because they were racially "unfit for citizenship."[89] Inheritors of a nineteenth-century discourse that championed "free labor" and the independent "producer" as the bulwark of the republic, organized labor linked the requirements of "citizenship" to economic and occupational "independence."[90] Not only were "Asiatics" unfamiliar with American political traditions, labor's spokesmen claimed, but a "servile" nature and the quasi-feudal system of contract labor under which they worked made them psychologically and economically dependent upon contractors and

employers. The introduction of such an antiquated labor system—
like the feudal doctrines of the injunction judges—might reduce
all workers to the status of a "serf" or "slave" unsuited for the rights
and duties of citizenship.[91]

Labor was by no means alone in its opposition to Asian immigrants. As Roger Daniels argues in his study of the anti-Japanese
movement in Progressive-era California, organized labor may
have "led the way," but Californians from all walks of life joined
the crusade.[92] As such, labor's public appeals often expressed a
bewildering mix of class consciousness and race consciousness.
Olaf Tvietmoe, an official in the Building Trades Council and
President of the Asiatic Exclusion League, mixed a language of
class conflict with equal parts patriotism and racism: "Capital,
greedy and soulless, wants cheap labor. Capital has no altar, no
home, no fatherland. Profit is its God; children's tears, women's
lives, and men's blood its food." Trade unionists, he insisted, were
"liberty-loving Americans" and "sentinels and guardians of Cau-
casian civilization," while the "captains of industry" were willing
"to sacrifice the entire country and its people on the altar of com-
mercialism." Yet labor leaders just as often appealed across class
lines, claiming that the Asian "menace" concerned "all white people." Demanding that Asians attend segregated schools, one San
Francisco trade unionist proclaimed that "the white taxpayer—
millionaire, merchant, or mechanic—does not wish his daughter
to associate with Asiatics" in the classroom.[93]

Organized labor's anti-Asian campaign no doubt reflected racist
beliefs that trade unionists shared with Californians of all classes,
but it also served the political needs of the labor movement.
Though only about one-tenth of California wage earners belonged
to unions in the Progressive era, organized labor claimed to speak
for *all workers* when it entered the political arena. Historians of
AFL politics have often stressed the disingenuous nature of this
claim, arguing that the AFL pursued only the narrow institutional
interests of organized white males while opposing reforms that
might have benefitted the entire working class. This view con-
tains more than a grain of truth, but it also oversimplifies. While

the California labor movement clearly used politics first and foremost to defend the rights and interests of trade unions, it also supported an array of social reforms that benefitted unorganized workers—even if such support was only a strategic effort to buttress organized labor's claim to speak for a wider constituency. So too did the anti-Asian campaigns allow organized labor to speak for the still broader constituency of all white Californians. Just as organized labor in California proudly declared itself "a leader" in progressive reform and the expansion of rights, so too did it unabashedly proclaim that "organized working people have been in the vanguard of this movement [for Japanese exclusion] just as they led in the struggle for Chinese exclusion."[94] And sadly, so they were.

CONCLUSION

Faced with the practical and ideological burdens of the labor injunction, California trade unionists had turned to the state legislature for relief. With the help of progressive allies and a political culture newly open to the pressure politics of organized interest groups, the CFL placed anti-injunction legislation atop a robust legislative agenda that sought to both limit and expand the powers of the state. In the end, however, labor lobbyists failed to persuade their progressive allies, and despite an impressive record of legislative success on most other matters, could not stop the courts from issuing injunctions. Yet, in the process, labor had constructed its own conception of law and rights—a "modern" and "progressive" alternative that defended collective as well as individual rights, dislodged property rights from their privileged position, and placed labor's rights of collective action on par with the property rights claimed by employers.

But as Christopher Tomlins has argued, it is one thing to construct an alternative legal discourse, quite another to make that alternative the *official* legal discourse.[95] Legal arguments, no matter how persuasive, could not change judicial behavior. Some California labor leaders tried to comfort themselves by maintaining that the most restrictive features of the *Pierce* ruling amounted to *obiter dicta*—that is, tangential or incidental statements in the judge's ruling that were not central to the disposition of the case.[96] In March of 1916 the San Francisco Labor Council's John O'Connell wrote to an official of the Ohio State Federation of Labor that, because violent threats had been made in the *Pierce* case, Judge Henshaw's suggestion that picketing *would have been* unlawful even in the absence of such threats was "mere dictum, and not binding on inferior courts." O'Connell even claimed that many Northern California jurisdictions allowed peaceful picketing despite the *Pierce* ruling. The truth was more complicated and less rosy than O'Connell suggested. On at least two occasions, Superior Court judges had indeed permitted peaceful picketing, but both times employers appealed and the appellate courts reiterated that the "weight of authority . . . and the governing tendency" was still "to regard picketing as inherently unlawful."[97] Moreover, when strike activity increased later in 1916, Superior Court judges in the same jurisdictions identified by O'Connell issued sweeping injunctions against all picketing, peaceful or otherwise.[98]

Failing to stop the "injunction mill" did not sour the California labor movement on politics or slow its pursuit of state-sponsored social reform. As the political arm of the labor movement, the CFL sought first and foremost to defend labor's preferred forms of collective action from state interference. According to many students of AFL politics, the effort to limit government interference in strikes "made it difficult for union leaders to turn around and advocate paternalist social legislation that would have placed workers as a class under the special protection of the state."[99] By this reasoning, state and local labor leaders, who encountered more legal hostility than did their national counterparts, should have made an especially hasty retreat from politics and government activism. Why then did the CFL—like so many other state labor federations—adopt a more positive view of politics and the state than did the AFL? Such differences did not reflect any sharp ideological divide. Labor leaders at both levels, after all, advocated both economic and political action and preferred the former to the latter whenever possible—however much they differed on the proper balance for any given policy issue.

The different political choices of state and national labor leaders had less to do with ideology than with the different incentives and opportunities at the state and national levels. First, the AFL and the CFL were formed for different reasons and served different constituencies.[100] Established in 1886, the AFL drew trade unionists who had become dissatisfied with the Knights of Labor. Whereas the Knights supported political action and state-sponsored reforms and used strikes only as the last resort, the trade unionists who formed the AFL wanted to reverse these priorities.[101] California trade unionists, on the other hand, formed the CFL in 1901 primarily to increase labor's political influence in the state legislature.[102] Furthermore, the AFL's policy-making structure gave a great deal of power to national and international unions, whose leadership was mostly concerned with collective bargaining issues. The CFL, on the other hand, gave greater voice to local union activists often linked to politically minded urban labor councils and trade federations. These local unionists had fought political battles over everything from street maintenance and city sewers to policing, public school reform, and municipal ownership.[103] The CFL provided an opportunity to carry this penchant for urban politics and reform to the state capital.

Perhaps the best explanation for the different political approaches of the AFL and CFL, however, lies in the nature of American federalism. Unlike, for example, the British Trade Union Congress, which could target a unitary British national state, the AFL had to work within a federal system that divided power and responsibility among national, state, and local governments. While the AFL, as a national organization, could and did lobby Congress for legislation favorable to trade union interests, it could not very easily lobby nearly fifty state governments. Not surprisingly, then, the AFL restricted its lobbying to issues over which Congress had some authority: immigration restriction, the hours of federal employees and inter-state railroad workers, and anti-trust law. But before the 1930s the American constitutional order left control over most social welfare and labor issues with the states. Quite simply, the CFL pursued a more ambitious social reform agenda than the AFL because state legislatures had jurisdiction over such matters while Congress did not.

While California labor leaders rejected the anti-statist voluntarism of the AFL, at least two factors prevented them from creating a truly class-based political movement. First, due to its limited constituency and the nature of interest group politics, organized labor could not secure legislation without allies. None of labor's most important allies—whether intellectuals, professional associations, women's clubs, reform-minded politicians, farm organizations, or the heads of government commissions—supported *all* of labor's positions, and they often expected labor to support some reforms that it did not always enthusiastically embrace. Though the CFL sometimes spoke of itself as an organization that represented the interest of all workers as a class, in practical terms it was drawn into progressive coalitions that claimed to rise above "class interests" to serve a broader "public interest." Moreover, once the political influence of labor's progressive allies waned, as we shall see in the next chapter, labor's political influence waned also.

A second obstacle to a truly class-based political movement in California can be seen in labor's anti-Asian crusades. Although a number of California labor historians have shown how the anti-Asian movements unified the *white* working class, those campaigns also suggest the limits of labor's progressive vision and the complexity of working-class political identity. While California labor leaders frequently employed a language of class to mobilize working-class voters, they also saw the political advantages—as did most politicians in the state—of exploiting the equally strong racial, ethnic, and religious identities of the working class. It was not simply that race divided the working class—though this is certainly true—but even more that "race" competed with, and sometimes supplanted, "class" as a source of political identity.[104] In this regard the California labor movement resembled other American social movements when it tried to broaden its political base by speaking on behalf of all citizens, with the implicit understanding that they were in fact speaking only on behalf of *white* citizens. As Michael Kazin reminds us, in "American history, those who invoke the rights and interests of 'the people' have usually been bound by a definition more ethnic than economic."[105] Too often, labor's defense of rights was similarly bound.

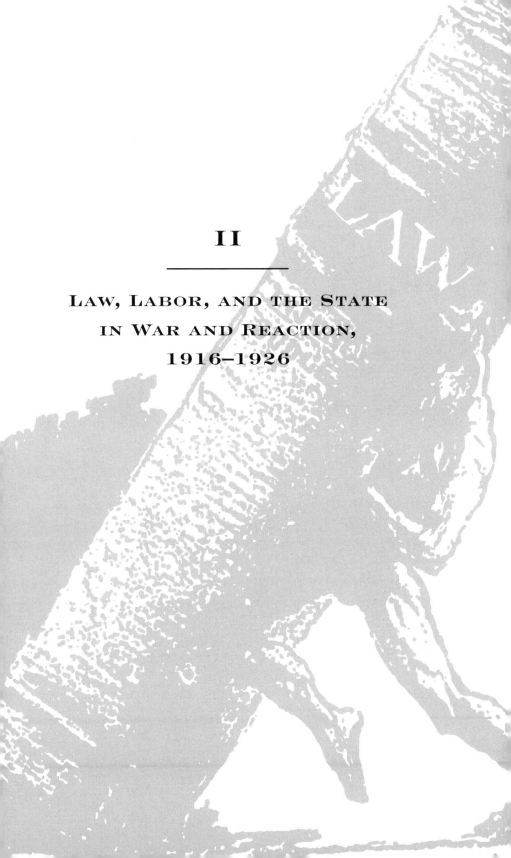

II

LAW, LABOR, AND THE STATE IN WAR AND REACTION, 1916–1926

Chapter 4

"LAW AND ORDER" AND THE WANING OF
LABOR'S POLITICAL POWER,
1916–1917

*Governor Stephens . . . has given notice that the progressive era [in California] has
come to an end.*

Coast Seamen's Journal
JUNE 6, 1917

Labor's Progressive-era campaign to secure anti-injunction legislation coincided with a period of relative labor peace and, ironically, the near-disappearance of the injunction in California labor disputes. After a decade of intense labor conflict, from the
1901 San Francisco waterfront strike to the unrest in Los Angeles at the end of the decade, labor relations in California entered
a period of relative stability that lasted from 1911 to 1915.[1] In
Los Angeles the absence of labor conflict reflected the weakened
state of the Los Angeles labor movement, a weakness aggravated
and exposed by the defeat of the San Francisco-led organizational
drive. Making matters worse, an economic downturn and an un-
relenting stream of new workers into the Los Angeles area produced high levels of unemployment and further eroded labor's
bargaining position.[2] In San Francisco labor peace reflected labor's
strength more than its weakness. By 1911, as Robert Knight noted,
most "employers showed little inclination to break ties" or need-
lessly pick fights with San Francisco's well-established unions. In
addition, when in 1911 Congress selected San Francisco to host
the Panama-Pacific Exposition (to mark the expected comple-
tion of the Panama Canal in 1914) both unions and employers understood that the event would bring tourists, construction

contracts, and other forms of capital to a city still rebuilding from the 1906 earthquake. Not wanting to threaten this promised economic stimulus, labor and capital declared an unofficial truce. From the first preparations in 1911 to the closing of the exposition in December of 1915, workers and employers in San Francisco temporarily put their differences aside and jointly profited from the event.[3]

But the era of good feelings soon ended. In California as throughout the nation, labor conflict emerged with new intensity when war in Europe stimulated a demand for American goods. War-born prosperity, labor shortages, and rapid inflation gave trade unionists both the confidence and the incentive to seek better wages and working conditions.[4] As in the past, a surge of labor activism aroused organized employers and produced new demands on local courts and police to restrict labor's methods. In Los Angeles employers turned as always to local police. In San Francisco, where a restrained police policy continued even after the Union Labor Party had fallen, employers looked to the courts. After "being idle for over ten years," the *Labor Clarion* warned in 1916, "the injunction mill promises to be working overtime again." The prediction proved all too accurate.[5]

This chapter examines some of the legal and political consequences of renewed labor conflict in California in the year preceding American entry into the First World War. Despite the political setbacks of the previous six years, the California labor movement continued to make the anti-injunction bill its top legislative priority. But at the local level a rejuvenated open-shop movement and well-publicized episodes of labor violence challenged labor's political power and left its legal status all the more precarious. By the time the United States entered the war in April of 1917, a new open-shop movement, under the guise of a "Law and Order Committee," had intervened in several strikes, secured a Los Angeles-style anti-picketing ordinance in pro-labor San Francisco, and defeated labor's nearly successful bid to win an anti-injunction law in the 1917 legislative session. An increasingly contentious legal and political environment did not diminish the California labor movement's passion for politics or state-sponsored reforms, but it did mean that labor's political program had to compete with more unified and politically aggressive employers.

"LAW AND ORDER" AND THE REVIVAL OF UNION ACTIVISM

Citing the inflation that accompanied war-induced prosperity, a handful of unions in Northern California extracted wage increases from their employers in 1916 without resorting to strikes.[6] Hoping to make similar gains, in early May of 1916 the Pacific Coast Division of the International Longshoremen's Association (ILA) requested wage increases and overtime pay from employers organized in the several Pacific Coast Waterfront Employers' Unions (WEU). When the employers refused, the ILA announced that longshoremen in all major West Coast ports would strike on June 1, 1916. Employers protested that the strike date violated a pre-existing agreement that either side would give sixty days notice before ordering a strike or lockout. Union leaders responded that rapid and unexpected inflation had rendered the old wage scale obsolete; in addition, they claimed, the contract required a sixty-day notice only should either side seek to *change* the terms of agreement, not if they sought to *cancel* the agreement entirely. Employers, the press, and even other union leaders found this distinction disingenuous. Indeed, both the Sailors' Union of the Pacific and the Teamsters' Union—the longshoremen's fellow members in the San Francisco's Waterfront Workers Federation— refused to support the strike on the grounds that it violated a collectively bargained contract. Despite this lack of support and charges of contract violation, the ILA proceeded with the strike. In all, some 10,000 longshoremen walked off the job, shutting down Pacific Coast ports from San Diego to Alaska.[7]

Because of the strike's impact on interstate commerce, the United States Secretary of Labor, William B. Wilson, intervened in the dispute. Wilson, himself a former trade unionist, charged the ILA with violating the contract, adding angrily that "the statement that you [the ILA] are not proposing to change the agreement but to cancel it deceives no one." Secretary Wilson then assigned Henry M. White, a federal immigration commissioner in Seattle, to mediate the dispute on behalf of the Department of Labor. White met with union and employer representatives in San Francisco and, within a few days, arranged a truce that sent workers back to work at the requested pay scale until negotiators reached a final settlement. Within a week San Francisco longshoremen, like their counterparts in most other Pacific ports, accepted the agreement and returned to work. The agreement applied to all longshoremen except the "lumber handlers," who were organized in separate ILA locals and employed by lumber mills and warehouses.[8]

In the Los Angeles harbors of San Pedro and Wilmington, where lumber handlers made up anywhere from one-third to one-half of the longshoremen, workers rejected the agreement and remained on strike. Lumber handlers typically earned much less than regular longshoremen and worked for the militantly anti-union lumber companies that ran mills and warehouses on the Los Angeles harbor. Because the lumber handlers made up such an unusually large portion of the longshoremen in Los Angeles, the local ILA stood by them and refused to accept the San Francisco-brokered deal. While longshoremen at other West Coast ports returned to work, nearly 1700 organized longshoremen in Los Angeles remained on strike. Despite the efforts of federal mediator White and the pleadings of the ILA local in San Francisco, the Los Angeles workers refused to accept the agreement so long as it excluded the lumber handlers.[9]

During the first week of the strike, even the usually hyperbolic *Los Angeles Times* reported almost "no disorder" and a "holiday air" at the harbor. Strikers came out "dressed in their best suits" to watch and poke "jibes" at the bosses and office personnel who attempted to load and unload passenger ships. Other than these passenger ships, the *Times* reported, "not a pound of cargo [was] loaded" or unloaded at the harbor. Yet as the strike wore on and

White's mediation efforts failed, employers became much more worried and announced plans to import "hundreds" of strikebreakers and forcefully "open the harbor."[10] Meanwhile, the M&M asked both the City Council and the Police Commission to appoint 500 special policemen. With the city facing a minor budget crisis, the Police Commission pointed out that the 300 special police already assigned to the harbor represented the maximum allowed under the city charter. While the City Council debated the M&M's request, however, Chief of Police C. E. Snively took matters into his own hands. Over the next few days, he dispatched 150 regular policemen to the harbor on the assumption that funding would be forthcoming. By early July, more than 200 regular police officers and as many as 300 specials kept watch on as few as 125 pickets.[11] The M&M did not get the 500 specials they had requested, but they certainly received more than adequate police protection.

With employers importing strikebreakers and strikers gradually drifting back to work, harbor shipping activity returned to near normal levels by early July. Still, sporadic violence between strikebreakers and remaining strikers prompted the six largest lumber companies to request an injunction from Los Angeles County Superior Court Judge Hauser. Coming only a day after the beating of a special deputy sheriff and a clash between policemen and pickets, Judge Hauser restrained all "interference," without defining exactly what this meant. Although the judge set a hearing date to determine whether the temporary injunction should become permanent, he allowed employers to repeatedly delay that hearing.[12] With the help of local courts and police, Los Angeles employers once again defeated an important strike. By early August of 1916, only 300 of the 1700 longshoremen who had walked out in June remained on strike. Although the union did not officially call off the strike until the following spring, by mid-August even the most ardent supporters admitted defeat. Strikers returned to work on the employers' terms and under open-shop conditions or drifted into other lines of work.[13]

Meanwhile, in San Francisco the truce that had sent the long-

shoremen back to work did not eliminate all conflict on the waterfront. First, despite union demands, the employers refused to
discharge all of the strikebreakers who had been hired during the
first week of the strike. In addition, longshoremen who worked for
the waterfront lumber companies remained on strike, resulting in
occasional skirmishes between strikers and strikebreakers. More
seriously, however, on June 18 an armed strikebreaker shot and
killed a member of the local Riggers' and Stevedores' Union. In
response, the ILA issued an ultimatum that if armed guards and
strikebreakers were not removed immediately, the strike would re-
sume. When the employers refused these demands, insisting upon
the right to hire whomever they chose, the ILA once again ordered its members out on strike. On June 22, the less than two-
week-old truce had come to an end.

Over the next few weeks, a flurry of waterfront disturbances
tested the policing policy of Mayor James Rolph. When elected
in 1911, Rolph had promised to continue the Union Labor Party's
policy of strict police neutrality during labor disputes, but before
1916 he had few opportunities to demonstrate his commitment.
Contrary to employer complaints, Rolph did not allow police to sit
by while strikers committed acts of violence against strikebreakers. Although Rolph refused employer requests to use regular police to escort strikebreakers or break up picket lines, he insisted
that police arrest anyone—striker or strikebreaker—who committed an act of violence. In all, dozens of strikers were arrested for
assaults on nonunion workers. Most of the attacks were minor—
some nothing more than the shouting of obscenities—and police court judges let most strikers off with light fines or simple
warnings.[14] When the Chamber of Commerce requested the appointment of 500 special police officers, however, Mayor Rolph
flatly refused the request, claiming that regular police could handle the few incidents of violence that occurred. Along with the
conservative San Francisco Chronicle and the business weekly Argonaut, the Chamber of Commerce condemned Rolph's refusal to
appoint the specials. Their anger only intensified days later when,
after meeting with members of the San Francisco Labor Council,
Mayor Rolph ordered regular police to search strikebreakers as

they entered and left the docks, disarming and arresting them if necessary.[15]

Meanwhile, federal mediator Henry White continued to work for a settlement. In mid-July White brought together members of the Waterfront Employers' Union and the ILA and reached an accord that sent the San Francisco longshoremen back to the docks at the wages prevailing at the beginning of the strike, with a final wage settlement to be worked out at conferences in August. (The agreement did not affect strikers in Los Angeles or the Pacific Northwest.) This meant, of course, that workers had agreed to return for lower wages than those agreed to in the original truce. But in exchange employers agreed to discharge all strikebreakers and remove armed guards from the waterfront.[16] Although the San Francisco longshoremen eventually received an upward revision of their wage scale and maintained the closed shop on the waterfront, the limited gains did not justify the costs of the strike. Much more than other labor disputes, waterfront strikes affected the entire community, for in a port city nearly all citizens depend upon the daily movement of goods through the harbor. Yet after a nearly two-month strike, the longshoremen had done little more than maintain the status quo and convince employers, the public, and even other unionists that they had violated a contract. Of even greater consequence, the strike aroused a San Francisco business community that, until this time, had grudgingly accepted unions as an unpleasant fact of life.

An "emergency meeting" called by the San Francisco Chamber of Commerce indicated just how aroused the business community had become. Called ostensibly in response to Mayor Rolph's refusal to supply struck employers with special police officers, the meeting became a call to restore the open shop and rid the city of the union labor "disease" that for too long had made San Francisco a "class-ruled city." According to most estimates, some 2,000 persons attended the meeting, hearing speeches by some of San Francisco's most powerful businessmen: Frederick Koster, president of the Chamber of Commerce; Frank Anderson of the Bank of California; Philip Teller of the San Francisco Commercial Club; and William Sproule, president of the Southern Pacific Railroad. All of the speakers decried the city's toleration for "lawlessness and violence, " and they repeated the by now familiar charge that San Francisco's "closed-shop" reputation discouraged new businesses and capital investments. More important than their predictable speeches, however, the participants created a "Law and Order Committee." In just one evening the Committee raised $200,000 to fund its work. Within a week it had raised $600,000, on its way to an eventual war chest of nearly one million dollars.[17]

Although its name recalled San Francisco's notorious nineteenth-century "vigilante" committees, the Law and Order Committee was in fact the most recent incarnation of an employers' open-shop movement. Like San Francisco's earlier Citizen's Alliance or the M&M in Los Angeles, the committee promised to organize employers, offer financial, legal, and moral support to those who faced strikes or boycotts, and pressure union employers to run an open shop. At first, labor leaders responded to the creation of the Law and Order Committee as so much bluff and bluster, with the Labor Clarion claiming that the Committee would keep San Franciscans "highly amused . . . by their ludicrous antics and loud boastings."[18] But the Law and Order Committee did more than boast. Over the next two years, it led a relentless publicity campaign against labor's methods and intervened in numerous labor disputes. It pressured both individual employers and employer associations to turn over management of their labor disputes to the Committee, so as to better prevent the "defection of weaklings."[19] Most importantly, the Committee orchestrated a political drive to secure an anti-picketing ordinance that surpassed the labor injunction in its repressiveness.

FROM PREPAREDNESS DAY TO THE ANTI-PICKETING ORDINANCE

The event that strengthened the Law and Order Committee more than any other involved neither the principle of the open shop nor the methods of organized labor. On July 22, 1916, with the Law and Order Committee less than two weeks old, a bomb exploded along the route of San Francisco's Preparedness Day Parade. The parade, like several others around the nation, promoted the cause of military preparedness in the event of United States entry into World War I. The Chamber of Commerce and its Law and Order Committee strongly supported military preparedness; organized labor, on the other hand, opposed the parade and all other signs of "militarism."[20] Two days before the parade, the San Francisco Labor Council sponsored a "peace meeting" at the city's Dreamland Rink. Labor leaders encouraged San Francisco citizens, and trade unionists in particular, to boycott the parade. Some labor leaders even warned that "an attempt may be made by the enemies of labor to cause a violent disturbance . . . and charge that disturbance to labor." This warning seemed eerily prophetic when shortly after the parade began a bomb exploded, killing six and wounding about forty others. Another four people eventually died from injuries sustained during the blast. Suspicion fell almost immediately upon organized labor, as the conservative press recalled the "inflammatory" speeches that had been made at labor's Dreamland Rink meeting.[21]

Within a few days police arrested labor organizers Tom Mooney, his wife Rena Mooney, Warren K. Billings, Edward Nolan, and Israel Weinberg. Authorities later dropped charges against Rena Mooney, Nolan, and Weinberg, but Tom Mooney and Billings were tried, convicted, and eventually given life sentences at San Quentin prison. The story of the Mooney-Billings "frame up" has been told well and often, and there is no need to repeat the details of the long and complicated legal proceedings or the contradictory evidence.[22] While many labor leaders and a number of sympathizers protested the unfairness of the trial, Mooney and Billings did not seem entirely unlikely suspects at the time. During a 1913 strike against PG&E, Billings had been convicted of transporting dynamite, and, more recently, Mooney had led an abortive streetcar strike, during which someone had bombed the electrical towers that served as a power source for the streetcars. Even many in the labor movement suspected Mooney. On the day before the bombing, the *Labor Clarion* had claimed that Mooney was "steeped" in the ideas of sabotage associated with the "mental defectives known as the Industrial Workers of the World."[23] Nonetheless, the overwhelming evidence now suggests that Mooney and Billings, if not framed, were at best falsely tried. Even the judge who tried the case and two federal commissions later concluded that Mooney and Billings had not received a fair trial and were sent to prison on perjured testimony.[24]

At the time, however, the suspected involvement of trade unionists in the Preparedness Day bombing had much the same effect as the *Los Angeles Times* bombing six years earlier: open-shop employers and other trade union opponents used the incident as evidence of labor's lawlessness. For the Law and Order Committee the bombing was the "natural, logical result of a long period of tolerance of lawlessness" and labor's "domination of courts, police, and elected officials." The business weekly *Argonaut* opined that there was "a difference only in degree between the outrage of last Saturday [the bombing] and the almost innumerable murders and assaults that have invariably disgraced our labor disputes."[25] Organized labor, for its part, condemned those who would use the incident to rile public opinion "for the scarcely veiled purpose of abridging [labor's] constitutional rights." Much to the delight of organized labor, Mayor Rolph condemned the Chamber's meeting and declared that "law and order" would be maintained by the "duly constituted" authorities, not by the self-styled vigilantes of the Law and Order Committee.[26]

While labor and employers exchanged barbs, a strike by the city's culinary workers provided the Law and Order Committee with an ideal opportunity to intervene in a labor dispute on behalf of the open-shop principle and to demonstrate its worth to the city's employers. In early July the unions representing the city's cooks, waiters, cook's helpers, and waitresses had submitted to the Restaurant Keepers' Association a new wage scale based on the eight-hour day. Early conferences between the unions and employers failed to reach an accord. Less than two weeks into the strike, Mayor Rolph proposed submitting the dispute to a fifteen-member arbitration panel, with five employer members, five union members, and five "public" members chosen from among the city's clergy. Labor accepted this proposal, no doubt encouraged by earlier statements by Catholic and Methodist ministers in support of the strikers. But the Restaurant Keepers' Association, at the urging of the Chamber's Law and Order Committee, rejected the Mayor's proposal.[27]

From the beginning of the strike, the Law and Order Committee made "violence" the cornerstone of an extensive publicity campaign that was highlighted by the publication of a nationally circulated forty-page pamphlet entitled *Law and Order in San Francisco: A Beginning*. The Committee published lists of violent "outrages," which on closer inspection revealed relatively few acts of physical violence. For example, a list based on police and hospital records alleged twenty-two confirmed acts of "violence" in the ongoing culinary strike. Yet the Committee's own evidence showed that most of these involved no physical violence. Of the twenty-two incidents, fifteen involved arrests for "disturbing the peace" or using "abusive" or "loud and boisterous" language, with no report of physical assault; three involved "assaults" of unknown severity; three involved nonunion men "beaten" by strikers, or alleged strikers; and one involved throwing a "stink bomb" into an unfair restaurant. Some violence, of course, did occur. Black workers, forced into strikebreaking because they were barred from the culinary unions, especially felt the sting of striker violence. As Douglas Daniels points out in his history of San Francisco's black community, African-Americans often found themselves the target of angry strikers and, not unlike the Law and Order Committee, routinely complained of "the dictation of the labor unions."[28]

In addition to publicizing "violence," the Law and Order Committee turned to local authorities to stop picketing. When pickets gathered at some restaurants during the first few days of the strike, employers appealed first to the police. Labor leaders, however, had already reached a voluntary agreement with the police whereby only four pickets worked a single establishment—thereby avoiding the large crowds that made even the most sympathetic policemen uncomfortable.[29] As in the past, when police measures failed to satisfy, organized employers turned to the courts for injunctions. Between mid-August and late-September of 1916, local judges issued more than 100, and perhaps as many as 200, restraining orders. The content of these injunctions varied considerably. Judge Hunt, who had issued forty of the sixty-eight injunctions still pending in late September, banned all picketing. Other judges allowed "peaceful" or "silent" picketing, or the carrying of signs near the struck establishment without shouting at, or approaching, replacement workers or customers.[30]

But the injunctions apparently did not go far enough for the Law and Order Committee and its allies. In early August of 1916 the San Francisco Board of Supervisors considered passing an anti-picketing ordinance submitted by Supervisor Emmit Hayden and drafted by the legal counsel of the Law and Order Committee. Modeled after the 1910 Los Angeles law, the proposed ordinance banned all picketing or "interference" with the employers' access to customers or workers. Violators of the law faced a $300 fine and up to six months in jail. Similar ordinances proposed by employer organizations in the East Bay had had been rejected by the City Councils of Richmond and Oakland in 1913 and 1915, respectively. Similarly, San Francisco Supervisors showed little inclination to pass an anti-labor measure in an election year. After a two-hour debate, they rejected Hayden's proposal by a seven-to-two vote. Not easily deterred, the Law and Order Committee then circulated petitions to have an anti-picketing initiative placed on the ballot in the upcoming November elections.[31] Ironically, in using the initiative process, the Law and Order Committee made use of a Progressive-era political reform that organized labor had only recently played a key role in enacting.

The campaign for the anti-picketing initiative put organized labor on the defensive politically and sparked an intense public debate. Frederick Koster, president of the Chamber of Commerce, emerged as the key spokesmen for the employers' position. Koster's own relationship with unions seemed contradictory. On the one hand, Koster's barrel manufacturing business ran on a closed-shop basis, and he had always enjoyed friendly relations with the Coopers' Union. On the other hand, in 1914 Koster helped form the Merchants' and Manufacturer' Association of San Francisco, which dedicated itself to the same open-shop principles as the M&M of Los Angeles and absorbed what remained of San Francisco's nearly defunct Citizen's Alliance. When Koster became president of the Chamber of Commerce in early 1916, he quickly moved the organization toward support of the open shop. Organized labor always contended that Koster and the executive committee of the Chamber of Commerce did not represent the thinking of most employers. Nonetheless, Koster's Law and Order Committee won the support of at least 100 leading businessmen, and membership in the Chamber of Commerce more than doubled between July and October of 1916. If the growing membership opposed Koster's policies, few protested.[32]

In an address to the California Commonwealth Club Koster stressed that the Chamber accepted unions that were "properly conducted" and objected only to the unlawful methods of the trade unions. In addition to the usual emphasis on the fundamental "right" of the employer to run his business as he saw fit, Koster borrowed from the republican rhetoric of California progressives, claiming that the Chamber of Commerce sought only to protect the "community interest." Only by eliminating San Francisco's reputation as a city dominated by unions, Koster claimed, could the city draw new businesses and investments and reach its economic potential. While Koster raised the specter of labor "lawlessness," he mostly stuck to his chosen theme of "industrial statesmanship." Koster accepted that in the modern era it was inevitable that workers and employers would organize, but he hoped that they might proceed in a spirit of harmony and cooperation.[33]

Despite the statesman-like quality of Koster's speech, the Law and Order Committee's publicity campaign adopted a much more belligerent anti-union tone. In a series of newspaper notices and circulars the Law and Order Committee merged reports of picket line violence, memories of Union Labor Party corruption, the Preparedness Day bombing, and the "monopolistic" intent and effect of the closed shop to demonstrate labor's disregard for the law. Campaign literature lifted whole phrases and passages found in restraining orders or in leading state and federal decisions upholding the use of labor injunctions. Borrowing from an often-quoted 1905 federal ruling, several of the newspaper notices and fliers declared in bold letters that there was "no such thing as peaceful picketing, any more than there is lawful lynching or peaceful mobbing."[34]

So that labor might respond to the criticisms leveled by Koster and the Law and Order Committee, the Commonwealth Club invited the CFL's Paul Scharrenberg to speak on the "labor side of the open shop conflict." Scharrenberg ridiculed Koster's contention that the Law and Order Committee accepted "properly conducted" unions. Like the earlier Employers' Association or the Citizen's Alliance, the Chamber of Commerce sought to destroy unions in the name of the "open shop" and "law and order." While earlier open-shop drives claimed to act on behalf of the employers' "right to run their business to suit themselves," the Law and Order Committee, "not showing any such frankness and sincerity," claimed to support the "community interest." But like the earlier open-shop movements, the Chamber's plan, according to Scharrenberg, "[was] to create a general impression . . . that the labor unions freely practice coercion, intimidation, and violence." Once "the public mind" had been "poisoned" and "prejudiced" against labor unions, "it will be so much easier to crush and annihilate them."[35]

As the municipal elections drew nearer, the Law and Order Committee used part of its million-dollar fund to hire nearly 400 women, working in two shifts with nearly 200 telephones, to call voters in the days preceding the election and persuade them to vote for the Chamber's initiatives.[36] In addition to the anti-picketing ordinance, which received most of the attention, the Chamber sponsored two other measures. One, a proposed charter amendment making police court judges appointed rather than elected officials, reflected the Chamber's belief that police court judges pandered to the labor vote by routinely dismissing charges against strikers or giving them only nominal fines.

Another measure required all public "soapbox" speakers to apply for a permit from the Police Commission before making speeches on public streets or in public parks. Although this measure seemed aimed more at socialists and Members of the Industrial Workers of the World, mainstream labor unions pointed to both proposals as further evidence that the Law and Order Committee sought to subvert American principles of democracy and free speech.[37]

On November 7, 1916, the anti-picketing ordinance won 52 percent of the vote citywide, with the vote running heavily against the measure in the working-class districts south of Market Street, and heavily in favor in the city's other districts. Undoubtedly, the Law and Order Committee's well-financed campaign, especially its pioneering use of the telephone to reach voters, contributed significantly to the passage of the anti-picketing ordinance. But the Committee's other two initiatives failed. The initiative making police court judges appointed rather than elected, which the Committee had backed with as much vigor as the anti-picketing ordinance, received only 33 percent of the vote. Voters apparently did not reflexively respond to the Chamber's campaign, but selected from among the three proposals. Voters did not passively accept the argument that police court judges treated strikers any differently than strikebreakers; nor did they embrace the Chamber's proposed restrictions on political speech. Voters did, however, elect to ban picketing. The Law and Order Committee's publicity, the Preparedness Day Bombing, two decades of sometimes violent labor conflict, and two decades of judicial pronouncements on the inherent "intimidation" and "coercion" of picketing apparently prompted a slight majority of voters to restrict labor's favored method of collective action.[38] Across the Bay in Oakland, voters passed a similar initiative the following spring, even though the Oakland City Council had rejected an anti-picketing ordinance in 1915.[39]

At first, labor leaders tried to soften the impact of the anti-picketing ordinance with optimistic claims that the courts would declare the law unconstitutional. But the state Supreme Court had already upheld the almost identical Los Angeles ordinance, and there was little reason to believe that any of the justices had changed their minds.[40] Within a month of the election, the San Francisco Labor Council instructed its members to obey the ordinance until such time as it could be legally challenged or removed from the books through another initiative.[41] Most importantly, the anti-picketing ordinance and the Labor Council's recommendation prompted the culinary unions to cease picketing and, eventually, to give up the strike. A delegate to the CFL convention reported that the culinary workers "lost heart and gave up the struggle after the anti-picketing ordinance was adopted."[42] Whereas the generally pro-labor San Francisco police formerly used discretion in drawing the line between acceptable picketing and unacceptable assaults or intimidation, the new ordinance obliged them to stop all picketing, and it carried penalties of up to $300 and six months in jail. Unable to risk such heavy fines and jail terms, the culinary workers officially admitted defeat in mid-December. For the first time since the 1901 strike, an employers' organization had won a clear and convincing victory over a well-established San Francisco labor organization.[43]

LABOR'S 1917 ANTI-INJUNCTION BILL

Flush from its victory in securing an anti-picketing ordinance, the Chamber of Commerce next turned to the state legislature, where CFL labor lobbyists continued to support a progressive reform agenda. At its 1916 convention, the CFL decided to focus its legislative efforts on a few measures deemed most important, and the anti-injunction bill stood at the top of this shortened list.[44] The 1917 anti-injunction bill was both stronger and weaker than its predecessors. It was stronger in that it brought into a single bill all of labor's proposals for limiting the power of the courts: it prohibited injunctions in any case growing out of a dispute between employer and employee; declared that "peaceful" picketing and assembly for the purposes of "persuasion" was lawful and could not be enjoined; and called for jury trials in any contempt of court case arising out of a labor dispute. But the 1917 bill was weaker in that it abandoned the narrow and controversial definition of "property" that excluded "the right to do business" as a property right.[45]

Without a definition of "property" that clearly excluded "the right to do business," the act's qualifying clause—"unless necessary to prevent irreparable damage to property or to a property right"—created the likelihood that judges would read the law as a statutory affirmation of judge-made law. When the bill passed both the Assembly and the Senate by narrow margins, organized labor responded as though pleasantly surprised. Paul Scharrenberg and the CFL's legislative agents attributed success to the hard work of the legislative agents and the decision to focus on just a few issues (strengthening the Workmen's Compensation Act and regulating private employment bureaus were the other two areas of concentration). But Chester Rowell, who had opposed the earlier anti-injunction bills, provided a more convincing explanation for the bill's success after six years of failure. Writing in the progressive *California Outlook*, Rowell claimed that the bill passed because, without the redefinition of property, it was an "emasculated" version of the earlier bills. Moreover, judicial interpretations of the Clayton Act had already suggested that such laws would not necessarily restrain the courts.[46]

While the *California Outlook* no longer saw the anti-injunction bill as a threat, the San Francisco Chamber of Commerce sent its attorney, Max Kuhl, to lobby for its defeat. Kuhl acted as the "authorized representative of a number of important business organizations throughout the state," including at least sixteen Chambers of Commerce and various merchants' and employers' associations from San Diego to Redding.[47] Kuhl's legislative agenda was threefold: to ensure the defeat of labor's anti-injunction bill; to secure an anti-boycott bill that would have effectively overturned the court's approval of secondary boycotts in *Parkinson*; and to pass a mandatory "arbitration" bill that would have effectively outlawed strikes against public utilities. But organized labor still carried some weight in the state legislature, and Kuhl failed to garner enough support for the anti-boycott and arbitration bills. When the anti-injunction bill finally passed both houses of the state legislature, Kuhl presented his case in a public hearing before Governor William Stephens.[48] Here, Kuhl would find more success.

Kuhl's argument before Governor Stephens showed that employers, like labor leaders, could infuse their political arguments with the language of both law and progressivism. Kuhl presented three basic objections to the anti-injunction bill. First, he objected to the phrase declaring that "human labor was not a commodity." Borrowed from the federal Clayton Act, the phrase reflected a moral sentiment among trade unionists more than a concrete provision. Conflating "commodity" with "property," Kuhl argued that labor power was the only commodity, or property, that the workman possessed: "What other property has the poor man except his labor?"[49] Most labor spokesmen would have agreed on this point; the nonunion worker had a right to sell his labor power, just as the union worker had the right to withhold labor and refuse to work with nonunion workers. But when labor leaders claimed that there was no property right in human labor—and that labor was not a commodity—they meant that the *employer* had no property right in the labor of his employees (or potential employees). Injunctions, after all, were almost always sought by the employer, not the nonunion replacement worker. When courts spoke of the "property" that the injunction protected from interference, everyone knew that it referred to the property rights claimed by the employer.[50]

Kuhl's second objection was that the bill threatened the legitimate authority of the courts. The legislature, according to Kuhl, had no constitutional authority to interfere with the equity jurisdiction of the courts. To allow this bill, Kuhl warned, would undermine the separation of powers built into both the California and the United States constitutions. He also argued that the provision calling for a jury trial would subvert the court's power to compel obedience to its orders. To grant persons charged with contempt of court a jury trial would, Kuhl claimed, "pyramid trial upon trial," as even acts of contempt during a jury trial could only be prosecuted with yet another jury trial.[51] (Labor responded to such claims by noting that, in injunction cases, there was never an initial jury trial for the contempt trial to be "pyramided" upon. If trade unionists were to be sent to jail, they were entitled to a jury trial at some point.)[52]

Third, Kuhl warned Governor Stephens that the bill threatened many progressive state and local laws. By making peaceful picketing lawful, the anti-injunction bill undermined local anti-picketing ordinances that had been adopted by initiative or referendum. Kuhl reminded the governor that these two forms of "direct democracy" were two of the great achievements of the progressive political reforms that had only recently swept California. As such, the anti-injunction bill undermined the "political revolution" that "[w]e have boasted [about] in California these last few years."[53] Moreover, by eroding the power of the courts, Kuhl claimed, the anti-injunction bill jeopardized other progressive reforms that relied upon judicial restraining orders for enforcement. As examples, he cited a Red Light Abatement Act that allowed judges to ban the use of certain properties for purposes of prostitution, and a conservation measure that allowed judges to shutdown iron smelters that damaged local vegetation.[54]

Kuhl concluded his plea to the governor by depicting the bill as a product of "those newly distilled liquors of syndicalism and anarchy." Kuhl maintained that "a feeling of true patriotism" and "reverence for [American] institutions" compelled him to oppose "the unbridled and unjust attacks upon the judiciary" implicit within the bill. What the *California Outlook* had seen as a tame and ineffectual bill, Kuhl portrayed as a wildly radical danger to the very fabric of society: "Some men, mentally frenzied by the belief that life has not yielded to them all of [the] material return which they feel they deserve, have sought . . . to shatter the entire structure of our social system." The time had come, Kuhl reasoned, "for the sober, intelligent, and patriotic people of this state to call a halt." By raising the specter of "syndicalism" and "anarchy," Kuhl deliberately linked the methods advocated by mainstream labor unions to the more radical doctrines of the IWW, who since 1915 had become more active in California.[55]

It is impossible to know whether Governor Stephens was at all moved by Kuhl's sometimes inflated rhetoric, but he did veto the bill. The governor's veto did not come as a complete surprise to labor. Only three years earlier, as a member of Congress, Stephens had voted against the 1914 Clayton Act. In a short press statement explaining his veto Stephens questioned the constitutionality of those parts of the bill that "diminish[ed] the power of the courts." For example, he claimed that "the provision as to trial by jury of contempt offenders gravely menaces the authority of the courts in injunction proceedings." Avoiding the labor issue altogether, Stephens claimed that the bill would threaten the courts' power to enforce orders in areas "not contemplated" by its authors, and he used Kuhl's example of the Red Light Abatement law.[56] An editorial in the next *Coast Seamen's Journal* blamed defeat on Kuhl and the business interests that he represented. After the "intimidation, threats, and bulldozing tactics" had failed them in the Senate and Assembly, the editorial claimed, "the would-be labor crushers" focused their attention on the governor's office. By siding with these "standpat forces," the editorial concluded, Governor Stephens "had given notice that the progressive era [in California] has come to an end."[57]

CONCLUSION

That the *Coast Seamen's Journal* saw the governor's veto as a symbol of progressivism's demise ignored the fact that most progressive reformers had never supported labor's anti-injunction bills. Still, in many ways the journal had accurately described the fate of progressivism. Progressivism did not exactly disappear, but it ceased to be a driving or innovative force in California politics.[58] By the time the United States entered the war in Europe in 1917, the labor-progressive alliance that had produced so many pro-labor reforms had begun to break apart. Governor Johnson had

left the governor's mansion for a seat in the U.S. Senate. For organized labor, Johnson and the progressives had been imperfect
allies, but allies nonetheless. Now the enemies of labor employed
the methods and rhetoric of progressivism to justify restrictions
on labor's rights. Throughout the nation, American entry into
the war redirected the progressives' crusading impulse away from
domestic concerns and toward Woodrow Wilson's effort "to make
the world safe for democracy." In the process progressivism's liberal language of reform gave way to a more conservative language
of patriotism and "100 percent Americanism."[59] In this new context and without progressive allies, labor's political agenda would
become increasingly defensive.

Even in San Francisco organized labor confronted an altered
political landscape. After failing to defeat the anti-picketing ordinance, labor leaders led an unsuccessful and divisive effort to
recall District Attorney Charles Fickert. Angered by Fickert's vig-
orous prosecution of Mooney and Billings, the California Federation of Labor and several union locals—especially San Francisco's
culinary unions—raised funds to defend Mooney and Billings and
finance a recall of Fickert. But more conservative labor leaders—
like *Labor Clarion* editor James Mullen and prominent members
of the San Francisco Labor Council—wanted to wash their hands
of Mooney and Billings and opposed the recall of Fickert. Like
the 1916 waterfront strike and Preparedness Day bombing, the
Mooney-Billings case and the Fickert recall united employers
while it divided labor. As Robert Knight has argued, these divisions coincided with splits on other issues, such as the debate
over craft versus industrial forms of organization and, as we shall
see, how best to take advantage of federal labor policies during
the war.[60]

Chapter 5

THE PROMISE OF FEDERAL PROTECTION:
THE AMBIGUOUS LEGACY OF
WORLD WAR I

No one can tell what is going to happen with respect to the labor question, for the Government is very powerful.

JUDGE ELBERT GARY,
1919

Despite the setbacks that the California labor movement suffered at the local level in 1916 and 1917, America's declaration of war inspired a new round of labor activism and promises of federal protection. In the six months following American entry into the war, the United States saw more than 3,000 strikes, nearly matching the total for all of 1916.[1] To prevent labor militancy from threatening vital wartime production, the federal government took a greater role in settling labor disputes. At first the Wilson administration attempted piecemeal mediation efforts through the President's Mediation Commission or industry-specific arbitration boards, such as the Shipbuilding Labor Adjustment Board. In April of 1918, with strike activity still at unprecedented levels, the Wilson administration centralized wartime labor policy by creating the National War Labor Board (NWLB). In exchange for labor's cooperation in the war effort, the federal government promised to protect labor's right to organize and bargain collectively.[2] For a labor movement that had faced ubiquitous hostility from local courts, police, and open-shop employers, these federal guarantees offered hope and opportunity.

Yet World War I promised more than it delivered. To be sure, with the help of the federal government, organized labor made substantial gains during the war: trade union membership nearly doubled; the eight-hour day became the norm in most industries; and many mainstream labor leaders earned a degree of prestige through service on national policy boards.[3] But a number of factors limited federal support. First, although many members of the wartime agencies genuinely supported labor, the overarching goal of federal labor policy was to ensure the smooth functioning of the war economy. Protecting labor's collective bargaining rights was a means to that end. Second, the Wilson administration's decision to respect "existing standards" meant that federal agencies would protect existing trade unions and union shop agreements from employer attacks, but by the same token they would not force union recognition or union shops where they had not existed before the war. Third, and most importantly, whatever the stated policies of wartime labor boards, they lacked adequate enforcement powers.[4] Finally, federal support of mainstream unions existed alongside a well-orchestrated attack on radical labor organizations, especially the Industrial Workers of the World. Federal policies gave mainstream labor unions and the principle of collective bargaining a much-sought-after legitimacy, but often at the cost of reining in rank-and-file militancy and radical dissent.[5]

Despite these limitations, as Joseph McCartin and Jeffrey Haydu have recently argued, federal policy had unintended and often beneficial long-term consequences for organized labor. In addition to sparking rapid gains in union membership, federal policy encouraged union activists and inspired more aggressive demands, especially on the part of newly organized workers. Even where federal intervention did not force union recognition, the promotion of "shop committees" in previously unorganized sectors of industry inspired worker solidarity and laid a foundation for industrial unionism in the 1930s. Most importantly, McCartin argues, World War I fueled a debate over the meaning of "industrial democracy." This term meant different things to different parties; but for workers it legitimated demands for a greater voice in the workplace and portrayed union organizing as an act of "good citizenship" rather than as an act of collective self-interest. "Far from suppressing labor unrest," McCartin contends, the language of industrial democracy "empowered the workers' movement in ways no one could have foreseen."[6]

For California organizer J. B. Dale, "Democracy of Industry," as he called it, meant the "right of men to organize into a union and deal collectively with their employer."[7] This chapter considers the extent to which federal interventions protected this right, and how in turn such interventions shaped the California labor movement's approach to politics and the state. I intend to show that California labor leaders continued to pursue a progressive, pro-statist political agenda in the state legislature, but when it came to protecting rights of collective action, they looked increasingly to the federal government. Even when federal authorities failed to enforce their pro-labor rulings or curb hostile actions of local courts and police, they remained labor's most likely ally. At the same time, federal and state prosecution of radical labor groups posed serious questions for mainstream labor unions and created a repressive climate that eventually affected "bona fide" as well as radical unions. By 1919, without federal support or progressive allies, even mainstream unions found themselves increasingly on the defensive organizationally, legally, and politically.

LOCAL CONDITIONS AND THE IMPACT OF FEDERAL INTERVENTION

Federal interest in labor disputes did not begin with World War I. Two years before the United States entered the war, the United States Commission on Industrial Relations issued a scathing report on the state on industrial relations in the country. Created partly in response to the bombing of the *Los Angeles Times* building, the Commission set out to investigate the "causes of industrial unrest." For two years the Commission held hearings across the country, gathering thousands of pages of testimony from more than 700 witnesses. Among the leading causes of labor violence and unrest, the Commission's *Final Report* concluded, were the unequal administration of the law and the denial of labor's "right of organization." The report condemned the actions of local courts and police and called for federal laws to foster mediation and, more importantly, to protect labor's rights of collective action.[8] Labor leaders in California applauded the report as confirmation of the arguments they had been making for nearly two decades.[9] Although the Commission lacked the power to translate its proposals into law, it nonetheless pushed the "labor problem" to the center of public debate, insisted that organized labor had "rights," and held out the prospect that if local and state governments could not protect those rights the federal government might be forced to do so.[10]

World War I brought about the federal presence that the Commission called for, but, as Jeffrey Haydu has argued, local conditions shaped the outcome of federal interventions. The relative strength of organized labor and organized employers, the local history of their relations with each other, and the nature of labor's demands all affected the willingness of federal mediators to intervene and what they accomplished once they did. In San Francisco, well-established unions—with the help of federal mediators— won wage gains without recourse to strikes or with relatively short strikes. In Los Angeles and some East Bay communities, on the other hand, weaker and upstart unions found that federal mediators were either unwilling or unable to secure their demands. For labor unions throughout California, federal support and favorable economic conditions led to gains in membership, but this did not always translate into an ability to bring employers to terms or shield labor from local court and police hostility.

San Francisco and Northern California

No California industry benefitted more from the war than shipbuilding. By war's end the number of workers employed in shipbuilding in the San Francisco Bay Area alone was more than ten times the number employed in the whole state only ten years earlier. This influx of workers added strength (and at times tensions) to the well-established metal trades unions that had organized most workers in the San Francisco shipyards.[11] Functioning much like an industrial union, the San Francisco Iron Trades Council (ITC) represented the several metal trades unions involved in shipbuilding. The ITC signed contracts with employers organized in either the California Metal Trades Association (CMTA) or the California Foundrymen's Association (CFA). Although the agreements between the ITC and the employer associations did not expressly demand a closed shop, the shipyards operated as closed shops in practice, with virtually all skilled metal tradesmen belonging to a union.[12] In September of 1917 the ITC demanded that employers increase the wages of all workers by one-third to keep pace with inflation. When both the CMTA and the CFA refused these wage demands as excessive, about 30,000 men walked off the job, making it the largest strike in Pacific Coast history up to that point. Appealing to the "patriotism" of both workers and employers, representatives of President Wilson's Mediation Commission arranged meetings between the Iron Trades Council, the CMTA, and the CFA.[13]

Within one week, both sides agreed to submit the dispute to a recently created Shipbuilding Labor Adjustment Board—popularly known as the "Macy Board," for its chairman, V. Everitt Macy. Until the Macy Board made its final ruling, workers received between 10 and 20 percent wage increases depending upon their job category. In its final settlement in November the Board granted a 30 percent increase to most workers. The ITC complained that this still did not match the rapid rise in prices, so the Board granted another 10 percent increase on all work done under federal contract. When the ITC then demanded that even those employers not filling government contracts meet the federal wage scale, the CMTA refused. But after a short strike in the final week of December, the CMTA agreed that all of its members would pay the wage rates established by the Macy Board, whether they worked under federal contract or not.[14]

Not all Bay Area shipyard workers benefitted equally from federal mediation, and unions divided over how best to take advantage of federal policies. While the ITC, dominated by skilled workers in the well-established San Francisco unions, sought wage increases, newer unions in the East Bay shipyards wanted federal mediators to support other demands—from union recognition and the closed shop to insisting upon a local unions' right to boycott nonunion materials. For example, the East Bay Boilermakers' Union (which was chartered as an offshoot of the San Francisco Boilermakers in 1917) criticized the leaders of the San Francisco-based ITC for not making more aggressive use of wartime conditions. In 1918 the Boilermakers defied the ITC by calling a strike against Alameda's Bethlehem Shipbuilding Corporation, demanding a forty-four hour week and the closed shop. Only the combined pressure of the ITC, the Boilermakers' international union, and federal mediators persuaded East Bay union leaders to back down. Even then, the Boilermakers' and a newly chartered Shipyard Laborers' Union staged a series of unauthorized half-day "strikes" on Saturdays and effectively established the forty-four hour week on their own terms. By 1919 employers finally accepted the forty-four hour week and granted a "half-holiday" on Saturdays.

In part the conflict between the older and newer unions in the Bay Area reflected the East Bay unionists' resentment at San Francisco's domination of the Northern California labor movement, but it also reflected more fundamental divisions within the labor movement. Not only did the newer East Bay unions seek the union recognition and closed shops that the San Francisco unions already enjoyed, but they believed that favorable economic conditions and federal support warranted more aggressive demands and more militant strike tactics. Federal policy, however, reinforced existing power relations within the labor movement and exacerbated tensions by requiring that local unions route their grievances through central bodies like the ITC.[15] As Robert Knight has suggested, the divide between San Francisco and the East Bay found expression on other issues as well, as East Bay unions were more likely to support the Mooney-Billings cause, industrial forms of organization, and independent political action. While federal intervention led to many real gains in wages and union membership, it also exacerbated tensions within the labor movement.[16]

Although shipbuilding received the most attention, federal mediators also secured wage increases and averted strikes in many other Bay Area industries. Ralph Merritt, the federal Food Production Administrator in California, negotiated a number of disputes before they reached the strike stage. Merritt's authority covered both food production and distribution, and from 1917 to 1918 his mediation efforts prevented strikes among cannery workers, teamsters, milk wagon drivers, butchers, and warehouse workers. In many other instances employers profiting from the wartime economy conceded wage increases even without federal intervention. Many open-shop employers temporarily set aside their antiunionism so as not to upset the profitable war economy.[17] Even Frederick Koster, who led the Chamber of Commerce in creating the Law and Order Committee in 1916, caught the cooperative spirit and voluntarily negotiated wage increases with the Coopers' Union during the war.[18]

In the South Bay city of San Jose in 1917, federal intervention brought wage gains to historically unorganized cannery workers. Neither the California Federation of Labor nor the IWW had had much success organizing the unskilled migrant laborers who moved seasonally from place to place and from harvesting in the fields to processing work in the canneries.[19] Yet in 1917 a rather obscure union organizer, E. B. Mercadier, organized the "Toilers of the World" and signed up as many as a thousand cannery workers in and around San Jose. Although employers routinely depicted the Toilers of the World as an IWW union—and no doubt a few IWW members had been involved—the union in fact received its charter from the AFL in the spring of 1917. When employers refused to grant the union's request for a 25 percent wage increase, Mercadier called the workers out on strike in late July of 1917. Employers, through their Canners' League of California, warned President Wilson's Mediation Commission that the strike threatened the production of canned foods vital to the war effort. Although the President's Mediation Commission did not intervene, federal troops stationed at Camp Fremont occupied San Jose canneries the day after the strike began as a matter of military expediency.[20]

It was not clear exactly what role the troops would play, but the crisis prompted the formation of an ad hoc mediation commission made up of Ralph Merritt, the Federal Food Administration's representative in California; Harris Weinstock, representing the California Governor's office; and W. T. Boyce, an Assistant U.S. Immigration Commissioner representing the U.S. Department of Labor. When the mediators convinced employers to offer a 20 percent wage increase, Mercadier agreed to call off the strike. While the settlement did not earn recognition for the union—as some union members apparently wanted—it nonetheless represented one of the rare instances in which farm or cannery workers effectively organized to win any gains. The following year the Toilers won another raise and overtime pay without resorting to a strike. Although Jaclyn Greenberg's study of cannery workers in the San Jose area stresses that federal mediators quashed more radical demands for union recognition in the name of securing "industrial peace," by her own reckoning the wartime agreements were impressive achievements given the repeated failures to organize farm or cannery workers in previous years.[21]

Los Angeles and Southern California

In Los Angeles, as in the San Francisco Bay area, shipbuilding became the focal point of wartime labor unrest. But the metal tradesmen who worked in the Los Angeles shipyards had never recovered from their defeat in the 1910 to 1911 strike. While San Francisco's skilled shipyard workers enjoyed the eight-hour day and a closed shop, their counterparts in Los Angeles labored nine to ten hours per day under open-shop conditions. As federal dollars poured into the Los Angeles shipbuilding industry, however, organizers from both the California Federation of Labor and the American Federation of Labor tried to exploit improved economic conditions and sudden labor shortages.[22] When the California Shipbuilding Company won contracts to build submarines and torpedo boats, the local Metal Trades Council demanded the eight-hour day for skilled workers, recognition of the International Association of Machinists (IAM) as the employees' bargaining agent, and the closed shop.[23] In addition, strikers demanded the reinstatement of five men allegedly discharged for union activity. Company owner John F. Craig and his managers refused to even talk with union representatives. On April 30, 1916, 300 workers walked off the job.[24]

Within three days, United States Secretary of Labor William Wilson appointed Charles Connell—an immigration commissioner in Los Angeles who would play a role in several wartime strikes—to mediate the dispute on behalf of the Department of Labor. But employers remained firm in their commitment to the open shop and refused to recognize the IAM. Unable to cajole employers, Connell abandoned his mediation efforts after about two weeks and the plant resumed operations with imported strikebreakers.[25] By June nearly half of the original 300 strikers had returned to work. Small numbers of unionists continued to picket the plant under the watchful eyes of city police, but by mid-July the strike had all but fizzled out. Even though the federal government was the major contractor, federal mediators could not force a determined open-shop employer to recognize a union. Labor did, however, gain some consolation when, the following January, the government canceled its contract with the California Shipbuilding Company. According to the *Citizen*, the government did not do so as a form of retaliation against a recalcitrant employer, but because of dissatisfaction with the quality of work performed by poorly trained strikebreakers.[26]

The following year metal tradesmen called another strike, this time against the Los Angeles Shipbuilding and Drydock Company owned by Fred Baker. As head of the open-shop Founders' and Employers' Association, Baker had played a key role in defeating the 1910 metal trades strike, and he remained firm in his commitment to the open shop. Baker's company, like many others that benefitted from wartime production, did not work directly under federal contracts and therefore did not grant the eight-hour day. Yet the Metal Trades Council insisted that all union members—whether working on federal contracts or not—deserved federal wage and hour rates.[27] After the union submitted its demands to Baker, federal mediator Charles Connell once again tried, and failed, to reach a settlement. When Baker discharged nine union molders, for reasons that union members found dubious, the Metal Trades Council approved a strike. The Council demanded reinstatement of the discharged workers, the eight-hour day, and recognition of the IAM.[28]

Only about one-fourth of Baker's 500 employees walked out. As the strike seemed unlikely to succeed on its own, local labor leaders turned to various agencies of the federal government for support, hoping that it might fulfill its wartime pledges. First, labor leaders sent petitions to the United States Navy, the Emergency Fleet Corporation (the government agency that granted contracts to private shipbuilders), and Labor Secretary Wilson asking that the federal government take over operation of the company as a wartime measure. Their petitions produced no response.[29] Although the strike seemed all but defeated, strikers earned one last chance to secure at least some of their demands in December of 1918 when the National War Labor Board (NWLB) agreed to hold hearings on the dispute. The NWLB did not rule favorably on any of labor's demands, pointing out that the "existing standards" policy could not force union recognition or the closed shop where they had not been the rule before the war.[30]

That federal intervention in Los Angeles failed to bring labor the kinds of gains it had brought in San Francisco reflected divergent local circumstances. From the very beginning the federal government's commitment to maintaining "existing standards" ensured that federal mediators would not challenge the clearly established open-shop conditions in Los Angeles. Moreover, differences in pre-war union success determined the nature of labor's wartime demands. San Francisco unions, which had already won recognition and closed-shop conditions, sought wage increases from employer associations with whom they had already established working relations. Los Angeles unionists, on the other hand, hoped to use wartime conditions to win the kinds of union security that the San Francisco labor movement already enjoyed. Federal mediators found it easier to reach accords in San Francisco, for while wage scales readily lent themselves to compromise, demands for union recognition or union shops were either granted or they were not. In addition, because San Francisco unions negotiated with employer associations rather than individual employers, their disputes threatened the entire industry and therefore demanded more immediate federal attention. In Los Angeles, where unions struck single employers with a few hundred employees, federal mediators approached the disputes with less urgency. Finally, Los Angeles employers knew that if their resistance to mediation led to a strike, they were still likely to win the support of the local press and local officials. Employers in San Francisco, on the other hand, could never feel so confident.

If the shipyard strikes showed the limits of federal intervention in Los Angeles, two strikes against the city's streetcar lines demonstrated that even when the National War Labor Board (NWLB) intervened on labor's behalf, employers could simply ignore its rulings and turn to more cooperative local authorities. Furthermore, the streetcar strikes revealed two other aspects of the complex nature of "federal" intervention in wartime. First, federal mediators did not constitute the whole of the federal presence. At times the military and federal courts also intervened, and their objectives were not always consistent with the aims of the executive branch. Second, despite the sometimes disappointing nature of federal intervention, local unionists and rank-and-file workers remained both militant and hopeful that federal intervention would benefit them. Wartime hostility did not push labor toward a philosophy of antistatist voluntarism; rather, it made them look to the federal government—despite its limitations—as the most likely guarantor of labor's rights.

Sprawling Los Angeles was served by two major streetcar systems: the inter-urban Pacific Electric Company and intra-urban Los Angeles Railway Company. Both systems had remained free from labor disputes since Henry Huntington crushed the streetcar unions in the 1903 strikes. Nonetheless, labor continued its efforts. By the spring of 1918 the Brotherhood of Railroad Trainmen (BRT) had signed up about 800 of Pacific Electric's 1500 employees and claimed that at least two-thirds of the workers would support a strike.[31] In late June the union demanded increased wages and union recognition and threatened to strike on July 2, 1918, if these demands were not met. On the day before the proposed strike, the Pacific Electric ran full-page newspaper notices questioning the union's patriotism, pointing out that a strike would greatly paralyze business activity and thus hamper war-related production. Managers at Pacific Electric made it clear that they would not grant union demands or even recognize the BRT as the employees' representative.[32]

Pacific Electric had anticipated the strike. Only two hours after the strike began, a federal district court judge in Los Angeles, Benjamin Bledsoe, enjoined all forms of "interference" with an employer's right to run a business and charged that picketing led inevitably to "violence and intimidation." Judge Bledsoe then went one step further: he ruled that, by agreeing to work for a company with a well-stated open-shop policy, employees had tacitly entered into an open-shop contract. Individual employees, of course, had a right to break this "contract" by quitting. But the union organizers, who were not themselves employees of the company, unlawfully induced employees into "breach of contract" when they asked them to join a union. Thus, not only did Judge Bledsoe's order enjoin picketing, it appeared to prohibit union organizing against any company with a well-established open-shop policy.[33]

Judge Bledsoe was not the only federal authority to intervene in the strike. Claiming that the streetcars were needed to bring workers to the shipyards to complete federal war orders, the Naval Commander of the submarine base at San Pedro placed four sailors on each Pacific Electric car with orders to prevent any disruptions.[34] With a federal judge and the United States Navy—in

addition to the Los Angeles police force and up to 250 private
guards—already in the service of the employers, the union reluctantly sent its members back to work just one day after the strike
commenced. Organized labor once again turned to federal mediator Charles Connell. But the Pacific Electric rebuffed Connell's
overtures, pointing out that President Wilson's orders on federal
labor policy clearly stated that employers who did not recognize
unions before the war "need not do so during the war."[35] Union
officials called off the strike indefinitely, and instead concentrated
on preparing a case to present to the NWLB.[36]

Meanwhile, as the BRT prepared its case for the NWLB, the
Amalgamated Association of Streetcar and Railway Employees
(AASRE) reported rapid strides in its efforts to organize workers
on the intra-urban Los Angeles Railway. Under the leadership of
Ben Bowbeer, an AASRE organizer from San Francisco, the union
had recruited nearly three-quarters of the carmen employed by
the Los Angeles Railway. In September of 1918 the union asked
the NWLB to hold hearings on its demands for the eight-hour
day, increased wages, and the reinstatement of two discharged
employees. Two months later the NWLB agreed to consider both
the Pacific Electric and the Los Angeles Railway cases together.[37]

When the NWLB finally reached a decision in April of 1919, it
granted the union's wage demands and ordered the reinstatement
of workers discharged for union activity. In addition, the NWLB
held that, if the employers did not recognize a union, then they
must at least meet with an employee-elected grievance committee. With the war over and the NWLB soon to disband, perhaps it
is not surprising that both companies ignored the NWLB ruling.
When the Los Angeles Railway eventually granted the wage demands in July of 1919, it insisted that it did so "voluntarily" and
not at the behest of the NWLB or the union. Both companies refused to rehire discharged workers or meet with employee-elected
grievance committees, claiming that the committees were dominated by union members. To recognize such a committee, the
employers feared, would be tantamount to recognizing the union.

When it became clear that neither company intended to honor
the NWLB decision, workers on both lines called a joint strike for
August 16, 1919.[38]

After ignoring the orders of the federal agency, Los Angeles employers turned as always to more cooperative local officials. In the
days before the strike the Los Angeles Railway secured fifty special
police from the city, and the Pacific Electric received thirty special
sheriff's deputies from the county. In addition, the Los Angeles
County Civil Service Commission appointed 300 special officers
to serve both companies. The city placed its 600-man police force
on twelve-hour shifts and called back all officers then on vacation.
Judge Bledsoe's injunction against the Pacific Electric workers remained in place, and two days after the strike began the Los Angeles Railway won a Superior Court injunction restraining all "interference" with the company's streetcars.[39] Union leaders decided
to ignore the injunctions, and strikers continued to approach the
streetcars and implore strikebreakers to quit. Over the next few
days they disrupted streetcar strikes and created a number of skirmishes, a few of which turned violent. The *Los Angeles Record*,
the only daily to support organized labor, called upon the city to
take over operation of the streetcar lines. Instead, the city ordered
its beefed-up police force to break up all gatherings of strikers and
strike sympathizers.[40]

These repressive actions, however, diminished neither labor's
war-induced militancy nor its confidence in federal authorities.
Chicano track-layers, once again shattering stereotypes that portrayed them as poor union material, were the first to walk out in
sympathy with the striking carmen. Within days, railroad workers
from as far away as Colton and Santa Barbara staged short sympathy strikes in support of the Los Angeles strikers. On August
26, 1919, more than a thousand railroad shopmen employed by
the Southern Pacific staged a one-day strike and marched to the
Los Angeles Labor Temple. In addition to expressing support for
the streetcar strike, the shopmen called for federal ownership of
the nation's railroads.[41] Once again, local labor leaders responded
to legal hostility not by embracing antistatist voluntarism, but

by calling for an expansion of federal power. Troubled by these displays of local militancy, the AFL leadership warned that any union engaging in a sympathy strike risked losing its charter, and the national Railroad Brotherhoods demanded that the local BRT call off the strike against Pacific Electric. Both the BRT and the AASRE continued to strike for several more months before conceding defeat. Although the BRT survived, the AASRE suffered such dramatic losses in membership that it relinquished its office space in the Los Angeles Labor Temple.[42]

The shipyard and streetcar strikes were only the most notable of the myriad defeats that the Los Angeles labor movement experienced in 1918 and 1919. According to E. L. Bruck, the CFL's vice president for the Los Angeles district, "all of the strikes" in Los Angeles during these years drew injunctions.[43] Bruck no doubt exaggerated, but not by much. Certainly the most important strikes of the war period prompted court and police intervention. In the fall of 1919 alone, with the war over and the NWLB disbanded, strikes by bartenders, tailors, telephone operators, longshoremen, and shipyard workers all witnessed either injunctions or police interventions, if not both, and all ended in defeat.[44] However much federal labor policy promised to promote collective bargaining and protect labor's rights—and however much labor expressed confidence in federal authorities—workers in Los Angeles still found themselves at the mercy of open-shop employers and local courts and police.

ANOTHER KIND OF INTERVENTION:
"BONA FIDE" UNIONS AND
CRIMINAL SYNDICALISM

World War I brought to California still another form of federal intervention: persecution and prosecution of labor radicals and dissenters. Unions affiliated with the AFL won favor from the Wilson administration by supporting the war, but the Industrial Workers of the World (IWW), Socialists, and many pacifists who opposed the war faced severe repression. Under the 1917 Espionage Act and the 1918 Sedition Act, radical dissenters faced arrest and sometimes deportation; the Postmaster General removed radical and pacifist literature from the mails; and the Department of Justice raided the regional offices of the IWW. In the post-war period, in the wake of the 1917 Bolshevik Revolution and communist uprisings in Europe in 1918 and 1919, the instruments of government repression turned from dissenters and pacifists to labor radicals, anarchists, and other assorted "reds." A 1919 strike wave, scattered bombings attributed to anarchists, and international events all fueled an hysterical search for "subversives." United States Attorney General A. Mitchell Palmer's famous "raids" of November 1919 and January 1920 led to the arrests of thousands of suspected radicals and the deportation of hundreds of aliens.[45]

As Robert Murray noted in his classic study of the post-war Red Scare, while "all branches of the federal government ultimately became involved in one way or another in anti-radical activity, the situation in the states was even worse."[46] Indeed, California participated vigorously in the wartime and postwar repression of the IWW and other labor radicals, from the extra-legal actions of vigilantes and local officials to the state legislature's 1919 Criminal Syndicalism Act. Attacks on the IWW came through the same network of private associations, local courts, and police that restricted the collective action of the mainstream labor movement. Most California labor leaders responded to this situation with ambivalence, opposing repressive acts and measures while at the same time clearly distinguishing their "bona fide" unions from the "irresponsible" methods and ideology of the IWW.

Before World War I mainstream labor leaders and the CFL had consistently, if cautiously, defended the rights of the IWW against attacks by local employers and public officials. For example, the CFL and other labor organizations from throughout the state condemned the actions of local police and vigilantes during the IWW's "Free Speech" fights in Fresno and San Diego in 1910 and 1912, respectively. In each case local employers' groups and vigilantes, often with the cooperation of local police, brutalized IWW orators. In San Diego, when the jails filled with Wobblies arrested for violating local ordinances prohibiting public speech without a permit, off-duty policemen and vigilantes carried suspected IWW members to the edge of the city, beat them, burned them with cigars, tarred and feathered them, and told them not to return to the city. While the leadership of the CFL had no love for the IWW, they recognized that the "self-termed 'law and order' men" committing the outrages were the same men who railed against trade unionists. The CFL condemned infringements of free speech and assembly, for it invoked these same freedoms to justify picket lines and boycotts.[47]

California labor leaders came to the defense of the IWW once again in 1913, when an IWW-led strike at a hops ranch in Wheatland, California, turned violent, resulting in the deaths of two strikers, a deputy sheriff, and the Yuba County district attorney. Two IWW organizers, Blackie Ford and Herman Suhr, were eventually tried and convicted for the murders of the deputy and the district attorney (no one was held accountable for the deaths of the two strikers). Although no evidence ever linked Ford and Suhr to the actual shooting, a jury found them guilty of second-degree murder on the grounds that their actions incited the fatal riot, even if they did not do the shooting. Although careful to distinguish their own "bona fide" and "legitimate" unions from the "irresponsible" IWW, the CFL and many local labor organizations vigorously condemned the prosecution of Ford and Suhr, charging that they had been "railroaded." Paul Scharrenberg worked both publicly and behind the scenes—albeit unsuccessfully—to persuade Governor Johnson to pardon Ford and Suhr.[48]

When the United States went to war in 1917, mainstream labor leaders learned that defending the IWW against state repression became more costly. As a wave of IWW-led strikes hit California's Central Valley farms and food processing plants, state and local officials in California grew alarmed. George Bell, Executive Secretary of the state Commission on Immigration and Housing, asked the Justice Department to hold suspected radicals in federal camps for the duration of the war. At the same time, Bell hoped that federal power might reinforce the Commission's efforts to clean up farm labor camps. In addition to seeking federal action against the IWW, Bell wanted federal authorities to force employers to improve the poor working and living conditions that had pushed farm workers into the arms of the IWW in the first place.[49]

The Justice Department did not follow Bell's suggestions, but not because they were unconcerned with the activities of the IWW. Even before receiving Bell's appeal, the federal government had already made plans to deal with the IWW. In addition to the strikes in California's agricultural regions, IWW-led strikes throughout the West threatened timber, mining, and other industries vital to the war effort.[50] In September of 1917 the Justice Department used the 1917 Espionage Act to launch simultaneous raids on IWW regional offices throughout the country, including offices in Fresno and Sacramento. Bell and the Commission of Immigration and Housing, however, did not find the federal approach to their liking; they complained that the high-profile raids only brought attention to the IWW and stirred up "class hatred," while Bell had hoped for a more "quiet" approach. In addition, the federal raids did nothing to force the growers to improve labor camp conditions.[51]

Even before the federal raids, California and a few other western states had attempted to thwart the IWW "menace" through state "anti-syndicalism" or "anti-sabotage" laws. Idaho and Minnesota passed the first such laws in 1917. The Idaho statute, which became the model for California's first "Criminal Syndicalism" bill in 1917, defined criminal syndicalism as any doctrine that "advocated crime, sabotage, violence, or other unlawful methods of terrorism as a means of accomplishing industrial or political reform."[52] Introduced by Assemblyman T. R. Finley, who represented an agricultural district in Santa Barbara County, the 1917 California bill not only outlawed "sabotage," but made it unlawful to advocate criminal syndicalism or to belong to any organization that advocated such doctrines. The bill drew its greatest support from the agricultural areas of the state, especially the Sacramento and San Joaquin valleys, where the IWW had led a number of strikes and showed signs of increased activism in 1917. The greatest opposition came from urban lawmakers from the San Francisco Bay area and other consistent supporters of organized labor. Some Assembly members, while not opposing the general intent of the bill—which clearly targeted the IWW—raised questions about the broad definition of "sabotage." Nonetheless, the Assembly passed the bill by a wide margin and sent it on to the Senate.[53]

Once in the Senate, the bill encountered the opposition of William Kehoe, chairman of the Senate Judiciary Committee. Kehoe, a progressive Republican from Eureka, routinely earned high marks from organized labor. Labor leaders who testified before Kehoe's committee complained that the vagueness of the bill's terms might subject the strikes and boycotts of all trade unions to prosecution under the Act. With little fanfare or explanation, Kehoe's committee voted unanimously to table the bill.[54] But this only stalled the drive for a criminal syndicalism law. In the next legislative session none other than Senator Kehoe introduced a slightly revised criminal syndicalism bill.

Between the defeat of the criminal syndicalism bill in April of 1917 and its reintroduction in January of 1919, the political climate had changed considerably. Most notably, the wartime attacks on dissenters had evolved into an anti-radical hysteria fueled by the press and government officials at all levels. In California, and in the West more generally, the IWW became the major target of concern, both during the war and after.[55] On December 17, 1917, just over two months after the federal raids on IWW headquarters, a bomb exploded at the Governor's mansion in Sacramento. While the blast caused no injuries and very little damage, it prompted one of the most celebrated trials in California history. Almost immediately, the Sacramento Chief of Police and most newspapers in the state blamed the IWW. Less than one week after the explosion, the Sacramento police arrested two Wobblies who, the police claimed, had received packages of dynamite though the mail.[56] In the weeks that followed local authorities raided IWW halls throughout Northern California. By mid-January of 1918, fifty-three Wobblies sat in the Sacramento County jail.[57]

Although a local agent of the Department of Justice questioned the basis on which the men had been arrested, California Governor William Stephens, Assistant Attorney General Raymond Benjamin, the president of the Sacramento Chamber of Commerce, and the publisher of the *Sacramento Bee* met with federal authorities in San Francisco and encouraged them to bring charges under the federal Espionage Act.[58] In February a federal grand jury indicted the jailed Wobblies on several counts of "conspiracy," including conspiracy to violate the Espionage Act, to disrupt West-coast shipping and industry, and to prevent the fulfillment of government war contracts. Four of the jailed Wobblies fell victim to the influenza epidemic, and one to tuberculosis, while awaiting trial. In January of 1919, a year after the original arrests, a jury took just over an hour to convict all forty-six defendants: forty-three received sentences ranging from one to ten years; two defendants from San Francisco who used attorneys received two months; and the one woman among them received a $100 fine.[59]

Only days after the verdicts, Senator William Kehoe—the chairman of the Judiciary Committee that had tabled the 1917 bill—introduced Senate Bill 660, the 1919 Criminal Syndicalism bill. Drafted by U.S. Assistant Attorney General Raymond Benjamin in consultation with Governor Stephens, Kehoe's bill differed from the 1917 version in that it more clearly defined "sabotage" as "willful and malicious damage or injury to property." In addition, where the 1917 bill had prohibited advocating violence or sabotage as a means of bringing about "industrial or political reform," the 1919 bill outlawed advocating such means to accomplish "a change in industrial ownership or control, or affecting any political change." Like the 1917 bill, the 1919 version also outlawed membership in any group that advocated violence or sabotage. The bill originally stipulated a sentence of not more than twenty years, but this was later reduced to fourteen years.[60]

In the two months between the bill's introduction and the final

Senate vote, California and the West experienced chronic labor unrest and almost daily reports of IWW "plots," as well as the Seattle General Strike. During this same period the press and many public officials attributed several bomb threats and the death of an Oakland woman to the IWW, although no evidence ever linked the Wobblies to the bomb threats and a confession later exonerated the IWW members accused of the murder.[61] Even many labor papers charged that "reds," "soviets," and "aliens" sought to undermine the mainstream labor movement. *Labor Clarion* editor James Mullen went so far as to condemn the San Francisco *Daily News* for its "red tinge" in labor reporting.[62] In this climate the criminal syndicalism bill received a unanimous recommendation from the Senate Judiciary Committee and passed on the Senate floor by an astonishing thirty-three to zero vote.[63]

In the Assembly labor lobbyists and their legislative allies worked to ensure that the bill would not harm the interests of "bona fide" trade unions. Given the political climate, CFL president Daniel Murphy and Paul Scharrenberg accepted the need for a criminal syndicalism law of some sort. But fearing that the law might be used against "legitimate" strikes or boycotts, they tried to amend the bill.[64] From their experience with injunctions, labor leaders and lawyers had learned that a broad definition of "property" gave judges a great deal of latitude. As such, they recommended changing "property" to "*physical* property" in the bill's definition of "sabotage." This would exempt labor's interference with an employer's "business" or expected profits (considered "property" in the injunction cases) from the law's meaning of sabotage. The Committee agreed to this change.[65] Wanting even more assurance that the law would not punish traditional trade union methods, labor's representatives proposed adding the following clause: "Provided, however, that the lawful purposes and acts of labor organizations in conducting strikes and boycotts shall not be construed to be a means of accomplishing a change of industrial ownership or control, or of affecting any political change as those terms are used in this act."[66] The Assembly rejected this amendment by a vote of fifty-three to sixteen, apparently agreeing with

Assemblyman Kasch of Mendocino County (home of a virulently open-shop lumber industry) that "if organized labor steps over the line . . . it should also be made subject to the penalties provided." After passing in the Assembly by a large margin, the bill was signed by Governor Stephens and became effective immediately.[67]

Labor leaders noted that "while [the act] should not affect the ordinary and lawful activities of labor unions," they nonetheless feared that "the enemies of Organized Labor [who] have great influence with the courts" would use the act's "uncertain and unusual legal phrases to harass . . . the legitimate trade-union movement." Although labor lobbyists tried to repeal the bill in the 1921 legislative session, labor had initially only asked for amendments. In addition, while the CFL's Executive Council agreed to fund the legal defense of any "trade unionist" charged under the law, it refused to support the left-leaning Labor Defense League, which would have defended IWW and "bona fide" unionists alike. The CFL's final report on the 1919 legislative session expressed grave doubts about the bill, but added that "as long as radicals show little or no regard for our laws and institutions, such legislation will probably have to be endured as a passing evil."[68]

Labor Politics and the 1919 Anti-Injunction Bill

A wartime and postwar climate that associated even mainstream labor with radicalism shaped labor's argument on behalf of the anti-injunction bill in the 1919 legislative session. As they had in the debates over the Criminal Syndicalism bills, labor and its supporters invoked the IWW's alleged disregard for the law. Labor's 1919 anti-injunction bill—its last such effort until the 1930s— was identical to the bill vetoed by Governor Stephens in 1917. While keeping up its attacks on the IWW and other labor radicals, the *Labor Clarion* tried to use the prevailing hysteria to marshal support for labor's rights, arguing that those who denied to labor "the right to organize" furthered the cause of "bolshevism" and "undermine[d] the faith of the people in the integrity and impartiality of the courts."[69] In the legislature labor's supporters used a similar tactic, defending the anti-injunction bill by contrasting "bona fide" unions with the lawless IWW. Senator Flaherty, a former union member and the bill's author, asked fellow senators to support the anti-injunction bill because, "unlike the I.W.W.s who sneer at all laws and assert that the end justifies the means," the CFL unions came before the senate "man-fashion declaring that they suffer under government by injunction judges."[70] But other senators either rejected Flaherty's distinction or found it beside the point. By a vote of twenty-three to seventeen, the Senate defeated the 1919 anti-injunction bill.[71]

Later that year Paul Scharrenberg tried to explain the defeat of the anti-injunction bill. Noting the "hysterical" debate surrounding the criminal syndicalism bill, he attributed the anti-injunction bill's defeat to the efforts of a "reactionary" legislature that made every effort to confound "trade union activities . . . with certain practices connected with radical propaganda."[72] If Scharrenberg's analysis were correct, the labor movement he represented was not entirely blameless. When trade unionists and their political allies defended rights of "bona fide" unions by invoking the IWW's disrespect for the law, they revealed a deep ambivalence, if not a contradiction; they opposed state repression of labor radicals while simultaneously contributing to the rhetoric that justified it.

Historians have interpreted labor's contribution to the postwar Red Scare in a variety of ways: the inherent conservatism of American workers; the iron-hand rule of conservative AFL leaders; the influence of an anti-socialist Catholic Church on a labor movement dominated by Catholics; and the narrow institutional interests of trade unions that competed with the IWW for the hearts, minds, and union dues of the American working class.[73] But the ambivalent stance of most California labor leaders had another source: the questionable legal status and charges of "lawlessness" that even "bona fide" unions had endured. After twenty years of court and police hostility, labor leaders tried to define the legitimacy of their methods and objectives in contrast to the alleged illegitimacy of the IWW. In the process they abandoned the more universal language of rights that had marked the earlier campaigns to curb interventions by courts and police. In the Progressive era, mainstream labor's determination to defend rights of collective action had led it to support the IWW Free Speech fights and to defend the rights of Ford and Suhr. During the Red Scare, however, supporting the rights of the IWW seemed too costly.

In addition to its efforts to pass an anti-injunction bill and limit the damage of the criminal syndicalism bill, the CFL continued to pursue progressive political reforms that benefitted organized and unorganized workers alike. After the anti-injunction bill, extending Workmen's Compensation to include agricultural workers and greater regulation of private employment agencies topped the CFL's list of legislative priorities. Even as the war seemed to drain the progressive reform impulse, the CFL still placed itself at the forefront of the "revolution in the political and economic affairs of our state." In the face of an increasingly "reactionary" state legislature and Governor's office, the CFL still stood for "progressive state government." As usual, the CFL's political platform bore little resemblance to the "antistatist voluntarism" of Samuel Gompers and the AFL. At its 1918 and 1919 conventions, the CFL joined the Farmers' Educational and Cooperative League and the Pacific Co-Operative League to endorse a farmer-labor platform that called for government support of cooperative enterprises, state ownership of public utilities, government health insurance, an expansion of the state's public employment bureaus, and support of the federal Plumb Plan, which sought to continue federal management of the railroads into the post-war period.[74]

1919: "Red with Revolution"

While labor continued to pursue a progressive political agenda, it did so without the support of progressive allies and in a climate that had grown increasingly hostile to labor activism. Despite their best efforts to distinguish themselves from the IWW, California labor leaders found that the postwar Red Scare endangered bona fide as well as radical unions. In the summer and fall of 1919 strikes by longshoreman in San Francisco and Los Angeles elicited accusations that trade unions had come under the influence of the IWW and other labor radicals. Labor now fended off charges of "bolshevism," "anarchy," and "radicalism" as well the usual accusations of "intimidation" and "coercion." Such charges came amid one of the greatest strike waves in the nation's history.[75]

Since 1916, San Francisco longshoremen worked under closed shop conditions for employers organized in the Waterfront Employers' Union (WEU). During the war the longshoremen won wage gains without resorting to strikes, but these gains were negated by rapid wartime and postwar inflation. In the late spring and early summer of 1919 the union notified the WEU of its intent to terminate the existing agreement. Reflecting the pattern of more aggressive wartime and postwar bargaining, union demands went beyond wage and hour issues to include union representation on the boards of directors of the WEU's member firms, a stock- and profit-sharing plan, and work rule changes reducing the amount of cargo that longshoremen handled per hour, effectively reversing a "speed-up" that the union had agreed to during the war. Attempting to exploit Red Scare hysteria to its own ends, the union warned that granting such demands was the "only way" to keep the country from "running red with revolution."[76]

The WEU rejected these demands as "extreme radicalism," offering a wage increase as a compromise. In a secret ballot union members first elected, by a narrow margin of 939 to 911, to accept the compromise. But in a "rising vote" a few days later, union members reversed themselves and rejected the offer. Employers complained that a "radical" minority within the union had called the "rising vote" to coerce and intimidate the "conservative and law-abiding" majority among the rank-and-file.[77] Taking a page from the Law and Order Committee's open-shop drive of 1916, the WEU and the Chamber of Commerce published full-page notices in the daily newspapers that cited every arrest and disturbance as another example of labor's "lawlessness," made charges of "anarchy" and "bolshevism," and warned "the law-abiding citizens of San Francisco" that the longshoremen's union had been taken over by a "radical and lawless minority."[78]

For two weeks the strike produced only "minor disturbances," but in time the waterfront erupted in violence. One union member was shot by a strikebreaker,' another—a union sheet metal worker possibly mistaken for a strikebreaker—was killed by a striker.[79] The worst violence occurred on November 15, when groups of strikers, sometimes numbering in the hundreds, roamed the waterfront and attacked nonunion workers throughout day. The attacks started in the morning when a group of strikers severely beat twelve African-American stevedores attempting to board a ferry to Oakland. Although the police did little to stop the morning assault, they responded more quickly when the attacks erupted again in the afternoon. By the end of the day, the police had arrested 119 union members, who were later released when the union paid the bail of $5 per person. As many as 150 nonunion workers required medical treatment. Employers pointed to the "riot" as more evidence of radical influence.[80]

The violence came as daily papers still carried headlines on a violent confrontation in Centralia, Washington, where only days earlier a parade celebrating the first Armistice Day ended in a bloody clash between American Legionaries and local Wobblies. In response to such reports local employer and civic groups warned that similar outbreaks might occur in California. Over the next few days the violence of the longshoremen's strike shared head-lines with stories about raids against IWW offices in Los Angeles and Berkeley, IWW arrests and an ordinance banning public as-semblages in Oakland, and a pronouncement by the Sacramento American Legion of plans to work with the local sheriff and police to combat IWW "espionage." Fears of IWW radicalism and strike violence converged when employers hinted that they would ask Governor Stephens to dispatch the militia to San Francisco.[81]

This proved unnecessary. In early December the WEU an-nounced that it had signed an agreement with a new union, the Longshoremen's Association of the San Francisco Bay Area. Ac-cording to employers, the new union had been formed by the "conservative and law-abiding element" who opposed the radical leadership of the Riggers' and Stevedores' Union.[82] Labor spokesmen, on the other hand, claimed that the new union was a "company union" formed by a foremen's group in cooperation with management. Nonetheless, the WEU claimed that a thousand longshoremen signed with the new Longshoremen's Association. From that time forward, the WEU only hired workers who joined the Longshoremen's Association, or the "Blue Book" union, as it came to be known. With little public support, and with even the San Francisco Labor Council divided on the merits of the strike and its demands, the longshoremen's strike ran out of steam by the end of the year. The Blue Book Union quickly displaced the Riggers' and Stevedores' Union, until the former was finally eliminated as a result of San Francisco's dramatic 1934 waterfront strike.[83]

In Los Angeles strikes by longshoremen and shipyard workers also brought charges of IWW domination. During the war a number of shipyard strikes, both large and small, ended in failure. Through the summer and fall of 1919 metal tradesmen and laborers in the shipyards, from San Pedro to Long Beach, tried once again to win wage increases from their employers, and again they failed. Employers in San Pedro and Long Beach won injunctions from local judges, but this alone did not defeat the strike. Rather, the cancellation of war orders produced layoffs at the very time that soldiers and sailors returned from the war, a combination that left the strikers with little bargaining power. Many shipbuilders simply ceased production during the strike. By November 8, 1919, the Metal Trades Council had called off the strikes, as Charles Piez, head of the wartime Emergency Fleet Corporation, visited Los Angeles and praised the open-shop conditions that prevailed in its harbor.[84]

While the shipyard strike was still in progress, San Pedro's Local 38–18 of the International Longshoremen's Association (ILA) also struck. Unlike the shipyard workers, the longshoremen won wage gains and added members during the war without resorting to strikes. Wages, however, had still not kept pace with inflation.

Wanting to test their strength, Local 38–18 demanded a wage in-crease from the Outer Harbor Dock and Warehouse Company in San Pedro. When the company refused wage demands, the long-shoremen struck on October 14, 1919. Except for a few attacks on strikebreakers, the first two weeks of the strike passed without the violence or large-scale disturbances that had marked the 1916 strike. Newspapers reported that the strikers places were quickly filled, and the M&M announced that it had the names and ad-dresses of 10,000 workers nationwide who wanted to move to the Los Angeles area.[85] From the beginning the strike showed few signs of succeeding.

Shortly after the strike began, the San Pedro Chamber of Com-merce issued a declaration in favor of the open shop. Much like the declaration issued by the San Francisco Chamber of Commerce in 1916, the San Pedro version claimed to recognize labor's right to organize "for the betterment of their condition along lawful lines," but added that the Chamber was "unalterably opposed" to the union's unlawful methods of "threats and intimidation." Unlike earlier open-shop arguments that condemned union "coercion" as an interference with an employer's right to run his establish-ment, members of the San Pedro Chamber of Commerce now stressed union interference with the right of nonunion workers to seek employment. "The pathways of San Pedro," a Chamber spokesmen declared, "should be made safe for those who desire to work without danger of assault from picketing." Members of the Chamber equated "slugging picketers" with "Bolshevistic ag-itators," while locating their position in the "flag and the Con-stitution of the United States and the right of every American citizen to pursue his chosen pursuit in a lawful manner without molestation." In addition to its declaration, the Chamber created a press relations committee to "create public sentiment in favor of the open shop."[86]

Labor leaders threatened to boycott any business that signed the open-shop declaration, which up to this point had only been adopted by voice vote at the Chamber of Commerce meeting that drafted the proclamation. Undeterred by the boycott threat, the

Chamber's Executive Council submitted the open-shop declaration to a vote of the entire membership through mailed ballots. Those who participated voted 378 to 29 in favor of the open-shop statement.[87]

The San Pedro strike took place at the height of the postwar Red Scare and a nationwide strike wave. Los Angeles newspapers carried almost daily reports of alleged IWW plots in the fall of 1919. In November, only days after the Centralia violence, about fifty men dressed in soldier's and sailor's uniforms raided IWW offices in Los Angeles, confiscated papers and other materials, and destroyed offices and furniture. Four IWW members inside the office at the time were beaten severely enough to require hospital treatment. Claiming not to know the attackers' identity, the Los Angeles police did not arrest any of the men who raided the offices; they did, however, arrest the four injured Wobblies and the wife of one of the injured men for violating the state's new criminal syndicalism law. The five were eventually tried and convicted with evidence confiscated by the unknown raiders. Increasingly, employers, the *Times*, and the full-page notices of a newly created "Industrial Freedom League," claimed that the IWW and Bolsheviks had infiltrated several Los Angeles labor unions. Like the longshoremen and shipyard workers, unions in the garment industry also faced charges of IWW influence, although Los Angeles labor historians Richard and Louis Perry claim that no more than 10 percent of the membership had anything to do with the IWW.[88]

Fear of union radicalism heightened in the late fall of 1919, when Los Angeles police officers threatened to form a union. For a few nervous weeks, the city braced itself for a police strike not unlike that which had rocked Boston earlier in the year. Newspaper editorials shuddered at the prospect of a police force "subject to the orders of the red unionite bosses," and the *Los Angeles Times* thought it a bad omen when police Captain Spellman of the San Pedro division reported that police officers "might be a trifle in sympathy with the strikers." Judge Works of the Los Angeles Superior Court alluded to heightened tensions and radical threats within the labor movement when he gave the maximum sentence of five days in jail *and* a $500 fine to two shipyard workers who had violated an injunction against picketing. "I think it is not going too far to say," Judge Works stated as he passed sentence, "that labor unionism is on trial before the world today." Works thought it "particularly necessary" to impose a maximum fine "at this particular time, when the world seems a mass of tinder and there is a lack of respect throughout the world for law and order and for courts." Works hoped that the maximum sentence would "send a message" to the unions to entrust their leadership to more "responsible" hands.[89]

As 1919 came to a close, the longshoremen and the shipyard workers joined the streetcar employees, journeymen tailors, telephone operators, bartenders, and many others in admitting defeat. After weighing labor's prospects, the Los Angeles Central Labor Council decided not to endorse any more strikes until at least the following spring. Attempting to save face, Joseph Taylor of the ILA's Pacific Coast division tried to persuade employers to allow striking longshoremen to return on terms that prevailed before the strike, but the employers refused.[90] Notwithstanding the accusations of employers and the *Los Angeles Times*, the IWW exercised only modest influence in the longshoremen's and shipyard unions before the 1919 strikes. It was, ironically, only after employers had defeated the mainstream unions that the IWW gained much ground among longshoremen and the harbor's unskilled laborers. At the end of the year, members of the San Pedro Laborer's Union voted to surrender their ILA charter and most moved into the IWW's Marine Transport Workers' Industrial Union.[91]

CONCLUSION

While the United States Commission on Industrial Relations had only proposed a program for federal protection of labor's rights, World War I provided an opportunity to implement such a program. President Wilson's proclamation creating the NWLB paralleled the Commission's recommendations in its formal recognition of labor's rights and its plan for federal intervention. For American workers who were showing signs of increased militancy as early as 1916, these promises provided still more incentive to form unions, make more aggressive workplace demands, and strike in unprecedented numbers. Yet the NWLB and other agencies reflected wartime expediency more than a lasting commitment to labor's collective rights. Both by policy and in practice federal intervention (and nonintervention) reinforced the status quo as often as it challenged it. When the NWLB ruled in favor of organized labor, local employers could, as they did in Los Angeles, ignore the rulings and turn to local courts and police to break strikes and stifle union demands.

Moreover, the war and its aftermath created a climate hostile to labor's organizational and political aspirations. A revived open-shop movement showed that it too could embrace the language of the law, defending the rights of employers and nonunion workers and linking the values of the open shop to the community's desire for "law and order." When labor unrest heightened postwar anxieties, open-shop employers exploited the situation by equating strikes and picketing with radicalism, lawlessness, and un-Americanism. Politically, CFL labor lobbyists found themselves on the defensive, seeking to mitigate harmful measures like the Criminal Syndicalism Act while looking to a diminishing corps of progressive allies to support labor's progressive reform measures. At times trade unionists added to their woes by genuinely opposing violence but committing just enough to lend credence to open-shop rhetoric and judicial presumptions. Finally, mainstream labor leaders contributed to the Red Scare by attacking the radicalism of the IWW in an effort to define their own legitimacy. This tactic backfired when employers charged that "a lawless and radical minority" influenced, if not controlled, even bona fide unions.

As Judge Elbert Gary noted in 1919, just how society answered the "labor question" would depend upon how the federal government used its considerable power. During World War I and in its immediate aftermath, the federal government displayed its power, but not in ways that clearly settled the labor question. Yet even when frustrated by federal intervention, labor leaders in California continued to express confidence in federal authorities.[92] For however disappointing the federal government's wartime labor policy worked out in practice, it at least formally recognized labor's rights of collective action. Given the record of local courts and police, the federal government still seemed the most likely guarantor of labor's rights. But for the time the promise of federal protection remained unfulfilled. As organized labor entered the 1920s, the legitimacy of its methods remained as tenuous as ever.

Chapter 6

The "American Plan" and Labor's Use of the Injunction
in the 1920s

*The American plan . . . [is] nothing more natural than . . . the open shop
movement . . . [the] re-establishment of American ideals, ethics, and institutions.*

C. A. Fultz,
Los Angeles Merchants' and Manufacturers' Association, 1922

*All the court injunctions on earth cannot make these black things white, cannot
make them just, cannot make them American.*

Paul Scharrenberg,
California, Federation of Labor, 1922

As labor historian Irving Bernstein observed, the nature of work
and the relations between employers and employees underwent
a profound transformation in the first two decades of the twentieth century. But when it came to labor law, Bernstein concluded,
"the dead hand of the past reigned supreme."[1] And so it was in
California. Nearly two decades of political agitation against police and court intervention had failed to free labor from the law's
ancient grip. Wartime agencies had encouraged the growth of labor unions, asserted labor's right to organize and bargain collectively, and provided a degree of legitimacy to a labor movement
constantly fending off charges of "lawlessness." Yet even federal
power could not lift the dead hand of the past. By the time the
dust of war and reaction had settled, labor's methods remained as
legally suspect as ever. As we shall see, continued legal hostility
did not dampen labor's enthusiasm for political action and state-
sponsored reform in the 1920s. With much justification, the California labor movement continued to see itself as a spearhead of
political, social, and economic reform in the Golden State, even

though an altered political landscape prevented any reproduction of labor's Progressive-era legislative achievements.

In addition to their legal and political woes, California trade unionists faced a postwar open-shop movement determined to turn back labor's wartime organizational gains. Playing upon a Red Scare obsession with "100 percent Americanism," organized employers dubbed their new movement the "American Plan," but to organized labor it was the old open shop idea with a new name, patriotism. Whether old or new, the American Plan posed a real threat to organized labor. As the open shop became the norm in both Los Angeles and San Francisco by the early 1920s, organized labor looked to the national level for solutions: first by supporting the third-party presidential campaign of Robert LaFollette in 1924, and second by asking the United States Attorney General to take action against the "coercive" tactics of the American Plan. Both of these efforts ended in failure, but unbeknownst to labor at the time they pointed a path to the future.

"ON THE DEFENSIVE": LAW AND LABOR POLITICS IN THE 1920S

By almost all accounts organized labor in California and throughout the nation fared poorly in the 1920s. To be sure, an expanding economy led to increased wages for many workers and reduced unemployment in most sectors of the economy. In the past such conditions had always stimulated trade union confidence, growth, and activism; but in the 1920s union membership and strike activity declined, employer-sponsored "company unions" replaced "bona fide" unions, and a renewed open-shop drive that lasted from about 1920 to 1924—dubbed "the American Plan"— attacked the closed shop wherever it had taken hold and preserved the status quo where it had not. Events in California mirrored national trends. But in addition to their organizational woes, California trade unionists continued to suffer from a hostile legal environment and found their political position greatly weakened. As historian Philip Taft put it, throughout the 1920s the California labor movement found itself "on the defensive" on almost every front.[2]

On the legal front, of course, defensiveness was nothing new for the California labor movement. Neither the Progressive-era anti-injunction campaigns nor federal intervention during World War I had abated judicial hostility toward labor's methods. Indeed, in 1921 the Supreme Courts of both the United States and California issued rulings that forcefully reiterated the most damaging ideological assumptions of judge-made law.[3] Some historians have portrayed these rulings as precedent-setting cases that signaled the "growing anti-labor posture of the court" in the 1920s.[4] But from the perspective of California trade unionists, these decisions did not establish precedents or reflect a "growing" hostility on the part of the courts; rather, they simply confirmed the existing thought and practices of the lower federal and state courts.

This is not to say that the high court rulings of the 1920s were insignificant. Indeed, the United States Supreme Court's 1921 trilogy of anti-labor cases wrenched from the 1914 federal Clayton Act virtually everything labor thought it had won. Organized labor had assumed that the Clayton Act exempted labor boycotts from prosecution under federal anti-trust law, prohibited injunctions in labor disputes, and protected peaceful picketing from judicial interference.[5] Samuel Gompers, like most labor leaders across the nation, welcomed the Clayton Act as "Labor's Magna Carta" and a "Charter of Industrial Freedom." But not everyone read the legislation in the same way. Many judges and legal scholars—including the former president and future Chief Justice of the Supreme Court, William Howard Taft—claimed that the law merely affirmed existing equity practice and procedure. Taft pointed, in particular, to the law's qualifying phrase—"unless necessary to prevent irreparable injury to property or a property right." This principle of equity, after all, had always provided the rationale for judicial intervention. For a half-dozen years after its passage, therefore, the meaning of the Clayton Act remained ambiguous at best.[6]

In 1921 the Supreme Court removed a considerable portion of this ambiguity in two important cases: *Duplex Printing Press Company v. Deering* and *American Steel Foundries v. Tri-City Central Trades Council*. In *Duplex* the high court ruled unequivocally that the Clayton Act did not exempt labor boycotts from anti-trust law or prevent the court from issuing injunctions in labor disputes.[7] While the *Duplex* decision left labor boycotts subject to judicial intervention, the Clayton Act still seemed to protect picketing as a form of peaceful persuasion and assembly. Yet in *American Steel Foundries v. Tri-City Central Trades Council*, Chief Justice Taft concluded—as had many state and federal judges before him—that there was no such thing as "peaceful picketing," pointing to the "necessary element of intimidation in the presence of groups of pickets." Taft suggested that some forms of "persuasion," such as a single person dispensing "information" at a factory gate, might be permissible. But even here judges might reasonably issue an injunction if the behavior of this single person transgressed "peaceful" and "lawful" behavior as defined by the courts. In sum, Taft's ruling reflected an opinion he had expressed as early as 1915—that the Clayton Act was "declaratory" of existing judicial practice.[8]

By interpreting the Clayton Act narrowly the *Duplex* and *American Steel* decisions protected the equity powers of the federal courts from Congressional interference. But what of attempts by state legislatures to limit the power of state courts? In *Truax vs. Corrigan*, also issued in 1921, the U.S. Supreme Court struck down an Arizona anti-injunction law on the grounds that it violated an employer's Fourteenth Amendment rights to "due process of law" and "equal protection of the laws." Justice Taft, once again writing for the majority, began with the familiar principle that "business is a property right" and that pickets, by interfering with business, damaged an employer's property. By removing an employer's ability to protect his property, Taft reasoned, state anti-injunction laws effectively deprived him of property "without due process of law." Moreover, by denying to one group in society (i.e., employers) a legal remedy available to all others, the state law denied employers "equal protection of the laws."[9]

Labor in California found the Supreme Court's 1921 rulings disappointing not because they set a "precedent" or marked a "growing" hostility, but because they reinforced the status quo. That same year the California Supreme Court reaffirmed the most restrictive features of its 1909 *Pierce* ruling, upholding the propriety of the injunction in labor disputes and portraying labor's methods as inherently lawless forms of "intimidation" and "coercion." In *Southern California Iron and Steel Company v. the Amalgamated Association of Iron, Steel, and Tin Workers*, decided four months before Taft's *American Steel* ruling, the California Supreme Court had delivered an opinion that all but eliminated the possibility of "peaceful picketing" and stood firmly by its 1909 *Pierce* ruling.[10] As the 1920s began, therefore, the highest courts of both California and the rest of the nation had confirmed existing judicial practices and the values and assumptions that anchored those practices. An employer's freedom to conduct his business without undue "interference" remained a "property right" that the courts, through their equity function, had an obligation to protect. Labor's methods, by contrast, remained suspect forms of intimidation and coercion.

While facing an all-too-familiar legal hostility, organized labor in California saw its political power wane in the 1920s. Though the CFL maintained its positive view of political action and state-sponsored reforms, it did so in a political climate much less amenable to reform. In California as elsewhere the war and Red Scare had dampened the progressive reform impulse and created a more conservative political climate. With the Republican Party recaptured by conservative "standpatters," the Democratic Party all but vanquished in California, the California Progressive Party defunct, and Hiram Johnson departed for the U.S. Senate, labor in California counted few political allies. In 1924 the CFL's *Official Yearbook of Organized Labor* looked back upon the achievements of the past decade and proudly proclaimed that organized labor had always been at the forefront of political and social reform in California. But in the 1920s a more conservative political climate checked labor's political power and forced alterations to its political program.[11]

Most notably, at its 1920 convention the CFL abandoned its decade-long struggle for anti-injunction legislation. In part this decision reflected the poor showing of the 1919 anti-injunction bill, but even more it reflected the state's changed political climate. Given the CFL's failure to pass an anti-injunction bill when it enjoyed the support of progressive allies, labor lobbyists saw little hope that the bill could pass in California's increasingly "reactionary" state legislature. Facing such poor prospects, the CFL's 1920 convention refused to expend any more political capital on a lost cause. If Paul Scharrenberg and the CFL legislative agents had any thoughts of reviving the bill in later sessions, those thoughts quickly evaporated when the U.S. Supreme Court struck down Arizona's anti-injunction law in the 1921 *Truax* ruling.[12]

While dropping the anti-injunction bill, the CFL nevertheless maintained its commitment to progressive reforms that benefitted both organized and unorganized workers. Labor played a prominent role in campaigns to expand University Extension courses for wage earners, abolish the poll tax, remove property qualifications for jurors, and increase funding for agencies charged with investigating workplace conditions and enforcing existing statutes. In its most concerted effort of the 1920s the CFL helped found the Progressive Voters' League, which spearheaded a campaign for state control of water resources and hydroelectric power. Although the water and power measures failed, they offered further evidence of the California labor movement's willingness to expand the power of the state in order to defend the interests of workers (both organized and unorganized), farmers, and consumers. Racism still constrained labor's progressive vision, as the CFL successfully joined with state farm organizations in 1920 to amend and strengthen the 1913 Alien Land Law and continued to petition Congress to exclude "Asiatic" immigration.[13]

Organized labor trimmed its legislative agenda in the 1920s, but this did not represent a retreat from its commitment to progressive reform. Rather, it reflected the greater attention and political resources that the CFL devoted to fending off attacks from a new employers' political organization, the Better America Federation

(BAF). Founded in Los Angeles in 1920, the BAF became a leading champion of the American Plan and unleashed a relentless
publicity campaign against union "radicalism."[14] But more threatening than its rhetoric, BAF lobbyists in Sacramento set out to repeal the many labor-backed reforms of the Progressive era and cut
the state budget. In the fall of 1920 the CFL resolved to funnel its
legislative resources into stopping the BAF attack on Progressive-
era labor legislation.[15] Thus, while William Forbath has shown
how Samuel Gompers and the AFL abandoned all other reforms
to pursue federal anti-injunction legislation, California labor leaders abandoned the anti-injunction bill to defend earlier reforms.
Throughout the 1920s CFL lobbyists fought to preserve the budgets of the Industrial Welfare Commission, the Bureau of Labor
Statistics, and the Commission of Immigration and Housing. Although the BAF failed to repeal Progressive-era legislation or drastically cut the state budget, it nonetheless prevented organized
labor from putting forth a more pro-active reform agenda.[16]

Perhaps the surest indication of labor's persistent progressivism
was its enthusiastic support of Senator Robert LaFollette's third-
party campaign for the presidency in 1924. By the early 1920s
conservatives had largely ousted progressive reformers from positions of influence in both major parties. In an effort to revive
the progressive reform impulse, in 1922 a diverse group of labor
leaders, farm groups, women's organizations, moderate socialists,
and progressives formed the Conference for Progressive Political
Action (CPPA). At first, the CPPA pledged to support "progressives" within the major parties. But in 1924, when Republicans
nominated the conservative Calvin Coolidge and Democrats the
Wall Street banker John Davis, the CPPA endorsed a Progressive
Party ticket headed by Wisconsin Senator Robert LaFollette, a
nationally known veteran of pre-war progressivism.[17]

California's most prominent labor leaders campaigned vigorously on LaFollette's behalf, even though a procedural techni-
cality forced LaFollette to run with the Socialist Party label in
California. LaFollette's support of public ownership of railroads
and utilities corresponded with the CFL's support of the postwar

Plumb Plan (for federal management of the nation's railroads) and the campaign for public control of water and hydroelectric power. But California labor leaders were most attracted to LaFollette's unequivocal support of labor's right to organize and his strong opposition to labor injunctions. With just a bit of hyperbole, the Santa Barbara *Union Advocate* claimed that LaFollette was labor's "only hope," for his platform alone openly guaranteed the "industrial workers' right to organize and bargain collectively through representatives of their own choosing."[18] Although LaFollette finished third in the nation, he finished second in California, well ahead of the Democratic candidate John Davis. More significantly, as the voting studies of John Shover and Michael Rogin have shown, LaFollette received his greatest support in working-class districts. In San Francisco LaFollette's greatest support came in those districts that had been most opposed to the Chamber of Commerce's 1916 anti-picketing ordinance.[19] Although the 1924 Progressive Party campaign failed, it demonstrated labor's continuing commitment to a dual program of pro-statist reforms and protection of labor's collective rights.

THE "AMERICAN PLAN" IN LOS ANGELES AND SAN FRANCISCO

While labor attempted to hold the line legally and politically, it suffered serious setbacks on the organizational front, as employers across the nation organized to preserve the open shop where it existed and restore it where it did not. Bursts of trade union activity had always produced concerted reactions from employers, so, not surprisingly, the wartime gains in union membership and the strike wave of 1919 produced a new open-shop drive in the early 1920s. In 1921 delegates representing the National Association of Manufacturers, the National Metal Trades Association, the League for Industrial Rights (formerly the American Anti-Boycott Association), and a host of like-minded local and regional open-shop associations met in Chicago and formally launched "the American

Plan."[20] With its very name playing upon the bombastic patriotism unleashed by war and reaction, this latest open-shop drive charged that trade unionism in general, and the closed shop in particular, subverted such traditional American values as "individualism" and "independence." Continuing the main themes of the 1919 Red Scare, the American Plan portrayed union "collectivism" as a "radical" and "foreign" idea. Not only did the open shop make good economic sense, one Los Angeles employer proclaimed, it was more consistent with "American ideals, ethics, and institutions."[21]

Despite the new name and more patriotic rhetoric, both advocates and critics of the American Plan used the term interchangeably with the term "open shop." Like earlier open-shop movements, the American Plan used a combination of anti-union tactics: establishing "employment bureaus" to import and provide strikebreakers; putting economic pressure on employers who tolerated unions; dismissing union "agitators" and exchanging blacklists; issuing "law and order" proclamations; invoking the language of the injunction to portray labor's methods as inherent forms of "coercion" and "intimidation;" and securing court and police protection when necessary. In addition, some employers devised new ways to supplant functions once performed by unions: employer-run schools to train apprentices for the skilled trades; internal employee representation plans and grievance procedures, ranging from "company unions" to personnel offices; and "fringe benefits" aimed at fostering the "harmony of interest" between employer and employee.[22]

While the American Plan had its national spokesmen and organizations, local employer associations did the bulk of its work. In Los Angeles implementation of the American Plan fell to the M&M, which formally adopted the American Plan in June of 1921 with the creation of its "Industrial Relations Committee." C. A. Fultz, who headed the new committee, declared that an "essential function" of the committee was to create "placement bureaus" to bring nonunion workers and open-shop employers together. Of course, the M&M had always done this on an ad hoc

basis, but Fultz and the M&M had in mind more permanent solutions, such as the Sea Service Bureau that the M&M set up in cooperation with the Shipowners' Association. After 1921 all longshoremen, sailors, and other seamen secured employment only
through the Sea Service Bureau (or "Fink Hall," as it was known
to unionists). Between 1920 and 1923 the M&M helped break
strikes by machinists, waiters, electrical workers, marble cutters,
mill workers, and building tradesmen. Most of these strikes ended
quickly and without recourse to courts and police. Exceptions included several injunctions brought against striking garment workers between 1921 and 1923, and the mass arrests made during the
IWW-led waterfront strikes in San Pedro in 1923 and 1924.[23]

Whereas the American Plan in Los Angeles had only to check
what remained of an historically weak labor movement, organized
employers in San Francisco still operated in one of the strongest
union towns in the nation. Yet by 1922 the open shop had reached
the core of the San Francisco labor movement: the waterfront
and the building trades. Longshoremen and shipyard workers had
lost the closed shop in the 1919 strike (see Chapter 5), and in
1921 a failed strike by the Sailors' Union of the Pacific and other
smaller maritime unions completed the demise of trade unions
on the waterfront and at sea. Both the private Shipowners' Association and the United States Shipping Board secured sweeping
federal injunctions against all picketing or interference with private shipping in San Francisco, and clashes between strikers and
city policemen marked a rare departure from the patterns that had
prevailed since the 1901 strike. By the summer of 1921 the Sailor's
Union and the smaller maritime unions returned to work on an
open-shop basis.[24]

That same summer, the once-powerful Building Trades Council also went down to defeat. When the San Francisco Builders'
Exchange (an association of building contractors) refused union
demands for increased wages, the San Francisco Mayor's office
and the Chamber of Commerce convinced both sides to submit
their dispute to an ad hoc arbitration board. When the board
recommended a 7.5 percent wage *decrease* in the spring of 1921,

the unions rejected the offer and called a strike against any contractor who accepted the board's ruling. The Builders' Exchange, in turn, locked out all union members and demanded that its members pay the reduced wage rate. Yet many of the individual contractors—most of whom had longstanding relations with the unions—continued to hire union members and pay the old union wage. With the strike and lockout stalemated, the San Francisco Chamber of Commerce intervened. First, the Chamber's Industrial Relations Committee created an adjunct "Citizens' Committee," which raised more than one million dollars from the San Francisco business community to help bring the open shop to the San Francisco building trades. Second, the Chamber and the Builders' Exchange established a "permit system" to bring all contractors into line. Under this system, a contractor agreed to run his business on an open-shop basis in exchange for a "permit" that allowed him to buy materials from suppliers who participated in the Chamber's American Plan. Contractors also needed a permit to receive loans from participating banks. Since most of the San Francisco business community participated in the Chamber's system, contractors either accepted American Plan guidelines or faced economic ruin. By late August of 1921 San Francisco building tradesmen, having lost the support of the contractors, returned to work at reduced wages and under open-shop conditions.[25]

But the Chamber of Commerce did not rest with this one victory. On November 8, 1921, the Chamber officially announced the formation of the Industrial Association of San Francisco, the direct lineage of which could be traced back to the Law and Order Committee.[26] From that time forward, the Industrial Association became the official caretaker of the open shop and the American Plan in San Francisco. Not only did the Industrial Association continue the permit system, it maintained an "inspection department" to visit work sites and ensure that each contractor make a "good faith effort" to keep at least one-half of his work force nonunion.[27] In addition, the Industrial Association started its own employment bureau and training schools, the latter of which usurped an apprenticeship function that once belonged exclusively to unions. Between 1921 and 1932 the Industrial Association's employment bureau placed 87,900 men on the job; its schools trained 1,700 apprentices; and its funds brought at least 5,000 nonunion construction workers to San Francisco.[28] Humbled by the concerted power of San Francisco's well-heeled and well-organized employers, the once-powerful Building Trades Council turned to a most unlikely weapon in its battle against the open shop.

"THE CASE OF A MAN BITING A DOG": LABOR'S USE OF THE INJUNCTION

Just over a year after the Industrial Association had forced the building tradesmen to accept the American Plan, representatives from the San Francisco Building Trades Council initiated a series of legal actions—including requests for injunctions—against the Industrial Association and its permit system. The BTC's action was just one of a number of instances nationwide in which unions attempted to turn the injunction against the "coercive" methods of open-shop employers in the 1920s. Most of these efforts ended in failure, and they drew quick opposition from Samuel Gompers and the AFL executive council. According to Gompers, not only were the courts unlikely to decide in labor's favor, but even if they did they would only grant legitimacy to the injunction as a weapon in labor disputes. In the long run, injunctions would do much more harm than good. Yet not all labor leaders heeded this advice. Both Sidney Hillman of the garment workers and the editors of *The United Mine Workers Journal* applauded labor's use of the injunction, with the latter arguing in 1922 that if "labor unions would fight . . . employers with their own kind of fire, it would not be long before the injunction process would be as unpopular with employers as it has always been with employees." Although labor's resort to the injunction was, as one labor periodical put it, "as unusual as the case of a man biting a dog," the courts did grant a small number of injunctions on labor's behalf—mostly to force employers to abide by the terms of an existing collective bargaining agreement.[29]

After two efforts to make the San Francisco Superior Courts take action against the employers' permit system had failed, labor turned to its wartime ally, the federal government. In 1922 members of the Building Trades Council and a sympathetic representative from the American Federation of Labor convinced United States Attorney General Harry M. Daugherty to approve a federal investigation of the Industrial Association and its permit system. Daugherty assigned John Williams, a U.S. District Attorney in San Francisco, to conduct the investigation. In early September of 1922 Williams sent his final report to Daugherty with a recommendation that the Department of Justice proceed against the combination. *Organized Labor*, the weekly journal of the BTC, demanded that Daugherty follow Williams' recommendations—especially given that earlier that year the Attorney General's office had initiated up to 300 restraining orders against workers during a nationwide strike by railroad shopmen. Daugherty proved he was a "man of action" in that case, an editorial in *Organized Labor* wryly noted. "Let us have government by injunction for all of the people," another editorial asked, "or government by injunction for none of the people."[30] Somewhat to labor's surprise, Daugherty instructed District Attorney Williams to proceed with the case, finding sufficient cause to believe that the Builders' Exchange and building material wholesalers had denied goods to the contractors for no other reason than the union status of their employees.[31]

In early May of 1923 District Attorney Williams and a team of federal prosecutors announced that they would seek an injunction against the permit system. Their complaint named the Industrial Associations of both San Francisco and Santa Clara counties, the Builders' Exchanges of San Francisco and San Jose, the Master Plumbers' Association, twenty-three corporations, and twenty-one individuals, including Atholl McBean of the Chamber's Industrial Relations Committee. In addition to stopping the permit system, federal prosecutors wanted to dissolve the Industrial Association. Invoking language once used against labor unions,

the complaint charged that the combination pressured employing contractors to adopt the American Plan "through coercion,
threats, and intimidation." Specifically, the defendants had denied building materials, bank loans, and other forms of credit to
employers who did not hire a specified proportion of nonunion
employers. Judge William Van Fleet of the United States District
Court for Northern California scheduled a preliminary hearing
for June 11, 1923.[32]

Judge Van Fleet did not, however, issue an *ex parte* restraining
order, as judges often did when enjoining labor unions. Instead,
he ordered a full trial before the district court, with John Williams
bringing a suit on behalf of the United States Department of
Justice. The trial lasted more than four months. In addition to the
charges relating to the permit system, the federal government also
charged the combination with inflating the price of materials by
refusing to bid against each other.[33] Yet federal prosecutors needed
to show that the combination had conspired to restrain *interstate*
trade and commerce. Most of the building materials involved were
manufactured and sold within California, but a few products, such
as plaster and plumbing materials, came from outside the state.
The defendants admitted to using the permit system, but they
claimed, without a hint of irony, that under the labor-backed
Clayton Act such methods were not subject to an injunction
when used in connection with a labor dispute. Furthermore, the
defense claimed that the permit system did not interfere with
interstate commerce, for the goods from out of state had come
to "rest" in local warehouses before going to the contractors, and
had become, therefore, a local commodity.[34]

Judge M. T. Dooling, who wrote the opinion for the federal district court in November of 1923, rejected the defense argument.
Although Dooling did not dissolve the Industrial Association, he
issued a temporary injunction against use of the permit system for
any item that came from outside the state. A month later Dooling
made the injunction permanent.[35] The BTC and the labor press
applauded the use of the injunction against the coercive practices
of the employers, even though the injunction applied only to the
withholding of interstate goods, while most building supplies were

produced and sold locally. Nonetheless, *Organized Labor* claimed that the decision prompted the abandonment of the permit system in Santa Clara and San Mateo counties and had adverse effects on the practice in San Francisco and Alameda counties.[36] More telling, the Industrial Association found the decision troublesome enough that it appealed to the United States Supreme Court. The high court accepted the case in its 1924 October term and heard arguments in the spring of 1925.[37]

More than two years after the federal government started pursuing the case, and nearly four years after labor had first protested the use the permit system, the United States Supreme Court issued its ruling. On April 23, 1925, Justice George Sutherland delivered the opinion for an unanimous court. Sutherland noted that the appellants sought reversal of the decree primarily on the grounds that the permit system did not constitute a conspiracy to restrain trade or a violation of the Sherman Act. Other issues had been raised by both sides, but Sutherland announced that he would consider only whether the permit system violated federal anti-trust law. On this point Sutherland accepted the Industrial Association's argument that goods from outside the state had "been brought to rest in salesrooms and warehouses and commingled with other goods and property, before being subject to the permit rule." Sutherland also noted that the "object" of the American Plan was the "open shop," and thus "entirely apart from any purpose to restrict interstate commerce."[38] Sutherland dismissed labor's arguments, concluding that to extend the Sherman Anti-Trust Act "to a situation so equivocal and so lacking in substance, would be to cast doubt upon the serious purpose with which it was framed."[39] With the unanimous consent of his colleagues, Justice Sutherland ordered the lower court to lift the injunction against the employers' permit system.[40]

CONCLUSION

Labor's turn to the courts exposed the ambiguous, if not contradictory, positions sometimes taken by both sides. For two decades or more, employers had based their opposition to the closed shop on the fundamental right of the employer to hire whomever he chose and to run his business as he saw fit. Yet the Industrial Association's permit system, by compelling contractors to cap wages or hire a certain proportion of nonunion workers, violated the very principles that open-shop employers claimed to hold so dear. Similarly, when organized labor supported injunctions against organized employers, it embraced the values, assumptions, and legal doctrines so often used against trade union activity. Labor charged employers with "coercion," "intimidation," and "un-Americanism," and the federal attorneys prosecuting the Industrial Association cited the same court cases that organized labor had once held in contempt.

Labor had always tried to turn the language and doctrines of the law to its advantage, but the actions against the Industrial Association marked a significant, albeit temporary, retreat from its Progressive-era campaign for anti-injunction legislation. In that effort labor spokesmen had offered a "progressive" alternative to the outmoded, even "feudal," doctrines of judge-made law. They had denied the privileged position of the employer's property rights and insisted upon equal recognition for labor's rights of collective action. But in the legal action against the permit system, labor defended the employing contractor's "right" to run his business free from outside interference. In a statement that could have appeared in a *Los Angeles Times* editorial condemning labor unions, a 1922 BTC pamphlet argued that the permit system did not allow "merchants, contractors, and builders to conduct their business free from dictation, coercion, or interference."[41] To use such language in a losing cause might seem to justify the warnings of Gompers and the AFL Executive Council that labor's use of the injunction was "a Snare and a Delusion."[42] But labor's turn to the courts in California was more an act of desperation than a capitulation to the judicial reasoning of its adversaries. Knowing that it had failed to persuade judges to accept labor's vision of law, organized labor could at least demand consistency from the courts.

But there is another, more significant story to tell about labor's resort to the injunction. After local courts had failed to take any action against the permit system, the Building Trades Council turned to the United States Attorney General and the *federal* courts for relief. For all of its brevity and limitations, federal labor policy during World War I, along with the continued hostility of local courts, had convinced organized labor that protection would most likely come from federal authorities. At the same time, labor turned its political attention to the national level. One year after a federal district court had issued a permanent injunction against the permit system—and only a few weeks after the United States Supreme Court agreed to hear the employers' appeal—the California labor movement threw its support to Robert LaFollette's third-party bid for the presidency. LaFollette may have lost in 1924, but his progressive platform, his constituency, and his commitment to labor's rights looked backward to the labor politics of the Progressive era, and forward to a new deal.

Conclusion

The absence of a labor party in the United States is not evidence that trade unionists have not been active politically. In fact, the American trade union movement has been particularly active politically, but it has been opposed to party or partisan political action.

JOHN FREY,
American Federationist, 1919

In 1919 John Frey, editor of the *Iron Molders Journal*, addressed the above comment to a growing movement within the AFL calling for a British-style labor party in the United States.[1] But Frey could just as easily have directed his comment to scores of historians who, ever since, have made the absence of a labor party the hallmark of "American exceptionalism." Just as Frey's unnamed critics lamented the "absence" of a labor party, most histories of American labor politics explicitly or implicitly try to explain the absence in America of the class-conscious, independent, and usually socialist labor politics that emerged in Europe in the early twentieth century. In his classic study of America's "liberal tradition," Louis Hartz invoked a causal chain of absences: the absence of feudalism explained the absence of class consciousness, which in turn explained the absence of socialism.[2] As most historians soon discover, however, it is difficult enough to find evidence to explain what *did* happen; not surprisingly, therefore, trying to explain what *did not* happen has led to a counterfactual *cul de sac*. Not only does Werner Sombart's well-worn question—"Why is there no Socialism in the United States?"—doom labor's political history to a narrative of failure, it also, as Karen Orren puts

219

its, risks "highlighting contrasts at the expense of common and arguably more fundamental tendencies."[3]

John Frey would have agreed. In responding to his critics, Frey claimed that American and European trade unionists sought common objectives through different political channels. Anticipating the arguments of later historians, Frey believed that legal hostility had shaped labor's approach to politics in both England and the United States. At the beginning of the twentieth century, he pointed out, "the trade union movements of both countries were confronted with a crisis." Like the injunctions issued by American courts, Great Britain's 1901 Taff Vale decision— which held unions liable for economic damages caused by a strike—"threatened the existence of effective trade unionism." This threat, Frey observed, "gave new life to the Labor Party in Great Britain." Through the efforts of its Labor Representation Committee—the forerunner of the British Labour Party—the British Trade Union Congress increased labor's representation in Parliament and secured passage of the 1906 Trades Dispute Act, which effectively overturned the Taff Vale ruling. In the United States, on the other hand, the AFL began a campaign in 1906 to elect its "friends" (from among both Republicans and Democrats) to Congress and then spent about eight years lobbying for the Clayton Antitrust Act, which exempted labor from anti-trust prosecution and restricted the use of injunctions in labor disputes. Frey could not have known that two years after he offered his comparison, the United States Supreme Court would gut labor's cherished Clayton Act. But as of 1919 he reasonably concluded that the American labor movement's nonpartisan political approach had been as successful as third-party politics in Great Britain.[4]

Frey also explained why labor's nonpartisan lobbying approach was more appropriate to the American context than the third-party approach of British unionists. "Our British brethren through their labor party have secured marked benefits," Frey admitted, but they had not managed to unite the British working class politically. While "the British Trade Union Congress reports over

4,500,000 dues-paying members," he noted, " the total vote for the Labor Party in the [most recent] election was but 2,374,385."[5] Having a labor party did not guarantee that all trade unionists, let alone all workers, would support it. Because American trade unionists did not compose a majority of voters in the nation at large or even in very many localities, Frey argued, they would always fare poorly in the American system of winner-take-all elections. But, he reminded his readers, trade unionists and working-class voters often possessed "the balance of power."[6] In the American context, therefore, organized labor could exert more influence by forging political coalitions and engaging in interest group politics.

Frey focused his attention on the national level, but his observation that legal hostility generated diverse but unmistakably political responses is even more apparent at the state and local levels. As we have seen, when confronted with legal hostility, an already politically active and pro-statist California labor movement intensified its political efforts. Far from explaining labor's aversion to third-party politics, legal hostility sparked the few third-party challenges that did occur. When these political movements succeeded in giving labor a degree of control over local police, as they did in San Francisco, employers turned to the courts for injunctions. But while court intervention frustrated labor's political efforts, it did not cause labor to retreat from politics. Taking advantage of Progressive-era changes in the "rules of the political game," organized labor lobbied the state legislature to eliminate the courts' power to issue labor injunctions. In the process, California labor leaders articulated a view of law and the state that simply cannot be squared with the "antistatist voluntarism" of the AFL's national leadership. California labor leaders constructed not a labor version of *laissez-faire*, but a complex political philosophy that demanded an expansion of the state's responsibility for social welfare while at the same time obliging the state to protect a sphere of voluntary collective action. Organized labor in California rejected the court's hodge-podge of feudalism and liberal individualism for its own vaguely defined "industrial liberty," a "progressive" (albeit racially exclusive) brand of liberalism more conducive to modern industrial conditions.

By the time the United States entered the European war in 1917, labor's political efforts had failed to win adequate protection for labor's rights. While the courts had come to accept trade unions as an inevitable part of an increasingly organized society and formally recognized the right to strike, they severely restricted the methods that labor might employ to realize that right. World War I had an ambiguous impact on labor's political struggle for collective rights. On the one hand, President Woodrow Wilson's administration made recognition of workers' rights a cornerstone of federal labor policy, and a number of federal agencies mediated labor disputes in a manner that most mainstream labor leaders found fair and just. On the other hand, federal agencies had little power to enforce their judgements and, at any rate, disbanded shortly after the war ended. Whatever legitimacy labor had accrued during the war was eclipsed by the anti-radical hysteria, labor unrest, and state-sponsored repression of the postwar period.

Although the war and Red Scare created a more hostile legal climate, weakened labor's progressive political allies, and demonstrated the potentially repressive powers of the state, labor in California continued to reject the antistatist voluntarism of Gompers and the AFL. Throughout the 1920s organized labor defended the budgets of Progressive-era commissions from conservative attacks, supported programs that enhanced the social welfare of both organized and unorganized workers, joined with other progressives in calling for state control of water and electric power, and in all other ways retained its commitments to progressive reform. Yet increasingly California labor leaders looked not to the state legislature or to state politics, but to the federal government and national politics. As we have seen, when local authorities refused to take actions against the coercive practices of the American Plan, labor leaders turned to the United States Attorney General and the federal courts for assistance. Asking the federal courts for injunctions in many ways marked a retreat from the progressive arguments of the anti-injunction campaigns, but it signaled a growing conviction that protection of labor's rights would have to come from the federal government.

Labor's local and state-level political activism in defense of collective rights; its advocacy of progressive state-sponsored reform even while it sought limits on the power of courts and police; and its warming to the federal government all help to explain what seemed to be a resurgence of labor's political activism in the 1930s. According to the traditional periodization, the politically active and reform-minded unionism of the late nineteenth century gave way to the apolitical and voluntarist outlook of Samuel Gompers and the AFL, which prevailed from the 1890s through the 1920s. In the 1930s, shaken by economic depression and encouraged by President Roosevelt, blue collar voters and organized labor shifted gears once again and actively supported the Democratic Party and the New Deal welfare state. How did the politically quiescent and resolutely antistatist labor movement of the 1890s to the 1920s suddenly become the core constituent of the New Deal coalition? To begin with, as this study has demonstrated, the political activism and pro-statist outlook of labor in the 1930s did not represent an entirely new departure. At the local and state levels, labor had always been politically active and looked to the state as a positive source of reform. Furthermore, as Michael Rogin and John Shover argued thirty years ago, the labor-progressive alliance that emerged in California in 1910 was essentially the same as that which supported Robert LaFollette in 1924 and New Dealers in the 1930s. "The political upheaval of the 1930s," Shover concluded in his 1969 study of voting patterns in California, "marked the augmenting and coming to power of the same groups that had sustained Johnson, Wilson, and LaFollette, buttressed Progressive reforms two decades earlier, and kept what remained of reform politics alive through the 1920s."[7] In the 1930s, therefore, California labor did not embrace a new political ideology so much as it shifted its gaze toward Washington.

Epilogue: Toward Washington and a New Deal

When President Franklin Roosevelt signed the 1935 Wagner Act, he placed the power of the federal government behind the right of workers to organize free from the "interference," "coercion," and "intimidation" of their employers. By establishing the National Labor Relations Board, the Wagner Act created a dual shift in the locus of labor relations law: from the local to the national level, and from the judicial to the executive branch of government. Most importantly, where local and judicial authorities from the 1890s to the 1920s had at best tolerated and at worst restricted labor's collective actions, federal authorities in the 1930s actively promoted organization and prohibited many forms of employer interference. Both a response to and a catalyst for the labor unrest of the 1930s, the Wagner Act gave organized labor the legitimacy it had long sought. Union organizers could tell workers that "the President wants you to join a union."[1] In the four years after the Wagner Act went into effect, trade union membership in the United States grew from about 3.8 million to 6.6 million, an impressive gain especially when one considers that in the past union membership had always declined during economic depressions. These impressive gains were just the beginning; by 1945 union membership had increased to almost fifteen million.[2]

However impressive the numbers, historians still vigorously contest the intent, consequences, and meaning of the Wagner Act and New Deal labor policy. For the most optimistic liberal historians, especially those who wrote some of the first histories of the New Deal, the Wagner Act represented the culmination of labor's desire for "industrial democracy" and allowed workers to bargain on roughly equal terms with their employers. Furthermore, the liberal view holds that labor and its liberal allies shaped the main features of New Deal labor policy over the objections of the business community. At the other end of the interpretive spectrum, more skeptical and pessimistic New Left historians told a tale of deceit and co-option. Ronald Radosh, for example, argued that "a group of farsighted industrialists," with the acquiescence of a few corporate-minded union leaders, masterminded New Deal labor policy in order to "integrate" labor into the corporate capitalist "system." In cahoots with Capital, New Dealers tamed a once-militant labor movement. Fortunately, most historians fall somewhere between liberal praise and New Left brooding, recognizing the complex motivations that informed the Wagner Act and the often ambivalent consequences of New Deal labor policy.[3]

Christopher Tomlins, who more than anyone else has reoriented and revitalized the field of labor law history, places New Deal labor policy in the broader context of labor relations law from 1880 to 1960. According to Tomlins, state institutions—whether local courts or federal agencies—have always conditioned the "legitimacy" of organized labor and its forms of collective action. While the Wagner Act guaranteed labor's right to organize and bargain collectively, it nonetheless offered only a "contingent legitimacy," one dependent upon the capacity of collective bargaining to foster the state's interest in maintaining the productivity, order, and stability of capitalism. Tomlins recognizes that the authors of the Wagner Act brought a complex set of motives to their task, that they sought both "industrial democracy" and "industrial stability." Yet the subsequent history of the Wagner Act, Tomlins claims, shows that all too often labor's desire for "industrial democracy" fell victim to the state's desire for "industrial stability." In the long run, Tomlins concludes, the New Deal formula granted labor the rights it had long sought, but at the same time made unions dependent upon the state, and thus "hostage to a power over which they had historically enjoyed little control."[4]

This study, based as it is on an examination of labor and the law from the 1890s to the 1920s within a single state, makes no pretense of entering the debate over the origins and effects of New Deal labor policy. But in assessing the significance of New Deal labor policy, it helps to remember what organized labor had endured in the previous decades. No doubt the Wagner Act did not usher in a period of legal bliss for labor, and perhaps in retrospect one could argue that federal protection also subjected labor to the potential constraints of federal oversight and regulation. Yet from the vantage point of the 1890s to 1920s, which many trade unionists vividly remembered, the Wagner Act provided a much-sought-after legitimacy. It protected union organization and collective actions from the kinds of court and employer hostility that this study has detailed. Section seven of the Wagner Act asserted workers' right to bargain collectively through agents of their own choosing, and it demanded that employers recognize union representatives and bargain in good faith. Section eight prohibited employers from engaging in a number of "unfair practices:" they could not discharge workers for union activity or engage in any other acts of "intimidation" against union workers; they could not exchange blacklists; they could not create company unions to compete with bona fide unions; they could not interfere with union elections. Subsequent decisions by the National Labor Relations Board prohibited other longstanding forms of "interference," such as using armed guards or labor spies to break up picket lines or disrupt union meetings.[5]

Employers openly resisted the Wagner Act, in part on the advice of lawyers who assured them that the court would surely find the Act unconstitutional. Only when the United States Supreme Court upheld the Wagner Act in *NLRB v. Jones and Laughlin* in 1937 did employers grudgingly come to terms with the Act. In upholding New Deal labor policy, the high court ruled that workers enjoyed a "fundamental right" to strike and engage in practices that made the strike effective, suggesting that the right to strike went beyond a mere statutory right. In upholding section eight of the Act, the court described the anti-union tactics of the employers in words once reserved for trade unions, condemning the "intimidation" and "coercion" that interfered with the employees' rights of "self-organization and representation."[6] In exchange for this support, organized labor—and indeed blue collar workers in general—became the core constituent of the New Deal coalition and helped usher in a political realignment that ended more than thirty years of Republican domination of national politics.[7]

In California the legal and political transformations of the 1930s produced even more impressive gains than they did in the nation at large. Even though the labor provisions in section 7(a) of the 1933 National Industrial Recovery Act lacked any means of enforcement, the promise of federal protection emboldened workers to take militant actions, which in turn facilitated the passage of the 1935 Wagner Act. In California the new militancy could be seen not only among workers with long histories of union experience, such as the San Francisco longshoremen, but also among California farm workers long ignored by the mainstream labor movement. In the five years between 1933 and 1938 union membership in the state tripled and the number of chartered locals doubled. Even in San Francisco, which was already a strong union city, New Deal labor policy helped to double union membership between 1933 and 1940. As Robert Cherny and William Issel argue in their political history of San Francisco, organized labor continued to play an active role in the city's politics, but when it came to matters of industrial relations, "labor's attention came to focus on Washington." Like other San Francisco voters, workers and trade unionists responded to the New Deal by shifting their political loyalties to the Democratic Party.[8]

Most impressively, the federal protections offered by New Deal labor policy allowed the Los Angeles labor movement, at last, to successfully challenge the open shop. Trade union membership in Los Angeles had always been sensitive to federal policy. Despite the limitations of federal intervention during World War I, between 1915 and 1919 union membership in the Los Angeles Central Labor Council increased from about 15,000 to at least 40,000. These gains quickly evaporated in the 1920s and early 1930s, as union membership stood at less than 12,000 by May of 1933. But the promises of federal protection in section 7(a) of the

National Industrial Recovery Act, despite its well-known loop-
holes and lack of enforcement powers, inspired unprecedented
union growth in open-shop Los Angeles. Within a few months,
the membership of the Central Labor Council nearly tripled, to
about 30,000. The Wagner Act inspired still more growth, as
union membership in Los Angeles climbed to 65,000 in 1936
and 120,000 in 1940. From its nadir in 1933, union membership
increased tenfold in only seven years. Moreover, this growth occurred despite the continued hostility of local employers, sporadic
local court and police interventions, divisions within the labor
movement, and a renewed open-shop offensive between 1937 and
1938. Federal protection, which both responded to and inspired
union activism, provided a framework that allowed labor in Los
Angeles to overcome longstanding obstacles. By 1941 an *American Federationist* headline could reasonably proclaim of Los Angeles, "An Open Shop Citadel Falls."[9]

Labor in California, as it did throughout the nation, expressed
its appreciation for the legal protections afforded by the Wagner
Act by abandoning all pretense of nonpartisanship and throwing its support to the Democratic Party of Franklin D. Roosevelt.
Moreover, as the late J. David Greenstone noted in his survey
of American labor politics, organized labor did not merely endorse Democrats; it became a Democratic party organization, providing substantial financial contributions and a dedicated army
of campaign workers. For some analysts, the alliance with the
Democratic Party marked labor's political coming of age, as the
Democratic Party effectively became the American version of a
labor party; for others, it was a "barren marriage" that foreclosed
more radical alternatives.[10] Certainly, labor has since learned the
limits of that alliance. By the 1980s it was no longer clear that organized labor could rely upon either the National Labor Relations
Board or the Democratic Party for consistent support. During the
presidential primaries of 1984, with most Democrats attempting
to distance themselves from "New Deal liberalism," Democratic
candidate Gary Hart attacked the AFL-CIO endorsement of his
rival Walter Mondale as evidence of Mondale's debts to the "old

arrangement."[11] From the perspective of a new century, with the American labor movement suffering from a list of woes too long to reproduce, it is tempting to take a dim view of labor's earlier political choices and wonder if it is not time for a "new arrangement." But for labor leaders who had fought a mostly frustrating political battle to defend rights of collective action in the first three decades of the twentieth century, the legal protections afforded by New Deal labor policy must have seemed a godsend.

Notes

1. "Report of the Vice President for District No. 1," California Federation of Labor, *Proceedings of the Annual Convention* (San Francisco: California Federation of Labor) [Hereafter, CFL *Proceedings*], 1911, p. 59.

2. Gompers quoted in William Forbath, *Law and the Shaping of the American Labor Movement* (Cambridge, MA: Harvard University Press, 1991), p. 2, fn. 3.

3. On greater incidence of state and local intervention, see Edwin Witte, *The Government in Labor Disputes* (New York: McGraw Hill, 1931), p. 84, and Chapters 3 and 5, passim. See also Forbath, *Law,* Appendix C. Witte found that two-thirds of all injunctions issued between 1880 and 1930 came from state courts. Given that local court injunctions were much more likely to be lost to the historical record, while virtually all federal court orders were reported, the proportion of state court injunctions is probably even greater than two-thirds, and of course this does not even consider other forms of local intervention, especially local police acting on the basis of local ordinances or their more general responsibility to maintain law and order. I discuss Witte's estimates at greater length in Chapter 2.

4. For example, see John Commons, *The Legal Foundations of Capitalism* (New York: Macmillan, 1924); Felix Frankfurter and Nathan Greene, *The Labor Injunction* (New York: Macmillan, 1930); and Witte, *The Government in Labor Disputes.* On the close relationship between Progressive labor history and the emerging field of industrial relations, see Ronald Schatz, "From Commons to Dunlop: Rethinking the Field and Theory of Labor Relations," in *Industrial Democracy in America,* edited by Howell Harris and Nelson Lichtenstein. Leon Fink, " 'Intellectuals' versus 'Workers': Academic Requirements and the Creation of Labor History," *American Historical Review* (1991): 395–431.

5. See for example Leon Keyserling's assessment in Louis G. Siverberg, ed., *The Wagner Act: After Ten Years* (Washington D.C: Bureau of National Affairs, 1945), pp. 5–33. Keyserling—who, as an aide to Senator Wagner, is widely recognized as the principle author of the Wagner Act—portrayed

the whole of American labor history before the New Deal as "a struggle for the right to organize and bargain collectively."

6. Leon Fink, "Labor, Liberty, and the Law: Trade Unionism and the Problem of the American Constitutional Order," *Journal of American History* 74 (December 1987): 904–925, quotes at pp. 906–907. Fink's observation that the law might help explain the AFL's turn-of-the-century divergence from European patterns is supported by Gerald Friedman's comparative studies of labor and the state in the United States and France. Friedman shows that, in the nineteenth century, the labor movements of both nations faced similar problems, shared a similar "republican" ideology, and devised similar political and organizational strategies. However, because political and economic elites were divided in France, the French labor movement was able to ally with French Republicans to create a system of government arbitration that fostered union growth, assertiveness, and political involvement. In the United States, by contrast, a unified economic and political elite dominated political and state institutions, making organized labor much more wary of government involvement in industrial relations. See Friedman, "The State and the Making of the Working Class: France and the United States, 1880–1914," *Theory and Society* 17 (May 1988): 403–430; and *idem*. "Capitalism, Republicanism, Socialism, and the State: France, 1871–1914," *Social Science History* 14 (Summer 1990): 151–174.

7. Forbath, *Law and the Shaping of the American Labor Movement*; Victoria Hattam, *Labor Visions and State Power: The Origins of Business Unionism in the United States* (NJ: Princeton University Press, 1993). For an earlier study that links the AFL's anti-statist outlook to legal hostility , see Christopher Tomlins, *The State and the Unions: Labor Relations, Law, and the Organized Labor Movement in America, 1880–1960* (New York: Cambridge University Press, 1985), Chapters 2–3, passim.

8. Hattam, *Labor Visions and State Power*, quote at p. 215.

9. Forbath, *Law*, Chapters 3–5, *passim*.

10. Ibid. See also Forbath, "The Ambiguities of Free Labor: Labor and the Law in the Gilded Age," *Wisconsin Law Review* (1985).

11. For an outstanding collection of essays comparing American and European labor movements in the nineteenth century, see Ira Katznelson and Aristides Zolberg, eds., *Working Class Formation: Nineteenth Century Patterns in Western Europe and the United States* (NJ: Princeton University Press, 1986).

12. My own assessment of the problems of the "exceptionalism" debate in American labor history owes much to Sean Wilentz, "Against Exceptionalism: Class Consciousness and the American Labor Movement, 1790–1920." *International Labor and Working Class History* 26 (1984): 1–24; and Aristides Zolberg, "How Many Exceptionalisms?," in Katzneslon and Zolberg, *Working Class Formation*; and the "Introduction" in Eric Arnesen, Julie Greene, and Bruce Laurie, eds., *Labor Histories: Class, Politics, and the Working Class Experience* (Urbana: University of Illinois Press 1998), espe-

cially pp. 6–7. On the problem of American exceptionalism more gener-
ally, see Daniel Rodgers, "Exceptionalism," in Anthony Molho and Gordon
Wood, eds., *Imagined Histories: American Historians Interpret the Past* (NJ:
Princeton University Press, 1998).

13. On working-class support for local socialist parties, see Robert Hoxie, "The
'Rising Tide of Socialism': A Study," *Journal of Political Economy* 19 (1911):
609–617; Errol Wayne Stevens, "Labor and Socialism in an Indiana Mill
Town, 1905–1921," *Labor History* 26 (Summer 1985): 353–383; John T.
Walker, "Socialism in Dayton, Ohio: Its Membership, Organization, and
Demise," ibid., 384–404; Chad Garfield, "Big Business, The Working Class,
and Socialism in Schenectady, 1911–1916," ibid., (Summer 1978): 350–
372; and Richard Oestreicher, "Urban Working Class Political Behavior
and Theories of American Electoral Politics, 1870–1940," *Journal of American History* (March 1988), p. 1270. On support for socialism within the
mainstream labor movement, see John H. M. Laslett, *Labor and the Left:
A Study of Socialist and Radical Influences in the American Labor Movement,
1881–1924* (New York: Basic Books, 1970).

14. Wilentz, "Against Exceptionalism," p. 17

15. Julie Greene, *Pure and Simple Politics: The American Federation of Labor
and Political Activism, 1881–1917* (New York: Cambridge University Press,
1998), p. 1. For a discussion on just how much Greene's work qualifies
Forbath's, see the exchange between the two authors in "Symposium on
Julie Greene: Pure and Simple Politics," *Labor History* 40 (1999), pp. 196–
206. Forbath does not deny that court hostility sometimes drove labor into
politics, but insists that labor's political goals were limited to the voluntarist
objective of improving labor's power of collective bargaining. Greene also
stresses the voluntarist and "antistatist" objectives of the AFL, but sees
court hostility as only one of many factors shaping labor's political strategy
and ideology.

16. Greene, *Pure and Simple Politics* and idem., "The Strike at the Ballot Box:
The American Federation of Labor's Entrance into Politics, 1906–1909,"
Labor History 32 (1991): 165–192. See also David Montgomery, "Industrial Democracy or Democracy in Industry?" in Howell Harris and Nelson
Lichtenstein, eds., *Industrial Democracy in America: The Ambiguous Promise*
(New York: Cambridge University Press, 1993), p. 34. Gwendolyn Mink
also shows that court hostility caused labor to forge stronger ties to both
the Democrats and the state; but where Greene plays down the importance
of immigration in the AFL's political agenda, Mink makes it the center of
her interpretation. See Mink, *Old Labor and New Immigrants in American
Political Development: Union, Party, and State, 1875–1920* (Ithaca: Cornell
University Press, 1986), Chapters 5–7. Elizabeth Sanders also argues that
the AFL became increasingly involved in politics and established ties to
the Democratic Party in the Progressive era. But in her telling of the story
labor played junior partner to more influential farm organizations. See Elizabeth Sanders, *Roots of Reform: Farmers, Workers, and the American State,*

1877–1917 (Chicago: University of Chicago Press, 1999). Despite significant differences between their interpretations, Greene, Mink, and Sanders all present a more politically engaged labor movement than in traditional interpretations. Also, they show that no matter how "anti-statist" the impulse of the AFL's political activism, they ended up supporting reforms that increased the power of the state.

17. Dubofsky, *The State and Labor*, Chapters 2–3. As Dubofsky puts it, "Judicial rulings may have shaped the political activities of the trade union movement, but not in quite the manner that has been suggested [by Forbath and Hattam]," pp. 49, 248 (fn. 51). Elizabeth Sanders also suggests that labor's alliance with the Democrats unintentionally helped to create the modern administrative state in the Progressive era. Sanders, *Roots of Reform*, especially Chapters 3 and 11.

18. For the most recent accounts of the wartime alliance see Joseph McCartin, *Labor's Great War: The Struggle for Industrial Democracy and the Origins of Modern American Labor Relations, 1912–1921* (Chapel Hill: University of North Carolina Press, 1997); idem., "'An American Feeling': Workers, Managers, and the Struggle over Industrial Democracy in the World War I Era," in Lichtenstein and Harris, eds., *Industrial Democracy in America*, pp. 67–86; and Dubofsky, *The State and Labor*, Chapter 3.

19. Gary Fink, "The Rejection of Voluntarism," *Industrial and Labor Relations Review* 26 (1973): 805–819. Eric Leif Davin has argued that state and local labor leaders offered greater support for political action—including independent political action—into the 1930s. See Eric Leif Davin, "The Very Last Hurrah? The Defeat of the Labor Party Idea, 1934–1936," in Staughton Lynd, *"We Are All Leaders": the Alternative Unionism of the Early 1930s* (Urbana: University of Illinois Press, 1996).

20. Dubofsky, *The State and Labor*, p. xvii.

21. For an outstanding discussion of the "new labor history" and the "new political history," and its geographic focus, see Richard Oestreicher, "Urban Working Class Political Behavior and Theories of American Political Development, 1870–1940," *Journal of American History* 74 (March 1988): 1257–1286.

22. Ira Cross, *A History of the Labor Movement in California* (Berkeley: University of California Press, 1935).

23. United States Bureau of the Census. *Twelfth Census of the United States* (Washington, DC: Government Printing Office, 1900), Vol. 1; idem., *Fourteenth Census of the United States* (Washington, DC: Government Printing Office, 1923), Vol. 1; idem., *Abstract of the Thirteenth Census of the United States, Statistics of Population, Agriculture, Manufacturing, and Mining . . . With Supplement for California* (Washington, DC: Government Printing Office, 1913), pp. 33, 63, 84–85, and especially Table 19, p. 95. Los Angeles also had a significant Latino population, consisting of both immigrants from Latin America (mostly Mexico) as well as the Spanish-speaking "Californios" who lived in California at the time it was annexed by the

United States. Because the United States census counted this population as "white" until 1930, it is virtually impossible to know the exact percentage of native-born Latinos for the preceding years. Most studies suggest, however, that Los Angeles' Latino population did not grow rapidly until the decade of the Mexican Revolution (1910–1920) and American entry into World War I. See Leonard Pitt, *The Decline of the Californios: A Social History of the Spanish-Speaking Californians, 1846–1890* (Berkeley: University of California Press, 1966); Mark Reisler, *By the Sweat of Their Brow: Mexican Immigrant Labor in United States, 1900–1940* (Westport, CT: Greenwood Press, 1976), pp. 3–17, 50–55; and Albert Camarillo, *Chicanos in a Changing Society: From Mexican Pueblos and American Barrios in Santa Barbara and Southern California* (Cambridge, MA: 1979).

24. United States Bureau of the Census. *Thirteenth Census of the United States*, Vol. 9: *Manufactures* (Washington, DC: Government Printing Office 1912), pp. 92, 94, 97; idem. *Fourteenth Census of the United States*, Vol. 9: *Manufactures* (Washington, DC: Government Printing Office 1923), Table 2, p. 83, Table 35, pp. 106–110. For an example of the Los Angeles promotional literature, see the several editions of Harry Billington Brook, *The City and County of Los Angeles in Southern California* (Los Angeles: Chamber of Commerce, 1899–1919), passim. Brook's tracts—which also appeared under the title *Land of Sunshine*—stressed both opportunity to live "the ideal country life" and the "openings for capital [and] . . . manufacturing enterprises." Later pamphlets included references to wage-earners, promising to the working man higher wages than he could receive back East, and to the employer an "efficient labor force." See Brook, *Los Angeles*, 1919 edition, p. 61. On the promotional efforts more generally, see Robert Fogelson, *Fragmented Metropolis: Los Angeles, 1850–1930* (Berkeley: University of California Press, 1967), especially pp. 69–75.

25. Compare, for example, Ray Stannard Baker, "A Corner in Labor: What's Happening in San Francisco Where Unionism Holds Undisputed Sway?," *McClure's Magazine* 22 (1904): 366–379, with John Fitch, "Los Angeles: A Militant Open Shop Citadel," *Survey* 29 (1913): 607–617, and Frederick Palmer, "Otistown of the Open Shop," *Hampton's Magazine* 26 (1911): 29–44. These contrasting images are invoked in two standard surveys of California labor history—Ira Cross, *A History of the Labor Movement in California* and David Selvin, *A Sky Full of Storm* (Berkeley: University of California Press, 1966)—and in popular general histories of California, such as Kevin Starr, *Inventing the Dream: California through the Progressive Era* (New York: Oxford University Press, 1986).

26. On union membership, see California Bureau of Labor Statistics [CBLS], *Biennial Report*, 1899–1900 through 1920–1921 (Sacramento: Superintendent of State Printing, 1900–1922); on strike activity and success in particular, see CBLS, *Twelfth Biennial Report*, 1905–1906 (Sacramento: Superintendent of State Printing, 1907), pp. 184–211. On comparison of wages see United States Department of Commerce, *Earnings of Factory Workers*,

1899–1927 (Washington, DC: Government Printing Office, 1929), Table 68, pp. 149–150 and Table D, p. 392. See also Thomas R. Clark, "The Limits of Liberty: Courts, Police, and Labor Unrest in California, 1890–1926" (Ph.D. dissertation, UCLA, 1994), Chapter 4, passim.

27. For reviews of this literature see Clark, "The Limits of Liberty," pp. 233–240; and Michael Kazin, "The 'Great Exception' Revisited: Organized Labor and Politics in San Francisco and Los Angeles, 1870–1940," *Pacific Historical Review* 55 (1986): 371–402.

28. Alexander Saxton, *The Indispensable Enemy: Labor and the Anti-Chinese Movement in California*, (Berkeley: University of California Press, 1971), pp. 258–265. Daniel Rodgers, *The Politics of Prejudice: The Anti-Japanese Movement in California* (Berkeley: University of California Press, 1962).

29. Michael Kazin, *Barons of Labor: The San Francisco Building Trades and Union Power in the Progressive Era* (Urbana: University of Illinois Press, 1987), pp. 19–21; idem. "The 'Great Exception' Revisited," pp. 379–380, 386.

30. Kazin, *Barons of Labor*, pp. 202–204; idem., "The Great Exception Revisited," p. 387.

31. Los Angeles had fewer unions and union members than San Francisco, but those unions were much more likely to strike. For example, between 1901 and 1905 Los Angeles had only one-fourth as many unions (and only one-tenth as many union members), but it had nearly one-half as many strikes. Put another way, Los Angeles accounted for 6 to 8 percent of the state's union members in this period, but it accounted for 18.3 percent of the strikes in the state. See California Bureau of Labor Statistics, *Biennial Report*, 1905–1906, pp. 210–211; and Clark, "The Limits of Liberty," pp. 228–233.

32. Kazin, "The 'Great Exception' Revisited," pp. 375–382.

33. Cherny and Issel, *San Francisco*, especially Chapters 4 and 8. William Issel suggests that San Francisco may have been better organized: "A city that did not experience the rapid business expansion of Los Angeles during the post-1900 years, *the more stable and tightly knit business community [of San Francisco] typically demonstrated uncommonly high degrees of unanimity on priorities for public policy means and ends*" [Emphasis added]. William Issel, " 'Citizens Outside of Government': Business and Urban Policy in San Francisco and Los Angeles, 1890–1932," *Pacific Historical Review* (1987): 117–145, quote at p. 140.

34. Howard Kimeldorf, *Battling for American Labor: Wobblies, Craft Workers, and the Making of the Union Movement* (Berkeley: University of California Press, 1999). For similar observations, see Melvyn Dubofsky, *We Shall Be All: A History of the Industrial Workers of the World* (Chicago: Quadrangle Books, 1969); David Montgomery in "The 'New Unionism' and the Transformation of Workers' Consciousness in America, 1909–1922,' in idem., *Workers Control in America: Studies in the History of Work Technology and Labor Struggles* (New York: Cambridge University Press, 1979); Bruce Nelson, *Workers on the Waterfront: Seamen, Longshoremen, and Unionism in the*

1930s (Urbana: University of Illinois Press, 1988); and David Brundage, *The Making of Western Labor Radicalism: Denver's Organized Workers, 1878–1905* (Urbana: University of Illinois Press, 1994).

35. "Report of the Vice President for District I," CFL, *Proceedings*, 1911, p. 59.

CHAPTER 1

1. Ray Stannard Baker, "A Corner in Labor: What's Happening in San Francisco Where Labor Holds Undisputed Sway," *McClure's Magazine* 22 (Feb. 1904), p. 377.

2. Samuel Gompers, "Police as Strikebreaking Agents," *American Federationist*, January 1914, pp. 44–46

3. Although not primarily concerned with policing or politics, a number of the labor community studies written in the 1970s suggested that policing was a hotly contested political issue and sometimes spurred support for third parties. See, for example, John Cumbler, *Working Class Community in Industrial America: Work, Leisure, and Struggle in Two Industrial Communities* (Urbana: University of Illinois Press, 1978), pp. 77–78, 179–181; Daniel Walkowitz, *Worker City, Company Town: Iron and Cotton Worker Protest in Troy and Cohoes, New York* (Urbana: University of Illinois Press, 1978), pp. 185, 192–199, 233–237; Alan Dawley, *Class and Community: The Industrial Revolution in Lynn, Massachusetts* (Cambridge, MA: Harvard University Press, 1976), passim, but especially pp. 105–110. Policing issues and local state repression also played an important role in the local political challenges of the Knights of Labor. See Leon Fink, *Workingmen's Democracy: The Knights of Labor in American Politics* (Urbana: University of Illinois Press, 1983), pp. 25–26, 30–31, 226–228 and Chapters 5 and 7, passim.

4. On the reluctance of police to intervene against labor, see Herbert Gutman, "The Workers' Search for Power," in H. Wayne Morgan, ed., *The Gilded Age* (NY: Syracuse University Press, 1963); Bruce Johnson, "Taking Care of Labor: The Police in American Politics," *Theory and Society* (1976): 89–117; and Eric Monkkonen, *Police in Urban America, 1860–1920* (New York: Cambridge University Press, 1981), pp. 8–9. For a critique of this work, see Sidney Harring, *Policing a Class Society: The American Experience* (New Brunswick, NJ: Rutgers University Press, 1983), pp. 6–7, 261–262 (and accompanying footnotes), and Chapter 6, passim.

5. *San Francisco Examiner* August 11, 1901.

6. Richard Oestreicher, "Urban Working Class Political Behavior and Theories of American Electoral Politics, 1870–1940," *Journal of American History* 74 (March 1988): 1257–1286, especially pp. 1278–1282. See also Sean Wilentz, "Against Exceptionalism: Class Consciousness and the American

Labor Movement, 1790–1920," *International Labor and Working Class History* 26 (1984): 1–24.

7. *San Francisco Examiner* July 15–19, 23–28, 30, August 1, 6, 1901; *Coast Seamen's Journal* July 24, 31, August 7, 1901; *Organized Labor* August 10, 1901; *Chronicle* July 24, 30, 1901; Tygiel, "Workingmen," pp. 305–307; Knight, pp. 77–79.

8. The *Examiner* printed labor's complaints on an almost daily basis throughout the strike; the most concise summary of these grievances appeared in the *Coast Seamen's Journal* August 7, 21, 1901.

9. *Call* September 4, 6, 1901; *Examiner* July 7, 27, August 7, 15, 28, September 26, 1901; *Coast Seamen's Journal* July 31, October 30, 1901; *Chronicle* July 27, 1901.

10. *Chronicle*, July 23–28, 1901; *Examiner* July 23, 28–August 1, 1901; Thomas Clark, "The Limits of Liberty: Courts, Police, and Labor Unrest in California, 1890–1926," Ph.D. diss., UCLA (1994), pp. 285–291.

11. On the "unusual calm" see all daily papers from August 2–15, 1901, but especially *Chronicle* July 31, August 3, 5, 9, 10, 12, 13, 15, 1901; *Bulletin* August 4, 7, 9, 10, 1901. Even the conservative business weekly reported that violence was insignificant, *Argonaut* August 12, 19, 26, 1901; on the "union patrols" see *Call* August 1–3,8, 1901; *Bulletin* August 8–10, 1901; *Chronicle* August 1, 1901; *Coast Seamen's Journal* August 7, 1901.

12. *Examiner* August 10, 1901; *Chronicle* August 10, 1901; *Call* August 10–11, 1901; *Bulletin* August 14, 1901; *Argonaut* August 19, 1901.

13. *Coast Seamen's Journal* August 7, 21, 1901; *Examiner* August 11–14, 1901; *Chronicle* August 14, 1901; *Call* August 14–15, 1901; *Argonaut* August 12, 19, 1901; *Bulletin* August 14, 1901.

14. *Examiner* August 15, 1901; Reed, "Private Employees/Public Badges: 'Additional Patrolman' in the Policing of Detroit," Unpublished paper presented to the Social Science History Association, 1986. On the fiscal conservatism of urban officials in San Francisco as elsewhere, see Terrence McDonald, *The Parameters of Urban Fiscal Policy: Socioeconomic Change and Political Culture in San Francisco, 1860–1906* (Berkeley: University of California Press, 1987), passim.

15. "Charter of the City and County of San Francisco," (1898), Sect. 4, ch. 3, art. VIII, in San Francisco Charters File, Bancroft Library, University of California, Berkeley. See also *Examiner* August 12, 15, 1901.

16. On Board of Supervisors hearings and actions, see Clark, "Limits of Liberty," pp. 313–320; *Coast Seamen's Journal* August 21, 28, September 18, 1901; *Examiner* August 20–27, September 4–12, 1901; *Chronicle* August 23, September 12–13, 1901; *Argonaut* August 26, September 9, 16, 1901.

17. *Examiner* July 7, August 7, 28, September 26, October 2, 1901; *Call* September 4, 6, 1901; *Chronicle* July 27, 1901; *Coast Seamen's Journal* July 31, October 30, 1901.

18. Clark, "Limits of Liberty," pp. 323–329; *Chronicle* September 2, 11, 14, 15, 17–21, 1901; *Argonaut* September 9, 16, 30, 1901. Around mid-September

some businessmen talked of starting a vigilante committee if Phelan did not step up policing or call upon the state militia. See *Call* September 18, 1901; *Chronicle* September 21, 25–28, 1901. However, not all businessmen thought this a good idea; see the *Argonaut*'s opposition, September 30, 1901.

19. On institutional obstacles to third parties, see Oestreicher, "Urban Working Class Political Behavior," pp. 1270–1276; Mark Voss-Hubbard, "The 'Third Party Tradition' Reconsidered: Third Parties and American Public Life, 1830–1900," *Journal of American History* (June 1999): 121–150; Peter Argersinger, "A Place on the Ballot: Fusion Politics and Anti-Fusion Laws," *American Historical Review* 85 (April 1980): 287–306; and Richard McCormick, *From Realignment to Reform: Political Change in New York State, 1893–1910* (Ithaca: Cornell University Press, 1981), pp. 260–263. On working-class support for socialists in San Francisco, see Thomas R. Clark, "Labor and Progressivism 'South of the Slot': The Voting Behavior of the San Francisco Working Class, 1912–1916," *California History* 66 (September 1987): 196–206.

20. John Buenker, *Urban Liberalism and Progressive Reform* (New York: Scribner, 1973).

21. On the political power of the Building Trades Council see Michael Kazin, *Barons of Labor*, passim. On the background of California's trade union politicians, see Alexander Saxton, "San Francisco Labor and the Populist and Progressive Insurgencies," *Pacific Historical Review* 34 (1965): 421–438.

22. Voss-Hubbard, "The 'Third Party Tradition' Reconsidered," p. 145.

23. Walton Bean, *Boss Ruef's San Francisco: The Story of the Union Labor Party, Big Business, and the Graft Prosecutions* (Berkeley: University of California Press, 1952), p. 20. On the Union Labor Party platform, see *Examiner* September 8, 1901. On urban reform politics in San Francisco see Robert Cherny and William Issel, *San Francisco, 1895–1932: Power, Politics, and Urban Development* (Berkeley: University of California Press, 1986), Chapter 6; George Mowry, *The California Progressives* (Berkely: University of California Press, 1951), Chapter 2.

24. *Examiner*, July 2, 15, 1901; *Coast Seamen's Journal* July 10, 1901; *Bulletin* October 18, 1901.

25. *Examiner* July 28, August 12, 18, 21, 21, September 4, 1901.

26. *Coast Seamen's Journal* September 11, 1901.

27. Ibid., October 30, 1901; *Bulletin* October 18, 1901; *Examiner* October 28–29, 1901.

28. On the close relationship between Phelan and the BTC's McCarthy, see Michael Kazin, *Barons of Labor*, pp. 36–45; William Issel, "Class and Ethnic Conflict in San Francisco Politics: The 1898 Charter Reform," *Labor History* 18 (1977): 341–359.

29. Such condemnations can be found in the labor press and the *San Francisco Examiner* (the daily most supportive of the strikers) throughout the summer and fall of 1901. But see especially *San Francisco Examiner* Au-

gust 21–22, 1901. Statement of Iron Trades Council quoted in Jules Tygiel, "'Where Unionism Holds Undisputed Sway': A Reappraisal of San Francisco's Union Labor Party," *California History* 62 (1983), p. 201.
30. Statement reprinted in *San Francisco Examiner* August 21, 1901.
31. Clark, "Limits of Liberty," pp. 351–352, 372 fn. 130.
32. On the candidates in the 1901 election see *San Francisco Examiner* October 13, 1901; Bean, *Boss Reuf's San Francisco*, pp. 18–27; Cherny and Issel, *San Francisco*, pp. 154–155. On Tobin's role on the Board of Supervisors, see Clark, "The Limits of Liberty," pp. 314–319.
33. Steven Erie, "The Development of Class and Ethnic Politics in San Francisco, 1870–1910: A Critique of the Pluralist Interpretation," (Ph.D. dissertation, UCLA, 1975), p. 213; Tygiel, "'Where Unionism Holds Undisputed Sway,'" p. 207; idem., "Workingmen," p. 369, Table 7.1; Clark, "The Limits of Liberty," pp. 349–352.
34. Austin Lewis, "The Day After," *International Socialist Review* December 1911, p. 358.
35. I discuss the policing of strikes under the ULP at greater length in "Limits of Liberty," pp. 376–388, 403–404, 420–427.
36. *Bulletin* October 4, 1901; see also Tygiel, "'Where Unionism Holds Undisputed Sway,'" p. 207; Erie, pp. 213–214; Clark, "Limits of Liberty," pp. 427–430.
37. On the nationwide Citizens' Alliance and other open-shop groups, see Robert Wiebe, *Business and Reform* (Chicago: Quadrangle Books, 1968), Chapters 2 and 7, passim; David Montgomery, *Fall of the House of Labor* (New York: Cambridge University Press, 1987), pp. 269–285.
38. (San Francisco) Citizen's Alliance, *A Few Good Things Done by the Citizen's Alliance* (San Francisco: N.p., N.d. [1905?]; idem. *The Open Shop* (San Francisco, N.p., N.d.); Herbert George, "Think it Out," in the Union Labor Pamphlet Collection, Bancroft Library, University of California, Berkeley. Quoted in Kazin, *Barons of Labor*, p. 119.
39. On Partridge's attempt to distance himself from the Citizens' Alliance, see *Chronicle* November 2, 4, 1905; See also Tygiel, p. 211; Bean, *Boss*, pp. 58–61; Knight, p. 163.
40. On McCarthy and BTC opposition to ULP see *Organized Labor* November, 1903; Kazin, p. 115.
41. *Labor Clarion* September 8, November 10, 1905; *Organized Labor* October 28, November 4, 1905.
42. On the 1905 election, see Knight, pp. 162–164; Bean, *Boss Reuf*, Chapter 5; Tygiel, "'Where Unionism Holds Undisputed Sway,'" p. 207; Clark, "Limits of Liberty," pp. 430–435;
43. Kazin, *Barons of Labor*, Chapters 5–7, quote at p. 115.
44. On the ULP corruption and graft trials, see Bean, *Boss Reuf*, passim; *Chronicle* March 16–19, 1907; *Argonaut* February–March, May 25–June 29, 1907; see also Clark, "Limits of Liberty," pp. 430–431, 435–443, 446–447.
45. Bean, *Boss Reuf*, pp. 227–230.

46. Tygiel, "'Where Unionism Holds Undisputed Sway,'" p. 207.
47. Kazin, *Barons of Labor*, pp. 133–139; *Town Talk* June 22, 1907; *Argonaut* September 14, 21, 28, 1907; Clark, "Limits of Liberty," pp. 473–476.
48. On Rolph's background see Moses Rischin, "Sunny Jim Rolph: The First 'Mayor of All the People,'" *California Historical Quarterly* 53 (1974): 165–172; Cherny and Issel, pp. 161–162; Knight, pp. 243–244. See also *Call* June 8–10, 1911; *Bulletin* August 17, 1911.
49. *Coast Seamen's Journal* August 3, 1911; *Chronicle* August 12, 27, September 8, 1911; *Examiner* August 25, September 1, 6, 8, 10, 1911; Kazin, *Barons of Labor*, pp. 197–202. On voting returns, see Tygiel, "'Where Unionism Holds Undisputed Sway,'" p. 207.
50. "Testimony of F. J. Zeehandelaar," USCIR, *Final Report and Testimony*, Vol. 6, pp. 5493–5498.
51. California Bureau of Labor Statistics, *Ninth Biennial Report* (1899–1900), pp. 92–97; idem., *Tenth Biennial Report* (1901–1902), pp. 67–77; idem., *Eleventh Biennial Report* (1903–1904); pp. 30–48.
52. Stimson, pp. 237–247, 256–269.
53. On the M&M's original purpose and its shift to the open-shop cause, see "Testimony of Felix Zeehandelaar," USCIR *Final Report*, Vol. 6, pp. 5493f.; See also *Times* January 20, 1903; *Labor Clarion*, July 1, 1904; and Stimson, pp. 255–258.
54. I discuss the policing of strikes in Los Angeles before 1910 at greater length in "Limits of Liberty," pp. 389–420. Zeehandelaar quoted in "Testimony of F. J. Zeehandelaar," in USCIR, *Final Report and Testimony*, Vol. 6, pp. 5496–5498.
55. On news of San Francisco carmen's victory in Los Angeles, see *Socialist*, May 3, 1902; *Times* April 27–28, 1902; *Record* April 27–28, 1902. For background on Huntington and his labor policies, see William B. Fredericks, "Capital and Labor in Los Angeles: Henry E. Huntington vs. Organized Labor, 1900–1920," *Pacific Historical Review* 59 (August 1990): 375–395.
56. Fredericks, "Capital and Labor," passim; on Huntington's comments to E. P. Vining, see San Francisco *Chronicle*, April 22, 1902.
57. On the failure of the early efforts to organize Los Angeles carmen, see Fredericks, pp. 378–379; Stimson, *Rise of the Labor Movement in Los Angeles* (Berkeley: University of California Press, 1955), pp. 237, 266–267. On the role of Shafer and Knox, see *Los Angeles Times* February 12, 20, March 13, 26, 29, 1903.
58. *Los Angeles Times*, March 29, 30, 1903; (Los Angeles) *Evening Express*, March 28, 1903.
59. *Times* April 26, 29, 30, May 1, 6, 8, 12, 1903; *Record* April 29, 30, 1903; *Evening Express* April 27–29, 1903.
60. *Times* April 30, 1903.
61. Ibid.; *Record* April 30, 1903; *Evening Express* April 30, 1903.
62. *Los Angeles Record*, October 6, 1903. (Excerpts from letter originally published in early May, but full text of Elton's response printed on October 6.)

63. Ibid., April 24, 1903; *Evening Express* April 24, 1903; *Times* April 25, 27, 28, 1903; Wollenberg, p. 361; Stimson, p. 257.
64. *Times* April 25, 1903; *Record* April 24, 1903; *Evening Express* April 24–25, 1903.
65. *Times* April 27, 1903; *Evening Express* April 25, 1903; *Record* April 25, 1903.
66. *Times* April 25, 1903.
67. *Times* April 25–29, 1903. On only one occasion did the police fail to keep strike sympathizers from reaching strikebreakers at their work. On April 28, a group of twenty-eight Chicano women, led by a rather mysterious woman known as "Santa Teresa," approached the work sites and induced some fifty men to leave their jobs and join the union. Although she denied being a saint, "Santa" Teresa Rodriguez had a reputation as a mystic and spiritual healer. Reports on her background were varied and incomplete, but she took an active role in the MFU strike. She also helped MFU secretary A. M. Nieto inform Mexican laborers in other areas about the strike in Los Angeles and persuade them not to come as strikebreakers. See *Record*, March 25, 27, April 28, 1903; *Evening Express* March 27, April, 28, 1903; *Times* April 28, 1903.
68. *Record* May 1, June 6, 1903.
69. Ibid., May 5, 1903; *Times* May 1, 6, 8, 1903.
70. *Times* April 15, May 1, 4–9, 1903.
71. Stimson, Chapter 9, passim, on 1890 printers' strike; on the printers' friendlier relations with other papers before 1906, see idem., pp. 176–178, 239, 298–99.
72. Ibid., pp. 278, 280–81; *Times* July 12, 1904; *Record* August 9, 1904.
73. *Union Labor News* December 29, 1905, January 26, 1906 (expressing concern over growing strength of Citizen's Alliance and open-shop forces in Los Angeles more generally); Stimson, pp. 278–279,298–299 (on the role of the Employing Printers' Association).
74. *Union Labor News* February 16, 23, March 2, 1906.
75. Ibid., February 16, April 13, 1906.
76. Stimson, p. 299; *Times* November 3, 1906.
77. *Citizen* May 3, 10, 1907; *Times* May 2–5, 1907; Stimson, pp. 310–311; see also *Record* March 23, 1907, for evidence that the Draymen's Association had initially conceded to union demands.
78. "Testimony of Mr. F. J. Zeehandelaar," USCIR, Vol. 6., pp. 5496–5498; *Citizen* May 3, 1910; *Times, May* 2, 3, 1907; Stimson, p. 311.
79. *Citizen* May 3, 10, 17, 1907; *Times, May* 2–11, 1907
80. Stimson, p. 311–312, fn. 63, p. 482
81. Ibid., p. 312.
82. Stimson, pp. 229–235.
83. Ibid.; *Los Angeles Socialist* January 25, March 29, May 17, 24, July 5, 26, August 2, 23, 30, September 27, October 11, 25, November 8, 22, December 2, 1901; *Los Angeles Record* September 4, 22, 1902.

84. Stimson, p. 234.
85. Police departments provided scores of patronage positions, and they generated revenue for local political machines through selective enforcement of vice laws.
86. On complex and contingent alliance between labor and reformers in Los Angeles, see Daniel Johnson, "A Serpent in the Garden: Institutions, Ideology, and Class in Los Angeles Politics, 1901–1911," Ph.D., diss., UCLA, 1997; Martin Schiesl, "Progressive Reform in Los Angeles, 1909–1913," *California Historical Quarterly*. On similarities between the political agendas of labor and the progressives in Los Angeles, see the platform of the labor-backed Public Ownership Party in *Union Labor News* August 3, 31, 1906; *Los Angeles Examiner* February 22, 1906. See also Stimson, pp. 306–308, 323–325.
87. On labor and Alexander, see *Citizen* March 5, 1909, December 3, 1909; *Times* December 9, 1909.
88. Clark, "Limits of Liberty," pp. 455–458; *Citizen* June 3, 10, 17, August 12, 1910. On the role of San Francisco unions, see General Campaign Strike Committee [GCSC], *Final Report*, p. 5, in "Los Angeles File," San Francisco Labor Council Records [SFLC Records], Bancroft Library, University of California, Berkeley. See also *Times* June 2–5, 18, 1910; *Citizen* June 24, 1910.
89. *Baker Iron Works v. Metal Trades Council, et al.* Case No. 75559, and *Lewellyn v. Metal Trades Council*, Case No. 75647, Los Angeles County Archives, Los Angeles Superior Court Building; *Citizen* June 24, July 1, 1910. On Harriman's role, see "Testimony of Job Harriman," USCIR, *Final Report*, Vol. 6, pp. 5796–5798; *Citizen* June 24, July 8, 1910. Harriman lists six injunctions, omitting the *Baker* injunction. In addition, he claims that the injunctions were dismissed on various dates in August, 1910; this, however, is either an error on his part or a typographical error in the USCIR reports, for according to the case files in the County Archives, the *Baker* and *Lewellyn* injunctions were not formally ended until 1912.
90. According to Job Harriman and the local labor weekly, strikers continued to picket, albeit on a more limited basis and somewhat removed from work sites. See "Testimony of Job Harriman," USCIR, Vol. 6, pp. 5796–5799; *Citizen* June 3–July 8, 1907, June 24, 1910.
91. *Times* July 2, 1910; *Citizen* July 1, 8, 1910. Text of ordinance reproduced in "Testimony of Job Harriman," USCIR, Vol. 6., p. 5799.
92. "Testimony of Job Harriman," USCIR, Vol. 6, pp. 5797–5800; *Citizen* July 8, 22, 1910.
93. "Testimony of Job Harriman," USCIR, Vol. 6, pp. 5797–5802; GCSC *Final Report*, pp. 4–5; *Citizen* April 14, 21, 1911.
94. *Citizen* July 1, 8, 15, 1910.
95. Ibid., July 1, 1910.
96. Ibid., August 5, 1910; Stimson, pp. 346–347.
97. *Times* July 2, 6–8, 15–18, 1910. See also the letter of Los Angeles banker

Jackson Graves to the *Los Angeles Times*, reprinted in *Citizen* August 19, 1910.

98. The debate could be followed in the Los Angeles labor press throughout the strike, but see especially *Citizen* June 3, 17, 24, July 1, 8, 22, 29, August 12, 19, 26–September 23, 1910. Quote from "Report of the Executive Council," California Federation of Labor, *Proceedings of the Annual Convention* [hereafter CFL *Proceedings*] 1910, pp. 53–54.

99. Louis Adamic, *Dynamite: The Story of Class Violence in America* (New York: Viking Press, 1930); Stimson, Chapter 21. For a more recent account, see Geoffrey Cowan, *The People v. Clarence Darrow: The Bribery Trial of America's Greatest Lawyer* (New York: Random House/Times Books, 1993).

100. CFL *Proceedings*, 1910, pp. 14f.; *Citizen* September 23, October 7, 14, 1910; *Times* January 1, 1912.

101. Stimson, p. 364; see also "President's Report," and "Report of the Committee on Reports of Officers," in CFL *Proceedings*, 1911.

102. For the traditional view that the McNamara confessions cost Harriman the election, see Starr, p. 269; Bean, *California*, p. 287; Stimson, pp. 400–406 and Chapter 21, passim.

103. On the claim that women voters contributed to Harriman's defeat, see James Kraft, "The Fall of Job Harriman's Socialist Party: Violence, Gender, and Politics in Los Angeles, 1911," *Southern California Quarterly* (Spring 1988), p. 50; *Citizen* December 8, 1911.

104. See, for example, Karl Klare, "Labor Law as Ideology: Toward a New Historiography of Collective Bargaining Law," *Industrial Relations Law Journal* (1981); and Raymond Holger, "Labor History and Critical Labor Law," *Labor History* 30 (1989): 165–192. For a critique of Dawley's view of politics, see Bruce Laurie, *Artisan into Worker: Labor in Nineteenth Century America* (New York, Noonday Press, 1989), pp. 8f.

105. On the power of "rights consciousness" in a variety of political and social movements, see the several essays in Part II of *The Constitution in American Life*, a special edition of *Journal of American History* 74 (December 1987) edited by Hendrik Hartog, et al.

CHAPTER 2

1. For a classic account, see Felix Frankfurter and Nathan Greene. *The Labor Injunction* (New York: Macmillan 1930). It is difficult to find a copy of the *American Federationist*—the AFL monthly—during this period that does not have at least one, if not several, articles on the evils of the labor injunction. An index covering the period from 1898 to 1914 shows more entries under "injunction" than any other category other than "strikes." Given that the latter category included cross references to the former, one could reasonably conclude that the injunction was *the* most discussed issue during these years.

2. William Forbath, *Law and the Shaping of the American Labor Movement* (Cambridge, MA: Harvard University Press, 1991), Chapter 4.

3. *Daily Alta Californian* November 20, December 14, 1890; *Coast Seamen's Journal* November 26, 1890, December 3, 1890.

4. Lucille Eaves, *A History of California Labor Legislation* (Berkeley: University of California Press, 1910), p. 394.

5. Witte, Chapters 5–6; Frankfurter and Greene, pp. 17–24; Forbath, *Law*, pp. 101–102.

6. "Report of the Committee on Resolutions," CFL *Proceedings*, 1906, pp. 14–15.

7. "Report of the Executive Council," California Federation of Labor, Proceedings of the 7th Annual Convention, (San Francisco: 1907), pp. 58f. [Hereafter, CFL Proceedings.]

8. Forbath, p. 193.

9. Edwin Witte, *The Government in Labor Disputes* (New York: McGraw-Hill, 1932). Witte's list for California in Edwin Witte Collection, Wisconsin Historical Society [hereafter, Witte, WHS], Boxes 120–121.

10. Forbath, *Law*, Appendix B, pp. 193–198; Clark, "Limits of Liberty," Appendix A, pp. 768–770.

11. Witte, WHS, Boxes 120–121; California Bureau of Labor Statistics [hereafter, CBLS] *Twelfth Biennial Report* (Sacramento: State Printing Office, 1907), pp. 184–207; Clark, "Limits of Liberty," Appendix B, pp. 769–772.

12. Clark, "Limits of Liberty," Appendix A; Forbath, *Law*, Appendix B.

13. On the injunction to remove an employer from a "fair" list, see *Sentous v. Los Angeles Labor Council*, Case number 43031, Los Angeles County Archives, Los Angeles Superior Court Building; *Times* December 2, 1903. Although I have been unable to find supporting court records or newspaper references, Grace Stimson cites a 1906 injunction issued against a strike at the Los Angeles Harbor in San Pedro, Stimson, *Rise of the Labor Movement in Los Angeles* (Berkeley: University of California Press, 1955), p. 303. On the decline of union activism after 1907 in both San Francisco and Los Angeles, see Stimson, pp. 318–320, and Robert E. L. Knight, *Industrial Relations in the San Francisco Bay Area* (Berkeley: University of California Press, 1960), Chapter 6. On strike statistics see California Bureau of Labor Statistics, *Biennial Report*, 1906–1907, pp. 184–213. The data for 1901–1905 show 111 strikes in San Francisco compared to 51 in Los Angeles, or a 2.2:1 ratio. Given that one or more injunctions were issued on at least thirty occasions (and probably many more) between 1897 and 1907, one would expect at least thirteen injunctions in Los Angeles over the same period if the injunction-to-strike ratio were the same in both cities.

14. See, for example, *James H. Aver[y] v. Carmen's Union of San Francisco, et al.*, San Francisco Superior Court, Case No. 11268, copy of injunction in "Law and Legislative Committee" file, Carton 24, SFLC Records. See also Witte, *The Government in Labor Disputes*, p. 91.

15. CBLS, *Biennial Report*, 1906–1907, pp. 210–211.

16. On the 1910–1911 injunctions in Los Angeles, see *Baker Iron Works v.*

Metal Trades Council et al., Case No. 75559 and *Lewellyn v. Metal Trades Council* Case No. 75647, both in Los Angeles County Archives, Los Angeles Superior Court Building. Several more are cited in "Testimony of Job Harriman," United States Commission on Industrial Relations [USCIR], *Final Report and Testimony* (Washington, DC: Government Printing Office 1916), Vol. 6, pp. 5796–5799. See also *Los Angeles Citizen* June 3, 10, 17, 24, July 1, 8, 1910.

17. On the greater likelihood that closed-shop and recognition strikes would draw injunctions or other forms of intervention, see William Forbath, *Law*, p. 62 and Appendix B, *passim*.

18. *Argonaut* August 8, 1904; Herbert Ready, *The Labor Problem* (San Francisco: N.p., 1904). On the efforts to seek injunctions in combination with efforts to import strikebreakers, see San Francisco Citizen's Alliance, *A Few Good Things Done by the Citizen's Alliance of San Francisco* (San Francisco: N.p., N.d. [1905?]), Union Labor Pamphlet Collection, Bancroft Library, Berkeley. The Citizen's Alliance boasted that, in 1904 alone, its legal department had secured nineteen injunctions and its "employment bureau" has placed 1800 workers in forty-eight different occupations.

19. Paul Scharrenberg, "Reminiscences . . ." Interview conducted in 1954. Typescript in Oral History Collection, Bancroft Library, University of California at Berkeley.

20. Forbath, *Law*, Chapter 3.

21. Before the mid-nineteenth century, the most important state court decisions had ruled that labor unions, by their very nature, combined to restrain trade and were therefore unlawful conspiracies. In *Commonwealth v. Hunt* (1842), however, Massachusetts Judge Lemuel Shaw ruled that unions were voluntary associations, whose members could be convicted of conspiracy only if they had combined for an unlawful "purpose" or employed unlawful "methods." Labor unions did not, by their very existence, constitute an unlawful conspiracy, Shaw reasoned, for such associations might be used for "useful and honorable" ends as well as for "dangerous and pernicious" ends. See Walter Nelles, "Commonwealth v. Hunt," *Columbia Law Review* (1932). For more recent analyses see Holt, "Labor Conspiracy Cases"; Tomlins, pp. 40–44; Hattam, [essay in Tomlins and King]; and Alfred Konefsky, " 'As Best to Serve Their Own Interest': Lemuel Shaw, Labor Conspiracy, and Fellow Servants," *Law and History Review* (1989).

22. On the "malice" and "just cause" doctrines, see Oliver Wendell Holmes, Jr., "Privilege, Malice, and Intent," in Holmes, *Collected Legal Papers* (New York, P. Smith, 1952). See also Witte, Chapter 3; Commons and Andrews, pp. 388–403, 409–417; and Frederick H. Cooke, *The Law of Combinations, Monopolies, and Labor Unions* (Chicago: Callaghan and Co., 1919). *Mogul Steamship Co. v. McGregor, Gow, & Co.* L.R. 23 Q.B.D. 598 (1889), affirmed by the House of Lords, A.C. 25 (1892). Reprinted in Sayres, pp. 252–259.

23. Ibid., p. 255.

24. *De Mincio v. Craig* 207 Mass. 593 (1911), reprinted in Sayre, pp. 147–150. See also Commons and Andrews, pp. 390–391.

25. *Karges Furniture Co. v. Amalgamated Woodworkers Union* 165 Ind. 421 (1905), reprinted in Sayre, pp. 264–268, quote at p. 266, cases cited at p. 267.

26. *Plant v. Woods* 176 Mass. 492 (1900), reprinted in Sayre, pp. 312–318, quote at p. 317.

27. Ibid., p. 318.

28. *National Protective Association of Steam Fitters and Helpers v. Cumming* 170 N.Y. 315 (1902), reprinted in Sayre, pp. 303–311.

29. Ibid., p. 304.

30. Commons and Andrews, pp. 390f. See also Frankfurter and Greene, pp. 24–26; Witte, Chapter 5, passim.

31. For the best discussion of this distinction, see Witte, pp. 31–38; Frankfurter and Greene, passim; and *Iron Molders v. Allis-Chalmers* 166 F. 45, U.S. Circuit Court of Appeals (1908).

32. *Vegelahn v. Guntner* 167 Mass. 92 (1896).

33. *Atchinson, Topeka, and Santa Fe RR v. Gee* 139 F. 582 (1905), reprinted in Sayre, pp. 212–213.

34. On "violence" and "intimidation" see the cases cited in Sayre, pp. 181–193.

35. Forbath, p. 62; Hurvitz, pp. 333f.

36. *Blacks Law Dictionary*, 5th edition (St. Paul, MN: West Publishing, 1979), pp. 484–485.

37. Forbath, *Law*, pp. 59–66; Hurvitz, pp. 333f.

38. Forbath, *Law*, pp. 81–85, quote at p. 85.

39. James Atleson, *Values and Assumptions in American Labor Law* (Amherst: University of Massachusetts Press, 1983), pp. 1–3. See also David Kairys, ed., *The Politics of Law: A Progressive Critique*, 2nd ed. (New York: Pantheon Books, 1990), p. 8.

40. Edward Johnson, *The History of the Supreme Court Justices of California*, 2 vols. (San Francisco: Bender–Moss, 1963–1965), provides useful biographical summaries of California's appellate court judges. For a general overview of the education of judges during this period, see Lawrence Friedman, *A History of American Law*, 2nd. ed. (New York: Simon and Schuster, 1985), pp. 525–538; and Kermit Hall, *The Magic Mirror: Law in American History* (New York: Oxford University Press, 1989), pp. 211–225.

41. Ibid., passim, quote at p. 5.

42. Daniel Ernst, *Lawyers Against Labor: From Individual Rights to Corporate Liberalism* (Urbana: University of Illinois Press, 1995), especially Chapters 1–3.

43. On the factors that mitigated the partisan nature of judicial elections in California and three other states, see Kermit Hall, "Progressive Reform and the Decline of Democratic Accountability: The Popular Election of State Court Judges, 1850–1920," *American Bar Foundation Research Journal* (1984); 345–369; idem., *The Magic Mirror* and Robert Gordon, "Legal

Thought and Legal Practice in the Age of American Enterprise, 1870–1920," in Gerard Gawalt, ed., *The New High Priests: Lawyers in Post–Civil War America* (Westport, CT: Greenwood Press, 1984).

44. *Ex Parte Kubak* 85, Cal 274 (1890); "Complaint of J. D. Bailey," in Case File No. 20680. Hereafter citations for the final decision refer to volume and page numbers of *California Reports*. Case File numbers refer to files in the Records of the California Supreme Court and the California District Courts of Appeal in the California State Archives, Secretary of State's Office, Sacramento and Roseville, CA. [Hereafter, CSA]. Case files, where available, include original complaints, lower court transcripts and rulings, and briefs filed before the appellate courts.

45. On the eight-hour and anti-Chinese movements in California see Alexander Saxton, *The Indispensable Enemy: Labor and the Anti-Chinese Movement in California* (Berkeley: University of California Press, 1971); and Lucille Eaves, *A History of California Labor Legislation* (Berkeley: University of California Press, 1910).

46. 85 Cal. 274 at 276. See also "Points and Authorities of Petitioner," and "Brief for Respondent," in Case File No. 20680, CSA.

47. *Ex Parte Jentzsch* 112 Cal. 468 (1896)

48. *Davitt v. American Bakers' Union* 124 Cal. 99 (1899), "Points and Authorities of Appellants," Case File No. S.F. 1177, CSA.

49. Ibid.; chronology reconstructed from miscellaneous documents in Case File No. S.F. 1177, CSA.

50. 124 Cal. 99 at 101. See also, "Points and Authorities of Appellants" and "Points and Authorities of Respondents," in Case File No. S.F. 1177, CSA.

51. For labor's response to the *Davitt* ruling, see the *Voice of Labor* April 1, 1899. That lawyers for each side read the ruling differently is apparent in the briefs filed in the cases discussed below.

52. Lucille Eaves, *A History of California Labor Legislation*, p. 145. The CFL executive committee claimed that the anti-injunction bill was "one of the most important bills introduced in the legislative session in the interests of labor." However, the paucity of comment or discussion elsewhere in the labor press on convention proceedings suggests that this claim may have been exaggerated. See "Legislative Report," CFL *Proceedings, 1901*.

53. Eaves, Chapter 19; *Davitt v. American Baker's Union* 124 Cal. 99 (1899).

54. On AFL sponsorship of anti-injunction legislation see Forbath, *Law,* pp. 147–149; and Marc Karson, *Labor Unions and American Politics* (Carbondale: Southern Illinois University Press, 1958).

55. "Report of the Law and Legislative Committee, Proposed Bill No. 1," CFL *Proceedings, 1903*. See also *Labor Clarion* January 23, 1903.

56. Ibid.; see also *Examiner* February 5, 1903.

57. Unless otherwise noted, the legislative history of the 1903 bill is taken from *Labor Clarion* January 23, 30, February 6, 13, 20, 1903; *Examiner* February 5, 10–12, 1903.

58. Ibid.

59. California State Legislature. *Final Calendar of Legislative Business* (Sacramento: Superintendent of State Printing, 1903), p. 88.

60. Eaves, pp. 422–426; Knight, pp. 145–146; Taft, pp. 21–23.

61. On the cases dropped, see Eaves, p. 425, fn. 95. See also Edwin Witte's list of California injunctions, Edwin Witte Papers, Wisconsin Historical Society, Boxes 120–121. On the 1903 strike total, see CBLS, *Twelfth Biennial Report, 1906–1907*, pp. 190–201.

62. On the cases dropped, see Eaves, pp. 522–526; on the federal injunctions see Witte, WHS, boxes 120–121; on the 1903 strike total see California Bureau of Labor Statistics, *Twelfth Biennial Report*, pp. 190–201.

63. On the Citizen's Alliance's national activities, see Phillip Foner, *History of the Labor Movement in the United States*, Vol. 3, Chapter 2, passim. On the Citizen's Alliance in California, see Knight, pp. 139f.

64. Citizen's Alliance, *A Few Good Things Done by the Citizen's Alliance of San Francisco*, passim; *Goldberg, Bowen & Co. v. Stablemen's Union* 149 Cal. 429 (1906); *Pierce v. Stablemen's Union* 156 Cal. 70 (1909). On labor's reaction to legal efforts of the Citizen's Alliance, see *Labor Clarion*, especially July 15, August 12, 26, October 8, December 9, 1904.

65. *Jordahl v. Hayda* 1 Cal. App. 696, passim.

66. 149 Cal. 429 at 432.

67. Ibid., at 429. The decision did not in all ways go against labor, but the concessions were paltry at best. First, McFarland rejected Finnell's argument that boycotts were unlawful by definition. The judge noted that in many of the cases cited by Finnell, the boycott "was enjoined without reference to the means used to carry it into effect." The California justices, however, saw "no necessity to go that far." The judges did not dismiss the possibility that a boycott might be unlawful in its purpose, but "in the case at bar" they ruled only that the "means" employed "[did] directly intimidate customers." Second, McFarland agreed with Lister as to the excessively sweeping nature of the lower court decree. "Some parts of the judgment seem to enjoin . . . the mere expression of an opinion," the court ruled. The lower court order had implied that the union could not publish claims about the employer anywhere. As such, McFarland modified the injunction to read that pickets could not carry placards or banners "in the immediate vicinity" of the employer's business. Ibid. at pp. 432, 434–435.

68. As Karen Orren has argued the courts continued to rely on doctrines of master-servant law to enforce a hierarchical and essentially "feudal" ordering of the workplace well into the twentieth century. See Orren, *Belated Feudalism: Labor, the Law, and Liberal Development in the United States* (New York: Cambridge University Press, 1991).

69. Commons and Andrews, pp. 390f; Frankfurter and Greene, passim.

70. *Parkinson v. Building Trades Council of Santa Clara Co.* 154 Cal. 581 (1908), Case File No. S.F. 4469; *Pierce v. Stablemen's Union* 156 Cal. 70 (1909), Case File No. 4092, CSA.

71. 154 Cal. 581 at 584–585. On Parkinson's position in the Citizen's Alliance, see *Labor Clarion* December 26, 1908.
72. Agreement between Parkinson and Council reprinted in 154 Cal. 581, at 590–591.
73. 154 Cal. 581, at 590–591.
74. Ibid., at 581–583
75. Ibid., at 593–595, 598–599.
76. Ibid., Shaw dissent at 612–623.
77. Ibid., Sloss concurring opinion at 605–610, quotes at 605, 610.
78. *Labor Clarion* December 26, 1908.
79. California judges were not alone in using language that equated moral and economic intimidation with physical intimidation, or in assuming that labor's methods inherently led to violence. For this tendency among federal judges, see Dianne Avery, "Images of Violence in Labor Jurisprudence: The Regulation of Picketing and Boycotts, 1894–1921," *Buffalo Law Review* Winter 1988/89: 1–117.
80. *Pierce v. Stablemen's Union* 156 Cal. 70 (1909) at 72–73; on the origins of the dispute in San Francisco Superior Court, see the San Francisco *Chronicle* August 3, 1905.
81. Ibid., at 74–77.
82. Ibid., at 77–79.
83. Ibid., at 78.
84. Ibid., Angellotti concurring at 80.
85. Ibid., Shaw dissenting at 80–81.
86. Eaves, pp. 394, 422–427. Although Eaves's study was not published until 1910, the preface and contents of her book indicate that she did not incorporate the *Parkinson* and *Pierce* rulings.
87. Ibid., pp. 422–437.
88. *Labor Clarion* September 15, 1916, p. 8.
89. Ernst, *Lawyers against Labor*, quotes at pp. 1, 212.
90. For a similar observation on the importance of the timing of legal actions against labor, see E. P. Thompson's discussion of the British Combination Acts in *The Making of the English Working Class* (New York: Vintage Books, 1963). Thompson notes that prosecutions against British trade unions— like the injunction in California—"struck at the unionists at critical moments, or at critical points of development . . . Such cases generally arose at times of widespread or successful organization." Thompson, *Making*, pp. 507–508.
91. Thompson, *Whigs and Hunters: The Origins of the Black Act* (New York: Pantheon Books, 1975), pp. 258–269.
92. *Labor Clarion*, 1904.
93. David Montgomery, *Workers' Control in America: Studies in the History of Work, Technology, and Labor Struggles* (New York: Cambridge University Press, 1979), especially Chapter one.
94. In response to Christopher Tomlin's argument that antebellum judges infused nineteenth-century labor law with the hierarchical principles of mas-

ter and servant law, David Montgomery has asserted that "one cannot conclude that employers' authority in the workplace was created by legal discourse." No doubt legal discourse did not "create" that authority, but it did legitimate that authority and enforced it with the coercive power of the law. See Montgomery, *Citizen Worker: The Experience of Workers in the United States with Democracy and the Free Market during the Nineteenth Century* (New York: Cambridge University Press, 1993), pp. 43–45.

95. Orren, *Belated Feudalism*, passim. Although they differ with Orren on certain points, Christopher Tomlins and Amy Dru Stanley also point to the persistence of master and servant law well into the nineteenth century. See Tomlins, *Law, Labor, and Ideology in the Early Republic* (Cambridge: 1994) and Amy Dru Stanley, "Beggars Can't Be Choosers: Compulsion and Contract in Postbellum America," *Journal of American History* 78 (March 1992): 1265–1289.

96. In the *Pierce* ruling only Justice Angelotti's concurring opinion challenged the employer's contention that workers' demands, regardless of method, amounted to nothing less than "surrendering control" of the business to the union. 156 Cal. 70 (1909), pp. 8of.

97. Sloss ruling in *San Francisco Chronicle*, July 1901; Furuseth, "Government by Injunction—The Misuses of Equity Power," copy in Carton 30, SFLC Records; idem. *Coast Seamen's Journal* March 22, 1911. Forbath, *Law*, pp. 88, 136–137.

98. Scharrenberg. "Reminiscences . . . ," p. 48; *San Francisco Examiner* August 15, 1901. On the "disfigurement" of labor, see Forbath, *Law*. P. 127,

99. Resolution No. 7, CFL *Proceedings*, 1909. See also "Report of J. B. Dale," ibid., pp. 56–59.

CHAPTER 3

1. Peter Filene, "An Obituary for the Progressive Movement," *American Quarterly* (1970).

2. For overviews of progressivism, see Stephen Diner, *A Very Different Age: Americans of the Progressive Era* (New York: Hill and Wang, 1998); Daniel Rodgers, "In Search of Progressivism," *Reviews in American History* 10 (1982); Arthur Link and Richard McCormick, *Progressivism* (Arlington Heights, IL: Harlan Davidson, 1983).

3. Richard Hofstadter, *The Age of Reform: From Bryan to FDR* (New York: Vintage Books, 1955).

4. Richard McCormick, "Public Life in Industrial America, 1877–1917," in Foner, ed., *The New American History*, revised edition (Washington, DC: American Historical Association, 1997). For an appreciation of the continuing relevance of Hofstadter's interpretation, see Michael Kazin, "Hofstadter Lives: Political Culture and Temperament in the Work of an American Historian," *Reviews in American History* 27 (June 1999): 334–348.

5. James Weinstein, *The Corporate Ideal in the Liberal State, 1900–1918* (Boston: Beacon Press, 1968); Gabriel Kolko, *The Triumph of Conservatism: A Reinterpretation of American History, 1900–1916* (New York: Free Press, 1963).

6. Louis Galambos, "The Emerging Organizational Synthesis in Modern American History," *Business History Review* 44 (1970): 279–290; Robert Wiebe, *The Search for Order, 1877–1920* (New York: Hill and Wang, 1967); Samuel Hays, "Political Parties and the Community-Society Continuum," in William Nisbet and Walter Dean Burnham, eds., *The American Party Systems: Stages of Political Development* (New York: Hill and Wang, 1967); and idem., "The New Organizational Society," in Jerry Israel, ed., *Building the Organizational Society: Essays on Associational Activities in Modern America* (New York: Scribner, 1972).

7. Important exceptions to this trend include J. Joseph Huthmacher, "Urban Liberalism and the Age of Reform," *Mississippi Valley Historical Review* 49 (1962): 231–241; and John D. Buenker, *Urban Liberalism and Progressive Reform* (New York: 1973), both of which stress the support that working-class immigrant communities gave to Progressive-era social reforms.

8. George Mowry, *The California Progressives* (Berkeley: University of California Press, 1951).

9. The most important general reevaluation remains Spencer Olin, *California's Prodigal Sons: Hiram Johnson and the Progressives, 1911–1917* (Berkeley: University of California Press, 1968). On labor's role in state legislation, see CFL's "Report[s] on the State Legislature," in CFL *Proceedings, 1901–1919*. See also Mary Ann Mason Burki, "The California Progressives: Labor's Point of View," *Labor History* 17 (1976): 24–37; and Mary Ann Mason, "Neither Friends Nor Foes: Organized Labor and the California Progressives," in Tom Sitton and William Deverall, eds., *California Progressivism Revisited* (Berkeley: University of California Press, 1994).

10. On labor and working-class support for progressives, see Alexander Saxton, "San Francisco Labor and the Populist and Progressive Insurgencies," *Pacific Historical Review* 36 (1964); John Shover, "The Progressives and the Working Class Vote in California," *Labor History* 9 (1969); and Michael Rogin, "Progressivism and the California Electorate," *Journal of American History* 55 (1968). For a view that stresses the more qualified nature of labor and working-class support, see Thomas R. Clark, "Labor and Progressivism 'South of the Slot': The Voting Behavior of the San Francisco Working Class, 1912–1916," *California History* 66 (1987).

11. For works that stress the limits of the labor-progressive alliance, see Mary Ann Mason, "Neither Friends Nor Foes," and Clark, "Labor and Progressivism 'South of the Slot,'" passim.

12. Walter Dean Burnham, "The System of 1896: An Analysis," in Paul Kleppner, et al., *The Evolution of American Electoral Systems* (Westport, CT: Greenwood Press, 1981). See also Daniel Rodgers, "In Search of Progressivism," *Reviews in American History* 10 (1982): 113–132.

13. On the strength of nonpartisanship in California and the West, see Paul Kleppner, "Politics without Parties: The Western States, 1900–1984," in Gerald Nash and Richard Etulain, eds., *The Twentieth Century West: Historical Interpretations* (Albuquerque: University of New Mexico Press, 1989); Robert Cherny, "Research Opportunities in Twentieth Century Western History: Politics," in Gerald Nash and Richard Etulain, eds., *Researching Western History: Topics in the Twentieth Century* (Albuquerque: University of New Mexico Press, 1997).

14. On the decline of the parties and the rise of organized interest groups in Progressive-era politics, see Burnham, "The System of 1896," Samuel Hays, "Politics and Society: Beyond the Political Party," in Kleppner, *American Electoral Systems*, Chapter 7; Richard McCormick, "The Party Period and Public Policy: An Exploratory Hypothesis," *Journal of American History* 66 (September 1979), especially pp. 295–298. A more recent version of this argument is found in Elisabeth Clemens, *The People's Lobby: Organizational Innovation and the Rise of Interest Group Politics in the United States, 1890–1925* (Chicago: University of Chicago Press, 1997). As Julie Greene has noted, it is possible to overstate the decline of the parties—for at the national level they continued to play an important organizing role. See Greene, "Dinner Pail Politics: Employers, Workers, and Partisan Culture in the Progressive Era," in Eric Arensen, Julie Greene, and Bruce Laurie, eds., *Labor Histories: Class, Politics, and the Working Class Experience* (Urbana: University of Illinois Press, 1998). But even Greene would agree that the parties' role in the policy-making process had been diminished by what she has elsewhere described as "the brave new world of interest group liberalism." See idem., *Pure and Simple Politics.*

15. Taft, passim; Michael Kazin, "The 'Great Exception' Revisited: Organized Labor and Politics in San Francisco and Los Angeles, 1870–1940," *Pacific Historical Review* 55 (1986): 371–402.

16. On labor's legislative initiatives, see "Report on the Legislature," CFL *Proceedings, 1911–1913*; Franklin Hichborn, *Story of the California Legislature of 1911* (San Francisco: James H. Barry Press, 1911–1913). On Governor Johnson's appointments of trade unionists, see Saxton, "San Francisco Labor," pp. 422f.

17. Caminetti's bill quoted in "Summary and Comment on Labor Legislation," in CFL *Proceedings, 1911*, pp. 87–88. Andrew Furuseth's argument on behalf of the bill before the Judiciary Committee is reprinted in CFL *Proceedings, 1911*, pp. 89–91. See also *Bulletin* March 10, 1911; *Coast Seamen's Journal* March 22, 1911; *Labor Clarion* March 10, 1911.

18. Labor's insistence on redefining "property" proved prescient, as the AFL would soon learn at the national level in its campaign to exempt labor from anti-trust prosecutions. Both the Pearre and Wilson bills, which preceded the Clayton Act, included a similar re-definition of property. This definition was dropped, however, from the Clayton Act, allowing judges to interpret the qualifying phrase—"unless necessary to prevent irreparable

damage to property"—as declaratory of existing law. See Felix Frankfurter and Nathan Greene, *The Labor Injunction* (1930).

19. "Judiciary Minority Report," quoted in Franklin Hichborn, *Story of the California Legislature of 1911*, p. 272, fn. 310. See also *Coast Seamen's Journal* March 22, 1911.

20. Hichborn, *Story of the California Legislature of 1911*, pp. 272–282 and Appendix, Table 4; "Report of the Legislative Agents," CFL *Proceedings*, 1911, pp. 94–95. The senators' antics during this all-night session were widely reported by the press. Apparently, the sheriffs of Sacramento and San Francisco counties searched for the missing members into the wee hours of the morning. The senators remained locked in until the next morning and the vote for reconsideration not taken until past noon. Newspapers expressed puzzlement and dismay at the senators' mischief: the sergeant-at-arms rounded up one or two senators and ordered them to the chamber only to discover that two more had slipped out of a window to get something to eat; Senator Gates was at one point "crowned with a waste-paper basket," while Senator Finn of San Francisco treated "friend and foe alike" to union-made cigars; actors from a Sacramento theater were allowed in to entertain the lawmakers; and, finally, in the early-morning hours the bored senators engaged in a lively game of "white men and Indians," using wads of paper and files "as ammunition" and the Senate president's desk as "a fort." See *Los Angeles Times* March 22–23, 1911; *San Francisco Chronicle* March 22–24, 1911; *Sacramento Union* March 22–24, 1911

21. Hichborn, *Story*, 1911, pp. 282–283, Appendix, Table 4; *Times* March 22–26, 1911; *Final Calendar of Legislative Business*, 1911, SB 54.

22. "Report of the Legislative Agent," CFL *Proceedings*, 1911, pp. 92–96; *Labor Clarion* March 24, 31, 1911; *Coast Seamen's Journal* March 22, 29, 1911.

23. "President's Report," and "Report of the Secretary-Treasurer," in CFL *Proceedings*, 1912, pp. 71, 90; *Labor Clarion* January 31, February 21, 1913.

24. "Report of Legislative Agent to the 40th Session of the California Legislature, [Hereafter McConaughy Report]," in Law and Legislative Committee files, Carton 24, Records of the San Francisco Labor Council, Bancroft Library, Berkeley, California [Hereafter SFLC Records].

25. "Report on Labor Legislation," CFL *Proceedings*, 1913, pp. 90f; *Labor Clarion* March 14, 28, 1913.

26. McConaughy Report, in Law and Legislative Committee files, Carton 24, SFLC Records.

27. Hichborn, *Story of the California Legislature of 1911*, passim; "Report of the Committee on Law and Legislation," CFL *Proceedings*, pp. 38–41.

28. "Report of the Secretary Treasurer," CFL *Proceedings*, 1915, p. 87.

29. "Report on Labor Legislation," CFL *Proceedings*, 1913, pp. 90–99. For a similar assessment by the legislative agent of the San Francisco Labor Council, see pamphlet titled "Report of the Legislative Agent for the 40th Session of the California Legislature," N.p., N.d., [1913?], in the Law and Legislative Committee files, Carton 24, SFLC Records.

30. Voting records are derived from the appendices of Franklin Hichborn's

Story of the California Legislature of 1911, Tables 1–6; ibid., 1913, Tables 1–2, 5–6; California Legislature, *Final Calendar of Legislative Business*, 1911 and 1913; and "Records of Senators," and "Record of Assemblymen," in CFL *Proceedings*, Appendices, 1911 and 1913.

31. Ibid. See also Clark, "The Limits of Liberty," pp. 163–165.
32. *Times* March 9, 1911.
33. "Report of the Legislative Agents," CFL *Proceedings*, 1911, p. 95; Mowry, pp. 144–147; Meyer Lissner to Hiram Johnson, March 23, 1911, Hiram Johnson Papers, Bancroft Library.
34. Mowry, *California Progressives*, pp. 145–147.
35. Fresno *Republican* March 23, 1911; *Bulletin* March 10, 1911.
36. On the working-class shift to Johnson in 1914, see Clark, "Labor and Progressivism South of the Slot"; and Rogin, "Progressivism and the California Electorate. "
37. CFL *Proceedings*, 1911, pp. 95–96; Scharrenberg, "Reminiscences," pp. 54–67; *Labor Clarion* March 3–April 17, 1911.
38. California Special Labor Commissioner [Weinstock, Harris] *Report on Labor Laws and Conditions in Foreign Countries in Relation to Strikes and Lockouts* (Sacramento: Superintendent of State Printing, 1910). On the fate of Weinstock's bill in 1911, see Hichborn, *Story of the California Legislature of 1911*, pp. 261–265 and Appendix, Table 3.
39. *California Outlook*, March 29, 1911.
40. Weinstock, *Report*, pp. 150–152; *California Outlook* March–May, 1911.
41. "Testimony of John Britton," in United States Commission on Industrial Relations, *Final Report and Testimony* [Hereafter USCIR], Vol. 6, pp. 5423f; "Testimony of Fred Baker," ibid., pp. 5566f.
42. Walter Macarthur, "Memorandum on Bill Providing for Public Investigation into Labor Disputes," pamphlet in Law and Legislative Committee files, Carton 24, SFLC Records.
43. Ibid., and "Report of the Secretary Treasurer," CFL *Proceedings*, 1911; Hichborn, *Story of the California Legislature of 1911*, pp. 261–265.
44. Macarthur, "Memorandum"; "Testimony of Andrew Gallagher," USCIR, Vol. 6, pp. 5444–5452.; and *Labor Clarion* February 17, 1911.
45. Macarthur, "Memorandum," passim.
46. Ibid.; Mullen "Picketing," Typescript in Carton 27, SFLC Records.
47. "Testimony of Fremont Older," USCIR, Vol. 6, pp. 5437–4542.
48. Ibid., p. 5437.
49. Older's distinction between "peace and harmony" and "justice" in many ways mirrors Christopher Tomlins' distinction between "industrial stability" (which is the state's primary interest) and "industrial democracy" (which is labor's primary interest). See Christopher Tomlins, *The State and the Unions: Labor Relations, Law, and the Organized Labor Movement in America* (New York: Cambridge University Press, 1985), pp. xii–xii.
50. Tomlins, *The State and the Unions*, pp. xi–xii and passim; Ernst, *Lawyers against Labor*, pp. 1–9.
51. Ibid.; on general changes in economic thought, see James Livingston, "The

Social Analysis of Economic History and Theory," *American Historical Review* 92 (February 1987).

52. Macarthur, "For Industrial Freedom," in *Labor Clarion* February 17, 1911. Emphasis added. See also Walter Macarthur, "Memorandum."

53. Mullen, "Picketing," Carton 27, SFLC Records. Emphasis added.

54. Daniel Rodgers, "In Search of Progressivism"; and Stephen Diner, *A Very Different Age*, Chapter 8. Elizabeth Sanders argues that both organized farmers and organized workers, who made critical contributions to the Progressive-era expansion of the American state, were nonetheless deeply ambivalent about increasing state power. See Elizabeth Sanders, *Roots of Reform: Farmers, Workers, and the American State, 1877–1917* (Chicago: University of Chicago Press, 1999), especially Chapter 11.

55. On the concept of "social unionism" see, for example, Alan Derikson, "Health Security for All?," pp. 1334–1335; Alice Kessler-Harris, "Trade Unions Mirror Society in Conflict between Collectivism and Individualism," *Monthly Labor Review*, August 1987; and Kim Moody, *An Injury to All: The Decline of American Unionism* (New York: Verso Press, 1988).

56. "Report of the Secretary-Treasurer," CFL *Proceedings*, 1911, pp. 96–97.

57. That the CFL's primary purpose was to develop labor's state-level legislative program is demonstrated in Philip Taft's comprehensive survey, *Labor Politics American Style: The California Federation of Labor* (Cambridge, MA: Harvard University Press, 1968).

58. "Testimony of Paul Scharrenberg," USCIR, Vol. 6, pp. 5040–5052; "Testimony of Austin Lewis," USCIR, Vol. 6, pp. 4999–5010.

59. "Testimony of Austin Lewis," pp. 5008–5010.

60. "Testimony of Paul Scharrenberg," pp. 5043–5046. See also "Report[s] on Labor Legislation," CFL *Proceedings*, Appendices, 1913–1917.

61. On the anemic efforts of CFL organizational efforts among migrant farm workers, see "Testimony of J. B. Dale," USCIR, Vol. 5, pp. 4972–4979; "Testimony of Paul Scharrenberg," ibid., Vol. 5, p. 5042. See also Taft, *Labor Politics American Style*, Chapter 2; Cletus Daniel, *Bitter Harvest: A History of California Farmworkers, 1870–1941* (Ithaca: Cornell University Press: 1981), pp. 76–81.

62. Alice Kessler-Harris, *Out to Work: A History of Wage-Earning Women* (New York: Oxford University Press, 1982), pp. 201–205, 212–215. See also Theda Skocpol, *Protecting Soldiers and Mothers: The Political Origins of Social Policy in the United States* (Cambridge, MA: Harvard University Press, 1992) especially Chapter 7.

63. Rebecca Mead, "'Let the Women Get Their Wages as Men Do': Trade Union Women and the Legislated Minimum Wage in California," *Pacific Historical Review* 58 (August 1988): 317–347.

64. Of course, there was nothing inconsistent about labor's opposition to the minimum wage law and its support for the IWC. To begin with, the IWC enforced not only the minimum wage law, but also other protective labor laws that the CFL had supported. Moreover, once the law had been passed,

it was in labor's interest to keep the minimum wage as high as possible and to support its enforcement. Mead, "'Let the Women Get Their Wages as Men Do,'" passim; and Jaclyn Greenberg, "The Limits of Legislation: Katherine Philips Edson, Practical Politics, and the Minimum Wage Law in California, 1913–1922," *Journal of Policy History* 5 (1993): 207–230.

65. Kessler-Harris; Mead; "Testimony of Paul Scharrenberg," "Testimony of Mrs. Katherine Philips Edson," USCIR, Vol. 6, pp. 5683–5693; and "Testimony of J. B. Dale," USCIR, Vol. 5, pp. 4972–4979 (on organizing farm workers).

66. On the tendency to conflate a "minimalist" view of politics and the state with "exclusiveness" as reinforcing ingredients of AFL conservatism, see, for example, Bruce Laurie, *Artisans into Workers*, Epilogue; Michael Rogin, "Voluntarism: The Political Functions of an Antipolitical Doctrine," *Industrial and Labor Relations Review* 15 (1962): 521–353; Leon Fink, "The New Labor History and the Powers of Historical Pessimism: Consensus, Hegemony, and the Case of the Knights of Labor," *Journal of American History* 75 (1988): 115–136; and Forbath, *Law*, pp. 96–97.

67. While individual trade unionists would have benefitted from such laws, they clearly did not benefit trade unions per se. For example, laws regulating payment of wages included requiring at least semi-monthly payments and the elimination of payments in script. These laws would only have benefitted unorganized, mostly unskilled, workers who did not work under collective bargaining agreements, especially migrant farm workers. On farm workers, see Paul Taylor; Cletus Daniel, *Bitter Harvest*; and Carlton Parker, "Report on the Wheatland Hopfield Riot," in *The Casual Laborer and Other Essays*. On CFL support for these measures, see "Report[s] of the Legislative Agent," CFL *Proceedings*, 1911–1915; Taft, *Labor Politics American Style*, Chapter 3.

68. "Testimony of Walton Wood," USCIR, Vol. 6, pp. 5818–5826.

69. Gerald Nash, "The Influence of Labor on State Policy, 1860–1920: The Experience of California," *California Historical Quarterly* 42 (1963), pp. 241–257, quote at p. 241.

70. Arthur Viseltear, "Compulsory Health Insurance in California, 1915–1918," *Journal of the History of Medicine* (April 1969): 151–182. On the opposition of Gompers and other national leaders of the AFL, see Samuel Gompers, "Voluntary Social Insurance vs. Compulsory," *American Federationist* May 1916, pp. 333–335. However, even some members of the AFL executive committee supported health insurance proposals, including Vice-President William Green, who replaced Gompers as AFL President in 1924. On Green, see Derikson, "Health Security For All?," passim.

71. CFL *Proceedings*. See especially "President's Report," CFL *Proceedings*, 1917, pp. 52–54; "Report of the Delegate to the 36th Annual Convention of A.F. of L.," [D. Haggerty], CFL *Proceedings*, 1917, pp. 69–75, noting that the AFL convention thought the issue should be given "greater consideration," but that if it ever was established, it "shall be voluntary not

compulsory." (p. 74). See generally the "Report[s] on Labor Legislation," "Report[s] of the Secretary Treasurer," and the "President's Report[s]" in the CFL *Proceedings*, 1915–1919. Andrew Viseltear's study of the movement for health insurance in California gives the false impression that labor opposed health insurance by citing the opposition of *Labor Clarion* editor James Mullen and conservative leaders of the San Francisco Labor Council. Viseltear, pp. 158–159. But the fact remains that most of the state's labor federations, and most importantly the majority and leadership of the CFL, consistently supported the Social Insurance Commission's recommendations. Moreover, at least some of those opposed to the plan did so not because it was compulsory, but because it excluded many categories of workers, most notably migrant farm workers. See "President's Report," CFL *Proceedings*, 1917, pp. 52–54.

72. *Labor Clarion*, April 18, 1913.

73. On the AFL leadership's embrace of a "court minted ideology," see Forbath, *Law*, passim.

74. Scharrenberg, "Address to the Commonwealth Club of California," reprinted in CFL *Proceedings*, 1916. California labor leaders, like their national counterparts, repeatedly stressed labor's role as an agent in securing a "larger liberty" or a "broader conception of human rights," and thereby advancing "progress" and "civilization." As one editorial put it, "the story of the struggle for the right to [strike] is the story of the struggle from barbarism to civilization." *Coast Seamen's Journal* June 5, 1901. But see also, for example, the Los Angeles labor papers. *Union Labor News* December 18, 1903, November 17, 1905; *Los Angeles Citizen* August 14, 1908; February 19, 1909; June 17, July 1, July 29, August 12, September 16, 1910.

75. Furuseth presented labor's case in the labor press and before state and federal legislative committees. For a sampling see *Coast Seamen's Journal* March 22, 1911, November 13, 1912, March 26, 1913; *Labor Clarion* March 3, 10, 1911, September 1, 1913. A good summary of the attack on the "ancient" and "feudal" assumptions of law can be found in his "Government by Injunction—The Misuses of Equity Power," in Carton 30, SFLC Records. At the core of Furuseth's position was his belief that the right of employers and employees to enter into relationships was a "personal" and not a "property" right. As such, the relationship could not be protected by equity, which only protected damage to property. For a more recent analysis of the law's feudal vestiges and labor's early-twentieth-century assault against it, see Karen Orren, *Belated Feudalism: Labor, the Law, and Liberal Development in the United States* (New York: Cambridge University Press, 1991).

76. Scharrenberg, "Address to the Commonwealth Club of California," reprinted in CFL *Proceedings*, 1916.

77. Walter Macarthur, "For Industrial Freedom," *Labor Clarion* February 17, 1911.

78. Mullen, "Picketing," Carton 27, SFLC Records. A version of this manuscript was printed in serial form beginning with the September 15, 1916,

issue of *Labor Clarion*. But for very similar arguments that individual rights could only be protected by protecting collective rights, see also Walter Macarthur, "For Industrial Freedom," *Labor Clarion* February 17, 1911; Paul Scharrenberg's "Address to the Commonwealth Club" and "Report of the Secretary-Treasurer," both in California Federation of Labor, *Proceedings*, 1916.

79. Mullen, "Picketing," Carton 27, SFLC Records; and "Testimony of Ira Cross," USCIR, Vol. 6, pp. 5412–5418, quote at 5418.

80. C. B. Macpherson, *The Political Theory of Possessive Individualism: Hobbes to Locke* (New York: Oxford University Press, 1962). According to Macpherson, "possessive individualism" conceived of "the individual as essentially the proprietor of his own person and capacities . . . The individual was seen . . . as an owner of himself." Walter Macarthur opposed any restrictions on the right of workers to strike, whether it came from a board of arbitration or from a court, as depriving "the workingman of control over the only thing he possess as a means of earning his livelihood—his power of labor." Where labor perhaps departed from "possessive individualism" was in its contention that, if the right to withhold this labor power were inherent in individuals, it was also inherent in any group of individuals. Macarthur, "Memorandum." *Op. Cit.* For similar arguments, see the articles by Andrew Furuseth in the *Coast Seamen's Journal* November 13, 1912, March 19, 1913, June 17, 1917.

81. Ibid., and Mullen, "Picketing," Carton 27, SFLC Records.

82. Alexander Saxton, *The Indispensable Enemy: Labor and the Anti-Chinese Movement in California* (Berkeley: University of California Press, 1971); and Roger Daniels, *The Politics of Prejudice: The Anti-Japanese Movement in California and the Struggle for Japanese Exclusion* (Berkeley: University of California Press, 1962), especially Chapter 2 on labor's role. But see also Asiatic Exclusion League, *Proceedings of the Asiatic Exclusion League, 1907–1913*, (San Francisco: Asiatic Exclusion League, 1907–1913), copy in California History Room, California State Library, Sacramento. [Hereafter, AEL, *Proceedings*.]

83. CFL *Proceedings*, 1918, pp. 77f; ibid., 1919, pp. 95f.

84. Paul Scharrenberg, "The Attitude of Organized Labor toward the Japanese," pamphlet in the "Japanese Pamphlets" collection, edited by V. S. McClatchy, Rare Book Room, California State Library, Sacramento, California. Scharrenberg's essay also appeared in the *Annals of the American Academy of Political and Social Science* 93 (January 1921): 34–38.

85. For works that stress the absence of competition between Japanese immigrants and white workers, see Yuji Ichioka, *The Issei: The World of the First Generation Japanese Immigrants, 1885–1924* (New York: Free Press, 1988), Chapter 4; Thomas Almaguer, *Racial Fault Lines: The Historical Origins of White Supremacy in California* (Berkeley: University of California Press, 1994), Chapter 7; and Daniel Rogers, *The Politics of Prejudice*, Chapter 2. For an opposing view, see Edna Bonacich, "A Theory of Ethnic An-

tagonism: The Split Labor Market," in Irving Horowitz, et al., *The American Working Class: Prospects for the 1980* (New Brunswick, NJ: Transaction Books, 1979), pp. 82–83. Bonacich claims that although there might not have been "direct competition," workers might still reasonably fear the *potential* of economic competition should immigration continue unabated.

86. One of the few instances in which the mainstream labor movement supported the organization of Asian workers occurred during the 1903 sugar beet strike in Oxnard, California. The Los Angeles Labor Council passed a resolution in favor of organizing Japanese workers who were already in the United States, but still steadfastly favored Asian exclusion. For brief discussions of the Oxnard Strike, see Ichioka, *Issei*, pp. 96–102; Almaguer, *Racial Fault Lines*, pp. 189–204. After the 1916 culinary workers strike in San Francisco—in which Japanese culinary workers honored picket lines even though they were formally excluded from the unions—some unionists sought to organize Japanese immigrants. Hugo Ernst of the Cooks and Waiters Union criticized the CFL for passing resolutions in favor of exclusion, and instead introduced a resolution calling for the organization of workers regardless of race. The resolution was defeated. See Ichioka, pp. 138–139.

87. Walter Macarthur, "Review of Exclusion History," AAAPS, January 1921. On Scharrenberg, compare Yuji Ochioka, *Issei*, pp. 131–144, with Scharrenberg, "The Attitude of Labor toward the Japanese," passim.

88. Yoell, who was Secretary of the Asiatic Exclusion League, quoted in AEL, *Proceedings*, December, 1908. For examples of labor's more ambivalent (but still negative) view of Southern and Eastern European immigrants, see *Labor Clarion* April 18, 25, and May 3, 1913. More generally, see Gwendolyn Mink, *Old Labor and New Immigrants in American Political Development: Union, Party, State, 1875–1920* (Ithaca: Cornell University Press, 1986).

89. *Labor Clarion*, April 25, 1913; AEL, *Proceedings*, August 1911, N.p. On the importance of "citizenship" in Progressive-era discourse, and organized labor's embrace of the term, see Michael Kazin, *The Populist Persuasion: An American History* (New York: Basic Books, 1995), Chapter 2.

90. On the "free labor" ideology, see Eric Foner, and for an application of how it continued to inform working-class racism in California, see Tomas Almaguer, *Racial Fault Lines*. Alexander Saxton also argued in *The Indispensable Enemy* that a "producer ethic" informed the early critiques of "coolie labor" in the anti-Chinese campaigns of the nineteenth century. More recently, David Roediger—although discussing black-white relations in the antebellum period—cites a "fear of dependency" and "wage slavery" as key elements in the formation of a white working-class identity. See Roediger, *Wages of Whiteness: Race and the Making of the American Working Class* (New York: Verso, 1991).

91. For an example of the argument on the dangers of a "servile race" and the threats to citizenship, see "Dr. Jordan and Cheap Labor," in AEL, *Proceedings*, April 1912. To a large extent, this line of reasoning was a continuation

that Alexander Saxton found in the arguments against the Chinese in the nineteenth century. However, by the early twentieth century labor made this argument much more selectively. That is, while at times the Japanese were alleged to be as "servile" as the Chinese, at other times they were accused of being overly "aggressive" and "ambitious" and "arrogant," traits that made them "more dangerous" than the "servile" and "docile" Chinese. But consistency was never a hallmark of the anti-Japanese movement. For a number of startling examples of such inconsistency—among labor and most other supporters of exclusion—see Roger Daniels, *The Politics of Prejudice*, passim.

92. Rogers, *The Politics of Prejudice*, passim.

93. One can find these types of arguments in almost any of the monthly *Proceedings* of the Asiatic Exclusion League between 1907 and 1913. Quotes from AEL *Proceedings*, January 1908, January 1909, and June 1911.

94. Paul Scharrenberg, "The Attitude of Organized Labor toward the Japanese," p. 35. Labor's use of racial politics was not an isolated phenomenon in the early twentieth century. In all parts of the nation—especially but not only in the South—race was an integral part of Progressive-era politics. See Michael Goldfield, *The Color of Politics: Race and the Mainsprings of American Politics* (New York: New Press, 1997), pp. 137–172.

95. Christopher Tomlins, *Law, Labor, and Ideology in the Early American Republic* (New York: Cambridge University Press, 1993), p. xiv, fn. 9. See also idem., "How Who Rides Whom: Recent 'New' Histories of American Labour Law and What They May Signify," *Social History* (1995): 1–21; and "A Mirror Crack'd?," *William and Mary Law Review* 32 (1991), pp. 364–365.

96. John O'Connell to Thomas Donnelly, March 29, 1916, Carton 27, SFLC Records. On the concept of *obiter dictum*, see *Black's Law Dictionary*, 5th edition (St. Paul, MN: West Publishing, 1975), pp. 409, 967.

97. For appellate court rulings upholding the restrictive reading of *Pierce*, see *Armstrong v. Superior Court* 173 Cal. 143 (1916); *Berger v. Superior Court of Sacramento* 175 Cal. 719 (1917); *Rosenberg v. Retail Clerks Association* 39 Cal. App 67 (1918), quote at 70. Of course that these appellate cases even exist suggests that at least a few California Superior Court judges must have allowed peaceful picketing, or did not go so far as employers wanted in barring the scope and place of strike activity.

98. O'Connell had identified, in particular, San Francisco, Oakland, Sacramento, and San Jose as jurisdictions that allowed peaceful picketing. But within a few months of his letter, sweeping injunctions against all picketing had appeared in San Jose and Sacramento. See the "Reports of the District Vice President[s]" for San Jose and Sacramento in CFL *Proceedings*, 1916–1918. And as we shall see in the following chapter, anti-picketing ordinances against even peaceful picketing were passed in San Francisco and Oakland in 1916 and 1917, respectively.

99. Skocpol, *Protecting Soldiers and Mothers*, p. 228. In support of this statement, Skocpol cites Forbath and Leon Fink, "Labor, Liberty, and the Law."

Yet, while this quote accurately represents the positions of Forbath and Fink, Skocpol's own view places much less emphasis on the ideological consequences of judicial hostility and much more on the political and institutional factors. Indeed, my discussion of the differences between the CFL and the AFL in the next few paragraphs has been greatly informed by Skocpol's analysis of labor politics and American social policy in Chapter 4 of *Protecting Soldiers and Mothers*.

100. Gary Fink, "The Rejection of Voluntarism"; idem., *Labor's Search for Political Order: The Political Behavior of the Missouri Labor Movement, 1890–1940* (Columbia: University of Missouri Press, 1973); Taft, *Labor Politics American Style*, Introduction; and Skocpol, *Protecting Soldiers and Mothers*, pp. 239–243.

101. On the ideological differences between the Knights and the AFL, see Gerald Grob, *Workers and Utopia: A Study of Ideological Conflict in the American Labor Movement, 1865–1900* (Evanston, IL: Northwestern University Press, 1961); and Victoria Hattam, "Economic Visions and Political Strategies: American Labor and the State, 1865–1896," *Studies in American Political Development* 4 (1990): 82–129.

102. Taft, *Labor Politics American Style*, p. 1.

103. The two best studies of labor and urban politics in San Francisco and Los Angeles, respectively, are Kazin, *Barons of Labor*, passim; and Daniel Johnson, "A Serpent in the Garden: Institutions, Ideology, Class in Los Angeles Politics, 1901–1911," (Ph.D. dissertation, UCLA, 1997).

104. For example, see Ira Katznelson and Margaret Weir, *Schooling for All: Class, Race, and the Democratic Ideal* (New York: Basic Books, 1985). In a comparative analysis of labor's effort to shape Progressive-era education reform in Chicago and San Francisco, Katznelson and Weir argue that, while the Chicago working class was just as divided by race and ethnicity as the San Francisco working class, the Chicago labor movement took a more inclusive, class-based approach and enjoyed more political success on issues of education reform. See also William Issel, "Class and Ethnic Conflict in San Francisco Political History: the Reform Charter of 1898," *Labor History* 18 (Summer 1977): 117–138.

105. Kazin, *Barons of Labor*, p. 170. Kazin develops this point at greater length in *The Populist Persuasion*, especially Chapter 3.

CHAPTER 4

1. Robert E. L. Knight, *Industrial Relations in the San Francisco Bay Area, 1900–1918* (Berkeley: University of California Press, 1960), Chapter 7; and Louis Perry and Richard Perry, *A History of the Los Angeles Labor Movement, 1911–1941* (Berkeley: University of California Press, 1963), Chapters 1–2. Exceptions to the overall industrial peace included the 1913 PG&E strike

and 1914 Stockton strike. On the Stockton strike, see Clark, "Limits of Liberty," pp. 173–176; United States Commission on Industrial Relations [USCIR], *Final Report and Testimony*, Vol. 5, pp. 4812f; and the "Stockton Lockout" File, Carton 33, SFLC Records.

2. Perry and Perry, pp. 22–52. Grace Stimson, *The Rise of the Labor Movement in Los Angeles* (Berkeley: University of California Press, 1955), pp. 420–430.

3. Knight, pp. 236–241, 294–298. Robert Cherny and William Issel *San Francisco, 1865–1932: Politics, Power, and Urban Development* (Berkeley: University of California Press, 1986), pp. 92–93, 167–170; Michael Kazin, *Barons of Labor*, pp. 217–231.

4. On increased strike activity nationally, see Florence Peterson, *Strikes in the United States, 1880–1936*, Department of Labor Bulletin No. 641 (Washington, DC: Government Printing Office 1936); and David Montgomery, *Workers Control in America: Studies in the History of Work, Technology, and Labor Struggles* (New York: Cambridge University Press, 1979), Table 2, p. 97.

5. *Labor Clarion* August 25, September 15, 29, 1916.

6. Knight, pp. 300–301.

7. For contemporary overviews of the waterfront strike by its combatants from the employers' perspective, see Waterfront Employers' Union [WEU]. *A Message from the Waterfront Employers' Union* (San Francisco: N.p., 1921); and from labor's perspective, Waterfront Workers' Federation, *The Longshoremen's Union Strike: A Brief Historical Sketch of the Strike Inaugurated on June 1, 1916, in Pacific Coast Ports of the United States* (San Francisco: N.p., 1916), copies in "Strikes" file, Carton 33, SFLC Records.

8. Wilson quoted in *Argonaut* June 24, 1916. See also *Labor Clarion* June 9, 1916; *Los Angeles Times* June 1, 1916; and Waterfront Employers Union [WEU], *A Message from the Waterfront Employers' Union* (San Francisco: N.p., 1921).

9. *Los Angeles Times* 13–14, 1916; *Citizen* June 16, 23, 1916.

10. *Los Angeles Times* June 2–9, 1916; *Labor Clarion* June 16, 1916

11. *Los Angeles Times* June 14, 16, 20–28, July 2, 4–7, 1916. Fred Wheeler, a socialist labor leader who had been elected to the City Council in 1913, was primarily responsible for the stalling on the part of the City Council. The *Times* harshly criticized the City Council's failure to provide funds for extra police and encouraged Chief Snively to dispatch the extras, posing a hypothetical question to the Chief: "If a mob should attack the First National Bank . . . and shoot down citizens . . . you would not wait for an order from the City Council before taking action, would you?" Ibid., June 24, 1916. See also *Citizen* June 23, 30, July 7, 1916; *Record* June 26, July 5, 1916; and Perry and Perry, pp. 177–178.

12. *Los Angeles Times* July 11–12, 19, 23, 25, 1916; *Citizen* July 14, 21, 28, 1916; Perry and Perry, p. 179.

13. "Report of the Secretary Treasurer," CFL *Proceedings*, 1916; *Los Angeles*

Times July 13, 15, 17–18, 24–25, August 9, 1916; *Citizen* July 21, 28, August 4, 1916; *Coast Seamen's Journal* July 19, 26, 1916; and Perry and Perry, p. 180.

14. San Francisco Chamber of Commerce, *Law and Order*, pp. 8–9; *San Francisco Chronicle*, June 29–July 8, 1916; *San Francisco Bulletin* June 29–July 8, 1916; *Argonaut* July 1, 1916.

15. *Labor Clarion* July 7, 1916; *Argonaut* July 8, 1916; *San Francisco Chronicle* July 6, 1916; and San Francisco Chamber of Commerce, *Law and Order*, pp. 14–16.

16. *Labor Clarion* July 7, 14, 21, 1916; Knight, pp. 306–307.

17. SFCC, *Law and Order*, pp. 14–19; *San Francisco Bulletin* July 11, 1916; *San Francisco Chronicle* July 11, 1916; *Argonaut* July 15, 1916; *Labor Clarion* July 14, 1916.

18. *Labor Clarion* July 14, 21, 1916.

19. Knight, p. 313: *Labor Clarion*, August 18, 1916; Clark, "Limits of Liberty," pp. 535–555.

20. On organized labor's response to the "preparedness" issue in the United States more generally, see Philip Foner, *Labor and World War I, 1914–1918*, Vol. 7 of *History of the Labor Movement in the United States*, (New York, International Publishers, 1987), pp. 64–74. [Hereafter, volume numbers for Foner's work refer to this series.]

21. Knight, pp. 309–311; *Labor Clarion* June 2, 9, July 14, 28, 1916; *Argonaut* July 29, 1916; SFCC, *Law and Order*, pp. 20–21; *Chronicle* July 23, 1916; *Examiner* July 23, 1916; *Bulletin* July 23, 1916.

22. *Examiner* July 27, 1916. A number of secondary works have dealt with the Mooney-Billings affair in whole or part. For example, see Foner, Vol. 7, Chapter 4; Richard Frost, *The Mooney Case* (CA: Stanford University Press, 1968); Curt Gentry, *Frame-Up: The Incredible Case of Tom Mooney and Warren Billings* (New York: Norton, 1967).

23. *Labor Clarion* July 21, 1916. For background on Mooney and Billings before the bombing, see Knight, pp. 268–270, 284–285, 293, 301, 307–311, 322–329.

24. United States National Commission on Law Observance and Enforcement [Wickersham Commission], *The Mooney-Billings Report*, (Montclair, NJ: Patterson-Smith, 1969). See also Knight, pp. 322–329, 347–350; and Foner, Vol. 7, pp. 93–95.

25. SFCC, *Law and Order*, pp. 20–21; *Argonaut*, July 29, 1916.

26. *Examiner* July 27, 1916; *Chronicle* July 27, 1916; *Labor Clarion* July 28, 1916; *Coast Seamen's Journal* August 2, 1916.

27. *Chronicle* August 10–13, 1916; *Labor Clarion* August 18, 1916; *Coast Seamen's Journal* August 23, 1916; *Argonaut* August 19, 1916; Knight, pp. 313–316; Edward Eaves, "A History of the Cooks' and Waiters' Union of San Francisco" (MA Thesis, University of California, Berkeley, 1930), pp. 61–73.

28. SFCC, *Law and Order*, "Forward," and pp. 30–32. On black strikebreakers,

see Douglas Henry Daniels, *Pioneer Urbanites: A Social and Cultural History of Black San Francisco* (Berkeley: University of California Press, 1990), pp. 36–42.

29. *Chronicle* August 1–2, 1916; Edward Eaves, p. 69.

30. *Chronicle* August 9, 25, September 7, 17, 1916; *Labor Clarion* August 11, 18, 25, September 15, 22, 29, 1916; *Argonaut* August 19, 26, September 16, 1916; Knight, p. 316; Edward Eaves, pp. 69–77.

31. SFCC *Law and Order*, pp. 34–36; *Chronicle* August 10–17, 1916; *Labor Clarion* August 11, 18, 1916; *Argonaut* August 12, 19, 1916; Knight p. 317. On the earlier efforts in Richmond and Oakland, see "Report of the Secretary Treasurer," CFL *Proceedings*, 1913, pp. 80–81; "Report of the Vice President for District 6," Ibid., 1915; "Report of the Vice President for District 7," Ibid. 1915; and "Report of the Vice President for District 6," Ibid., 1917.

32. For background on Koster, see Knight, pp. 304–306, 312. On the growth of the chamber—from 2,500 to 6,000 members, see Knight p. 318.

33. Copy of Koster's address in "Chamber of Commerce" file, Carton 16, SFLC Records.

34. Campaign literature in "Chamber of Commerce" file, Carton 16, SFLC Records. The quote was from *Atchinson, Topeka, and Santa Fe RR v. Gee* 139 F. 582 (1905). A similar phrasing had been used in California's *Pierce* ruling. See Chapter 4, above.

35. Scharrenberg's speech in CFL *Proceedings*, 1916, pp. 53–59.

36. SFCC, *Law and Order*, pp. 35–37.

37. San Francisco Board of Election Commissioners. *Proposed Ordinances and Charter Amendments to be Submitted November 7, 1916*. Copy in "Elections" file, Carton 28, SFLC Records. See also *Labor Clarion* October 6, 13, 27, November 3, 1916.

38. Municipal Record, "Official Vote of San Francisco, November 7, 1916," copy in "Elections" file, Carton 28, SFLC Records; "Statement of Voters, San Francisco City and County." Ledgers located at the Office of the Registrar of Voters, City Hall. See also *Bulletin* November 8, 1916; *Labor Clarion* November 10, 1916; and Thomas Clark, "Labor and Progressivism 'South of the Slot': The Voting Behavior of the San Francisco Working Class, 1912–1916," *California History* 66 (1987), 197–207.

39. "Report of the Vice President for District 6," CFL *Proceedings*, 1917, p. 59.

40. *Labor Clarion* November 10, 17, 1916; *In Matter of J. J. Williams* 158 Cal. 550 (1910) (upholding the Los Angeles anti-picketing ordinance of 1910).

41. *Labor Clarion* December 8, 1916.

42. "Report of the Vice President for District 9," CFL *Proceedings*, 1917.

43. Ibid., December 22, 1915; Knight, pp. 317–318, Edward Eaves, pp. 85–86. Eaves estimates that, in addition to losing the strike, union membership decreased by 50 percent following the defeat.

44. On the legislative agenda, see "Report[s] on Labor Legislation," CFL *Proceedings*, 1916–1919, passim. See also Philip Taft, *Labor Politics American*

Style: The California State Federation of Labor (Cambridge, MA: Harvard University Press, 1968), pp. 55–56, 75–79.
45. California Federation of Labor, *Essence of Labor's Contention on the Anti-injunction Abuse* (San Francisco: N.p., [1917?]), in "Law Notes" File, Carton 30, SFLC *Records*.
46. *California Outlook* May, 1917. Although the Supreme Court would not completely eviscerate the labor provisions of the Clayton Act until 1921, such prominent jurists as William Howard Taft—the former president who would later serve on the United States Supreme Court—had asserted in writings and public speeches that the labor provisions of the Clayton Act were "declaratory of existing law." See Dallas Jones, "The Enigma of the Clayton Act," *Industrial and Labor Relations Review* 10 (1957): 201–221; Stanley Kutler, "Labor, The Clayton Act, and the Supreme Court," *Labor History* 3 (1962): 19–38. On Taft's position and the view that the Clayton Act was declaratory of existing equity practices, see Dianne Avery, "Images of Violence in Labor Jurisprudence: The Regulation of Picketing and Boycotts, 1894–1921," *Buffalo Law Review* 37 (Winter 1988/89): 1–117, especially pp. 18–36, 61–70 and fn. 366, p. 81.
47. Max Kuhl, *Argument on the Anti-Injunction Bill Before Hon. Wm. D. Stephens, Governor of California, Monday, May 21, 1917*, (San Francisco: Chamber of Commerce, 1917). A Forward was later added and sent to other business organizations throughout the country in line with the Chamber's "policy of disseminating information of importance to the industrial community."
48. *Coast Seamen's Journal* January 31, 1917; "Report on Labor Legislation," CFL *Proceedings*, 1917, p. 106.
49. Ibid., pp. 6–12.
50. See, for example, Andrew Furuseth's response to Governor Stephens's veto message, reprinted to "Report on Labor Legislation," CFL *Proceedings*, 1917. See also "Report of the Secretary Treasurer," CFL *Proceedings*, 1916. See also Scharrenberg's address to the Commonwealth Club, reprinted in CFL *Proceedings*, 1916, pp. 53–59.
51. Kuhl, pp. 12–16, 22–24.
52. For labor's general position on the contempt of court issue, see Forbath, *Law and the Shaping of the American Labor Movement* (Cambridge, MA: Harvard University Press, 1991), pp. 67, 101, 108, 203.
53. Kuhl, pp. 19–25. Kuhl's analysis ignored the fact that the Los Angeles anti-picketing ordinance had been passed by the City Council, not by a popular initiative.
54. Ibid., pp. 24–25, 40–44.
55. Ibid., pp. 16–18, 45–47.
56. Governor Stephens's veto message printed in CFL "Report on Labor Legislation," CFL *Proceedings*, 1917.
57. *Coast Seamen's Journal* June 6, 1917.
58. On progressivism's continued relevance into the 1920s, see Jackson Put-

nam, "The Progressive Legacy in California: Fifty Years of Politics, 1917–1967," in William Deverell and Tom Sitton, eds., *California Progressivism Revisited* (Berkeley: University of California Press, 1994); idem., "The Persistence of Progressivism in the 1920s: The Case of California," *Pacific Historical Review* 35 (1966). Yet Putnam shows primarily that neo-progressivism left an *institutional* legacy in California state politics, most notably nonpartisanship and the continued work of Progressive-era commissions. These institutional legacies, for example, provided an important avenue for women to continue to pursue politics outside of the political parties. See, for example, Judith Raftery, "Los Angeles Clubwomen and Progressive Reform," in Deverell and Sitton. But the innovative period of progressivism had passed, and labor and many other progressive politicians found themselves defending past achievements rather than proposing new initiatives.

59. Richard Hofstadter, *The Age of Reform: From Bryan to FDR* (New York: Vintage Books, 1955). For the war's impact on the progressive impulse in California, see Spencer Olin, *California's Prodigal Sons: Hiram Johnson and the Progressives, 1911–1917* (Berkeley: University of California Press, 1968), pp. 156–182; and George Mowry, *The California Progressives*, pp. 274–301. In addition to the impact of the war, both Olin and Mowry suggest that California progressivism had been so closely tied to the person of Hiram Johnson that his departure marked a defeat for California progressivism in general. According to Michael Kazin, labor had gained much from the alliance with progressives, but they had abandoned an autonomous class-based political movement, and "when the reform wave receded and organized business turned hostile, labor activists found themselves isolated." *Barons of Labor*, pp. 284–288, quote at p. 286.

60. On the politics of the Fickert recall, see Knight, pp. 322–332, 347–350; Kazin, *Barons of Labor*, pp. 241–242.

CHAPTER 5

1. Melvyn Dubofsky, *Industrialism and the American Worker, 1865–1920* (Arlington Heights, IL: Harlan Davidson, 1985), p. 120.

2. Valerie Conner, *The National War Labor Board: Stability, Social Justice, and the Voluntary State in World War I* (Chapel Hill: University of North Carolina Press, 1983), pp. 18–34; Philip S. Foner, *Labor and World War I, 1914–1918*, Vol. 7, of *History of the Labor Movement in the United States* (New York: 1987), pp. 174–176.

3. Dubofsky and Dulles, *Labor in America* (Arlington Heights, IL: Harlan Davidson, 1984), pp. 215–220; Dubofsky, *Industrialism and the American Worker*, pp. 116–129.

4. Conner, passim, but especially pp. 22–34, 95–100 on the "existing standards" policy. See also Foner, Vol. 7, p. 175 for a concise summary of
the limitations of federal support. Grovesnor Clarkson, who served as research director of the Wilson administration's National Council of Defense, also stressed the limitations and missed opportunities of the NWLB.
See Clarkson, *Industrial America in the World War: The Strategy behind the
Line* (Boston: Houghton Mifflin, 1924), pp. 276–292.
5. Foner, *Labor and World War I*, passim; and David Montgomery, *Fall of the
House of Labor: The Workplace, the State, and American Labor Activism,
1865–1925* (New York: Cambridge University Press, 1987), Chapters 7–9.
6. Joseph McCartin, *Labor's Great War*; and idem., "'An American Feeling':
Workers, Managers, and the Struggle over Industrial Democracy during
the World War I Era," in Nelson Lichtenstein and Howell Harris, eds.,
Industrial Democracy in America: The Ambiguous Promise (New York: Cambridge University Press, 1993), pp. 67–86, quotes at pp. 73–74, 75–76. For
a similar argument on how wartime labor policy inspired labor activism
and rank-and-file militancy—even while attempting to strengthen more
established, conservative trade union leaders—see Jeffrey Haydu, *Making
American Industry Safe for Democracy: Comparative Perspectives on the State
and Employee Representation in the Era of World War I* (Urbana: University
of Illinois Press, 1997).
7. "Report of Organizer J. B. Dale," CFL *Proceedings*, 1917, p. 65.
8. USCIR Final Report.
9. Thomas Clark, "The Limits of Liberty."
10. On the Commission of Industrial Relations, see Graham Adams, *The Age of
Industrial Violence: The Activities and Findings of the United States Commission
on Industrial Relations* (New York: Columbia University Press, 1966). For
recent discussions of the Commission's significance for national labor politics, see Joseph McCartin, *Labor's Great War*, pp.18–37, and Julia Greene,
Pure and Simple Politics, passim.
11. Robert Knight, *Industrial Relations in the San Francisco Bay Area, 1900–1918*
(Berkeley: University of California Press, 1960), pp. 336–338.
12. Ira Cross, *Collective Bargaining and Trade Agreements in the Brewery, Metal,
Teaming, and Building Trades of San Francisco, California* (Berkeley: University of California Press, 1918), pp. 280–285; Knight, pp. 336–340; Haydu,
Making American Industry Safe for Democracy, p. 128;
13. *Labor Clarion* September 21, 28, 1917; *Chronicle* September 18, 1917; *Examiner* September 18, 1917; Knight, pp. 340–341.
14. *Labor Clarion* November 9, 1917; *Chronicle* December 26, 1917 through
January 1, 1918; *Examiner* December 26, 1917; Knight, pp. 341–342.
15. On the requirement that local unions take their grievances through the
ITC, see Haydu, p. 140.
16. Knight, pp. 339–342, 360–365.
17. *Labor Clarion* May 3, 1918.
18. Knight, pp. 342–344, 351–365.
19. On the half-hearted efforts of CFL organizers, see "Testimony of J. B. Dale,"

USCIR, *Final Report and Testimony*, Vol. 5, pp. 4972–4979; Cletus Daniel, *Bitter Harvest*, pp. 76–81.

20. Elizabeth Reis, "Cannery Row: The AFL, the IWW, and the Bay Area Italian Cannery Workers," *California History* 64 (1985), pp. 175–191; Foner, *Labor and World War I*, pp. 169–170; Knight, pp. 343–344.

21. Jaclyn Greenberg, "Industry in the Garden: A Social History of the Canning Industry in the Santa Clara Valley, California, 1870–1920," (Ph.D. dissertation, UCLA, 1985), Chapter 6, pp. 209–226.

22. Perry and Perry, pp. 106–116, 122–124.

23. The 1916 Federal Shipping Act created the United States Shipping Board and the Emergency Fleet Corporation to oversee the purchase, construction, and operation of commercial shipping. See David Kennedy, *Over Here: The First World War and American Society* (New York: 1980), pp. 301–305. On the contracts awarded at Los Angeles harbor, see Perry and Perry, pp. 124–125.

24. Ibid., pp. 124–125; *Times* May 1–2, 1916; *Evening Express* April 30, May 1, 1916.

25. *Citizen* May 19, 26, 1916; *Times* May 4, 21, 1916; Perry and Perry, p. 125.

26. *Citizen* June 2–30, 1916, January 12, February 9, 1917; *Times* July 28–29, 1916; Perry and Perry, p. 125.

27. Perry and Perry, p. 134.

28. *Times* June 11, 1918; *Citizen* June 14, 21, 1918.

29. *Times* June 11–12, 16–19, 1918; *Citizen* June 21, 1918; Perry and Perry, pp. 134–135.

30. *Times* December 24–25, 1918; *Citizen* December 20, 27, 1918; Perry and Perry, pp. 135–136.

31. Perry and Perry, pp. 70–75.

32. Ibid., pp. 78–80; *Times* July 1, 1918.

33. *Montgomery v. Pacific Electric Railway* 258 Fed. 382; *Los Angeles Times* July 3, 1918; Perry and Perry, p. 81. In support of his ruling, Judge Bledsoe cited *Hitchman Coal Company v. Mitchell*, which ruled that the United Mine Workers' efforts to enroll West Virginia Miners who had signed "yellow dog" contracts (i.e. where workers agreed not to join unions as a condition of employment) amounted to an inducement to breach of contract and was therefore subject to an injunction.

34. *Times* July 3, 1918; a copy of Commander Poundstone's order in *Montgomery v. Pacific Electric Railway* 258 Fed. 382.

35. *Times* July 3–6, 1918; *Citizen* July 5, 1918.

36. Perry and Perry, p. 83.

37. Ibid., pp. 75–76.

38. *Times* April 12, June 30, July 1, 4, 1919; *Citizen* April 18, July 4, 11, 18, 1919; Perry and Perry, pp. 84–85.

39. *Times* August 12–20, 1919; Perry and Perry, pp. 84–86.

40. *Times* August 19–21, 1919; *Record* August 16–20, 1919; *Citizen* August 15, 22, 19, 1919.

41. *Times* August 27, 1919; Perry and Perry, pp. 87–88.

42. Ibid., August 29–31, October, 19, 30, November 19, 1919; *Citizen* September 5, December 5, 1919; Perry and Perry, pp. 90–92.

43. "Report of the Vice President for District No. 2," and "Report of Organizer J. N. Buzzel," in CFL *Proceedings*, 1919, pp. 77–78, 86–87.

44. Perry and Perry, pp. 137–162, on the fate of several other strikes in 1919; on the longshoremen's and shipyard strikes of 1919, see discussion below.

45. The most comprehensive study of the Red Scare is still Robert Murray, *Red Scare: A Study in National Hysteria, 1919–1920*, (New York: McGraw-Hill 1955), passim. For concise overviews, see William Leucthenberg, *The Perils of Prosperity, 1914–1932* (Chicago: University of Chicago Press, 1958), pp. 66–83; Samuel Walker, *In Defense of American Liberties: A History of the ACLU* (New York: Oxford University Press, 1990), Chapters 1–2; Kennedy, pp. 75–87, 278–292.

46. Murray, p. 231.

47. On the IWW Free Speech Fights and mainstream labor's response, see Grace Miller, "The IWW Free Speech Fight: San Diego, 1912," *Southern California Quarterly* 54 (1972): 211–238; Harris Weinstock, *Report of Commissioner to Investigate Recent Disturbances in the City of San Diego and County of San Diego* (Sacramento: Superintendent of State Printing, 1912); "President's Report" and "Report of the Vice President for District No. 9," CFL *Proceedings*, 1912.

48. On the causes of the Wheatland riot, see Carlton Parker's report for the California Commission of Immigration and Housing, reprinted as an appendix in Carleton Parker, *The Casual Laborer and Other Essays* (New York: Harcourt, Brace, and Howe 1920), pp. 171–199. See also the clippings and related material in the "Wheatland" file, Simon J. Lubin Papers, Bancroft Library [hereafter, Lubin Papers.] On labor's response see "President's Report," "Report of the Secretary Treasurer," and "Appendix: Government Johnson's Statement Denying a Pardon for Ford and Suhr," all in CFL *Proceedings*, 1915, pp. 49–50, 79–87, 96–99. See also "President's Report" and "Proposition 36," in ibid., 1917, pp. 42–43, 52–54.

49. On the increasing activity of the IWW in 1917, see *Pacific Rural Press* November 14, 1917. On George Bell's effort to secure federal action in 1917, see the "IWW Investigation" file, Lubin Papers, and the following correspondence: Bell to Lubin, June 19, 1917; Bell to President Wilson, July 26, 1917; Bell to J. Harry Covington, September 1, 1917; Bell's letters to eight Western governors, July 6, 1917; and Lubin to Governor Campbell of Arizona, July 11, 1917. All in "Commission's Correspondence" files, in Lubin Papers.

50. President's Mediation Commission. *Report of the President's Mediation Commission* (Washington, DC: Government Printing Office, 1918; first published in May 1917), pp. 13–19. This report blamed the poor working conditions and employer intransigence for the unrest as much or more than it blamed the IWW, but it saw the strikes, whatever their cause, as a threat to the nation's economic mobilization.

51. On the federal raids of September 5, 1917, see Foner, Vol. 7, pp. 297–299; Dubofsky, *We Shall Be All: A History of the Industrial Workers of the World* (Chicago: Quadrangle Books, 1969), pp. 405–409; and William Preston, Jr., *Aliens and Dissenters: Federal Suppression of Radicals, 1900–1933* (Cambridge: Harvard University Press, 1963), pp. 118f. Even before the raids, Dell and the Commission expressed displeasure with the federal agents in California. See Bell's telegrams to Governor Lister of Washington, August 17, 18, 1917, and his letters to the eight Western governors, August 27, 1917, in Lubin Papers.

52. Eldridge Foster Dowell, *A History of Criminal Syndicalism in the United States* (Baltimore: Johns Hopkins Press, 1939), especially pp. 89–91 and Appendix II. For a complete history of the California Criminal Syndicalism Act and its early implementation, see Woodrow Whitten, "Criminal Syndicalism and the Law in California, 1919–1927," (Ph.D. dissertation, University of California, Berkeley, 1947). An abridged version of this dissertation appeared under the same title in *Transactions of the American Philosophical Society*, New Series, Vol. 59, Part 2, 1969. Subsequent page citations refer to the abridged version.

53. Whitten, p. 14. See also, *Times* April 22, 1917; California Assembly, *Journal of the Assembly*, 1917, pp. 776, 1679, 2006; Dowell, p. 90.

54. *Times* April 26, 1917; Sacramento *Bee* April 26, 1917; Whitten, p. 15; California Senate, *Journal of the Senate*.

55. On the IWW in the West, see Dubofsky, *We Shall Be All*; Foner, Vol. 7, Chapters 12–14.

56. *Bee* December 18, 1917; Sacramento *Union* December 18–19, 23, 1917; Whitten, pp. 17–18. For general accusations that "bomb plots" throughout the state were the work of the IWW, see *Times* December 34–30, 1917; *Chronicle* December 25, 1917; *Union* December 23, 1917.

57. *Chronicle* December 24, 1917, January 10, 1918; *Bee* December 23–24, 1917, January 20, 1918; San Francisco *Examiner* December 23, 1917. Unless otherwise noted, the following discussion of the trial and its consequences draws heavily from Whitten, "Criminal Syndicalism and the Law in California," passim.

58. *Bee* December 29, 31, 1917; *Chronicle* January 2, 1918; Whitten, p. 20.

59. For a brief overview of the Sacramento trial, see Weintraub, pp. 148–154; Whitten, pp. 20–22. See also the accounts in the *Union* and the *Bee* from December 10, 1918, through January 18, 1919; and San Francisco *Examiner* January 17–18, 1919.

60. *Labor Clarion* March 28, 1919; *Times* April 20, 1919; Whitten, pp. 22–23. On Benjamin's role in drafting the 1919 bill, see Dowell, pp. 52 (fn. 23), 66, 86 (fn. 287).

61. *Times* February 6–23, 1919; *Chronicle* March 20–28, April 28, 1919; Whitten, pp. 23–24.

62. The *Labor Clarion* under Mullen carried weekly attacks on labor radicals during this period; see issues for February 14–28, March 7–28, April 11–25, 1919.

63. Senate *Journal*, 1919, pp. 584, 608, 800, 832; *Chronicle* March 25–26, 1919; *Labor Clarion* March 28, 1919.

64. *Labor Clarion* March 28, April 25, May 2, 1919; "Report on Labor Legislation," in CFL *Proceedings*, 1919, pp. 111–119.

65. *Labor Clarion* May 2, 1919; Assembly *Journal*, 1919, pp. 946–947, 1807, 1849; *Times* April 19–20, 1919. The San Francisco Labor Council proposed inserting the word "physical" in the definition of sabotage; see "Law and Legislative Committee" files, Carton 24, SFLC Records.

66. Quoted in Whitten, p. 25.

67. Assembly *Journal*, pp. 2017–2019; *Union* April 23–24, 1919; Whitten, p. 25.

68. "Report on Labor Legislation," CFL *Proceedings*, 1919, p. 119. See also Proposition and Resolution No. 13, Propositions 71 and 73, ibid., pp. 23f, 50f; and "Report of the President," ibid., 1920, p. 58.

69. *Labor Clarion* April 4, 25, 1919.

70. "Report on Labor Legislation," CFL *Proceedings*, 1919.

71. Ibid., p. 121.

72. Ibid., pp. 112–119.

73. John Laslett and Seymour Lipset, eds., *Failure of a Dream? Essays on American Socialism* (Garden City, NY: Anchor Press, 1974), passim; Marc Karson, *American Labor Unions and Politics* (Carbondale: Southern Illinois University Press, 1958), passim; Foner, Vol. 3, Chapter 5 (on the Catholic Church); Michael Rogin, "Voluntarism: The Political Functions of an Anti-Political Doctrine," *ILRR* 15 (1962).

74. See, for example, "Report of the Committee on Reconstruction" CFL *Proceedings*, 1918, pp. 94–96; "Report of the Secretary Treasurer," ibid., 1918, pp. 77–86; "Report of the President," ibid., 1919, pp. 72–74; "Report of the Secretary Treasurer," ibid., 1919, pp. 94–102; and "Report on Labor Legislation," ibid., 1919, pp. 111–113. See also Taft, pp. 75–79.

75. The connection between the 1919 strike wave and the Red Scare was not unique to California; see also Murray, pp. 92–98, 106–112, 267–269. Attacks on radical influence in the labor movement appeared almost daily in the *Times* throughout 1919, but see especially the nearly daily attacks on the garment workers' strike in October and November, 1919. More generally, see Howard Ambramowitz, "The Press and the Red Scare, 1919–1921," in Ronald Edsforth and Larry Bennet, eds., *Popular Culture and Political Change in Modern America* (Albany: State University of New York Press, 1991). The *Labor Clarion* also made regular attacks on alleged radical influence, especially in the Laundry Workers' unions. See, for example, *Labor Clarion* May 23 and June 13, 1919.

76. WEU, pp. 18–22; *Labor Clarion* August 15, 1919; *Chronicle* August 7, September 20, 1919.

77. WEU, pp. 18–20; *Labor Clarion* August 22, September 12, 26, 1919; *Chronicle* August 20–22, September 20, 26, 1919.

78. *Chronicle* September 16, 20, 26–30, November 15, 1919; *Labor Clarion* September 19, 26, October 31, December 5, 1919; *Bulletin* September 24, 30, 1919; WEU, pp. 19–22. See also Bruce Nelson, *Workers on the*

Waterfront: Seamen, Longshoremen, and Unionism in the 1930s (Urbana: University of Illinois Press, 1990), p. 52; and Robert Francis, "A History of Labor on the San Francisco Waterfront," (Ph.D. Dissertation, University of California, Berkeley, 1934), pp. 164–165.

79. WEU, pp. 20–21; *Chronicle* September 26–30, October 3, November 15, 1919.

80. *Chronicle* November 16, 1919; *Bulletin* November 16, 1919; *Labor Clarion* November 21, December 5, 1919.

81. On the Centralia incident, see Foner, Vol. 8, pp. 214–225. On the response in California, see *Times* November 13–20, 1919; *Evening Herald* November 12–15, 1919; *Chronicle* November 12–17, 19, 1919.

82. WEU, pp. 20–21; Paul Eliel, *The Waterfront and the General Strike—San Francisco, 1934: A Brief History* (San Francisco: N.p., 1934), pp. 1–2.

83. *Labor Clarion* December 12, 1919, December 30, 1927, May 2, 1931; Nelson, pp. 53, 127–155, 163; Cherny and Issel, pp. 94–95; Francis, pp. 174–182.

84. On the defeat of the 1919 shipyard strike in Los Angeles, see *Times* October 18, 27, 29–31, November 6, 9, 11, 19, 1919; *Evening Herald* November 8, 10, 1919; Perry and Perry, pp. 129–132.

85. *Times* October 15, 18, 1919; *Evening Herald* October 14–15, 1919; Perry and Perry, pp. 181–181.

86. *Times* October 24–25, 29, 31, November 5, 1919.

87. Ibid., October 25, November 5, 20, 1919.

88. Ibid., October 20–23, 28, November 5, 13, 15, 17–18, 20, 1919; *Evening Herald* November 6, 12–16, 1919; Perry and Perry, pp. 149–150.

89. *Times* October 31, November 19, 1919. On the police union, see September 2, 16, October 12, 16, 31, November 4–11, 1919; Perry and Perry, pp. 159–160.

90. *Times* November 4, 11, 1919. Returning soldiers and sailors contributed greatly to the defeat of several 1919 strikes. Their use as strikebreakers was facilitated by both public and private employment bureaus: the private San Pedro Stevedoring Company and the quasi-public Soldiers and Sailors Bureau, supported by the City Council. These organizations claimed to have found jobs for an estimated 13,000 World War I veterans between January 18, 1919, and November 4, 1919. See *Times* October 25, November 5, 1919.

91. On the growing influence of the IWW among rank-and-file waterfront workers in San Pedro, especially after the 1919 defeats, see Perry and Perry, pp. 131, 164–165, 181–191; Nelson, p. 61.

92. See, for example, "Report of the President, " CFL *Proceedings*, 1919, p. 74.

CHAPTER 6

1. Irving Bernstein, *The Lean Years: A History of the American Worker, 1920–1933* (Boston: Houghton Mifflin, 1960), p. 189.

2. The best overview of labor in the 1920s is still Irving Bernstein's *The Lean Years*. See also Frank Stricker, "Affluence For Whom? Another Look at Prosperity and the Working Class in the 1920s," *Labor History* (1983), which raises questions about the extent and distribution of the 1920s' "prosperity." On California, see Taft, *Labor Politics American Style: The California Federation of Labor* (Cambridge, MA: Harvard University Press, 1968).

3. *Duplex Printing Press Company v. Deering* 254 U.S. 443 (1921); *Truax v. Corrigan* 257 U.S. 312 (1921); *American Steel Foundries v. Tri-City Central Trades Council* 257 U.S. 184 (1921).

4. Melvyn Dubofsky and Rhea Foster Dulles, *Labor in America: A History*, 4th. ed. (Arlington Heights, IL: Harlan Davidson, 1984), Chapter 14; James Green, *The World of the Worker: Labor in Twentieth Century America* (New York: Hill and Wang, 1980), p. 123; Bernstein, p. 194. None of these fine studies claims that court hostility alone, or even primarily, caused labor's defeats in the 1920s, but each treats the courts as a significant factor.

5. On the Clayton Act, see Stanley Kutler, pp. 19–38; Robert Murray, "Public Opinion, Labor, and the Clayton Act," *The Historian* 21 (1959), pp. 255–270; Dallas Jones, "The Enigma of the Clayton Act," *Industrial and Labor Relations Review* 10 (1957), pp. 201–221; Dianne Avery, "Images of Violence in Labor Jurisprudence: The Regulation of Picketing and Boycotts," *Buffalo Law Review* (Winter 1988/89), pp. 1–117; and Charles Gregory, *Labor and the Law*, 2nd revised edition (New York: Norton, 1958), pp. 159–174. The Clayton Act's controversial sections 6 and 20 are printed in Gregory, Appendix A.

6. Gregory, Appendix A, sections 6 and 20; Samuel Gompers, "The Charter of Industrial Freedom," *American Federationist* (November 1914), pp. 971–972; Kutler, pp. 20–24; Jones, pp. 214–28; Gregory, pp. 159– 166; Avery, p. 81, fn. 366.

7. *Duplex v. Deering* 254 U.S. 443; good, concise analyses of the Duplex case include Kutler, pp. 30–34; Avery, pp. 61–70 and passim; Jones, pp. 218–219.

8. *American Steel Foundries v. Tri-City Central Trades Council* 257 U.S. 184, at 203–207; Taft's statement that "peaceful picketing was a contradiction in terms" actually appeared in *Truax v. Corrigan* 257 U.S. 312 (1921), at 340. However, he was simply reiterating the point that "[t]here is and can be no such thing as peaceful picketing" made by a federal court judge in *Atchison, Topeka, and Santa Fe Railroad v. Gee* 139 F. 582 at 584. See Avery, pp. 12, 96–97.

9. 257 U.S. 312 (1921), at 321–338; see also Avery, pp. 102– 103.

10. *Southern California Iron and Steel Company v. Amalgamated Association of Iron, Steel, and Tin Workers, et al.* 186 Cal. 604 (1921). Original and amended complaints for this case printed in California Supreme Court, *California Supreme Court Records* Vol. 5109, in the Law Library of the California Courts Building and State Library, Sacramento. I discuss this case at greater length in "Limits of Liberty."

11. CFL. *Official Yearbook of Organized Labor—1924* (San Francisco: N.p., 1924). See also CFL, *Ten Years' Achievement* (San Francisco: N.p., 1923); and Taft, p. 84.

12. "President's Report" and "Report of the Secretary Treasurer," in CFL *Proceedings, 1920.*

13. Paul Scharrenberg, "How Labor Views the Power Situation in California," offprint from *The Annals of the American Academy of Political and Social Science*, March 1925, copy in Paul Scharrenberg Papers, Box 4, Bancroft Library, University of California at Berkeley. See also "Report[s] of the Executive Secretary" and "Report[s] of the Legislative Committee," in CFL *Proceedings, 1920–1924*; Franklin Hichborn, *The Story of the Session of the California Legislative Session of 1921* (San Francisco: Press of James H. Barry, 1921); and Russell M. Posner, "The Progressive Voters League, 1923–1926," *California Historical Society Quarterly* 36 (1957): 251–261. The 1920 amendments to the 1913 Alien Land Law prohibited renting as well as owning land made it more difficult for Issei to put land in the names of American-born children. See Roger Daniels, *The Politics of Prejudice: The Anti-Japanese Movement in California* (Berkeley: University of California Press, 1962), Chapters 6–7.

14. Better America Federation of California. *A Brief Outline of Arguments* (Los Angeles: N.p., N.d. [1920?]) copy in Carton 27, SFLC *Records*. See also George West, "Good News From California," *Nation* June 22, 1921, pp. 867–869.

15. "Report of President," CFL *Proceedings*, 1920, pp. 57–59; "Report of President," ibid., 1921, pp. 52–53; "Report of President," ibid., 1922, p. 57; see also California Federation of Labor. *Points of Difference between Organized Labor and the Better American Federation* (San Francisco: N.p., N.d.), copy in Carton 27, SFLC *Records*.

16. Hichborn, p. 297; Edward Layton, "The Better America Federation: A Case Study in Superpatriotism," *Pacific Historical Review* 30 (May 1961), pp. 137–147. See also Philip Taft, *Labor Politics American Style: The California Federation of Labor* (Cambridge, MA: Harvard University Press, 1968), Chapter 5. Not only did the BAF fail to cut the state budget, but during Governor Stephens's term (1917–1922), the state biennial budget actually doubled, as the Progressive-era commissions survived conservative attacks. Stephens's successor, Friend Richardson (1923–1926) did initially cut the state budget, but after the 1924 election, a less conservative legislature restored the cuts and actually increased state spending. See Jackson Putnam, "The Persistence of Progressivism in the 1920s: The Case of California," *Pacific Historical Review* 35 (1966): 399–404; idem., "The Progressive Legacy in California," in Sitton and Deverell, eds., *California Progressivism Revisited* (Berkeley: University of California Press, 1994), pp. 250–252.

17. For a general overview of LaFollette's 1924 campaign in California, see John L. Shover, "The California Progressives and the 1924 Campaign," *California Historical Society Quarterly* 51 (1972): 58–74.

18. "Why you should vote for LaFollette," in Santa Barbara *Union Advocate*.

Special 1924 Convention Edition, September 19, 1924, p. 8. Copy in Paul Scharrenberg Papers, Box 4, "California Federation of Labor Publications."

19. John Shover and Michael Rogin, *Political Change in California: Critical Elections and Social Movements, 1890–1926.* (Westport, CT: Greenwood Press, 1970), Chapters 2–3.

20. On the early years and national dimensions of the American Plan, see Irving Bernstein, *The Lean Years,* especially Chapter 3.

21. For statements by several American Planners in California, see *Pacific Industries* February, 1922, and miscellaneous materials in the "American Plan" files, Carton 27, SFLC *Records,* Bancroft Library.

22. Bernstein, Chapter 3, passim.

23. Louis Perry and Richard Perry, *A History of the Los Angeles Labor Movement* (Berkeley: University of California Press, 1963), pp. 197–211; see also *Los Angeles Times,* June 3, August 6, December 17, 1921, January 19, 1922, May 2, October 12, 22, 1923, January 9, February 19, 1924. On the brutal repression of the IWW-led waterfront strike, see Clark, "Limits of Liberty," pp. pp. 663–676.

24. Clark, "Limits of Liberty," pp. 663–665, 677–684. See also Bruce Nelson, *Workers on the Waterfront: Seamen, Longshoremen, and Unionism in the 1930s* (Urbana: University of Illinois Press, 1990), pp. 54–60.

25. For the most complete overview of the Building Trades' strike and its consequences, see Frederick Ryan, *Industrial Relations in the San Francisco Building Trades* (Norman: University of Oklahoma Press, 1936), pp. 134–172; Kazin, *Barons of Labor,* pp. 253–262. See also *Organized Labor* May 21, 28, June 4, July 23, 30, September 3, 10, 1921; *Labor Clarion* May 6, August 5, 1921; *San Francisco Chronicle* May 4–9, July 20–22, August 3, 4, 27–30, 1921.

26. On the origins of the Industrial Association, see Ryan, pp. 167–172; Robert Cherny and William Issel, *San Francisco, 1865–1932: Politics, Power, and Urban Development* (Berkeley: University of California, 1986), pp. 95–96. See especially, however, the several documents in the "Industrial Association" files, Carton 29, and "American Plan" files, Carton 30, SFLC *Records.*

27. The Industrial Association and the Builders' Exchange sent notices to employers pointing out the ratio of union to nonunion workers, informing them that, "in carrying out the American Plan, the proportion should be nearer 50 percent of each." Copy of notice printed in San Francisco *Daily News,* April 13, 1922, clipping in "American Plan" file, Carton 27, SFLC *Records.* See also *Industrial Association of San Francisco v. United States* 268 U.S. 64 (1925), passim; and Ryan, pp. 167–170.

28. Ryan, pp. 172–173; Cross, p. 252–253.

29. On the AFL's opposition to the use of injunction, see AFL Executive Committee, "Use of the Injunction by Labor a Delusion and a Snare," reprinted in *Organized Labor* June 17, 1922; and Samuel Gompers, "What about Injunctions? Shall We Fight Them, Use Them, or Violate Them?," *Labor Age* 15 (1926), pp. 15–18. On the incidence of labor's use of the injunction in

the 1920s, see Edwin Witte, "Labor's Resort to the Injunction," *Yale Law Journal* 39 (1930), pp. 374–375. Quotes from Alpheus T. Mason, "Labor Turns to the Injunction," *North American Review* 231 (1931), pp. 246–250. Forbath cites Hillman's willingness to use the injunction, where Gompers would not, to demonstrate that at least a minority of union leaders, especially the more left-leaning ones, were willing to make "positive uses of politics, law, and state power." Forbath, *Law*, pp. 118–125, quote at 119.

30. Ibid., September 16, 23, 1922

31. Daugherty's statement printed in *Organized Labor* January, 13, 1921.

32. *Organized Labor* June 2, 1921; Ryan, pp. 176–177.

33. *Organized Labor* June 23, 1923; Ryan, p. 177.

34. *United States v. Industrial Association of San Francisco, et al.* 293 Fed Rep 925. Copy of court records in "American Plan" files, Carton 27, SFLC *Records*. See also the summary of the defense argument in James R. Kelly to John O'Connell, November 13, 1923, Carton 27, SFLC *Records*.

35. 293 F. 925 (1923); *Organized Labor* December 8, 22, 1923; Ryan, pp. 177–178.

36. *Organized Labor* December 8, 1923.

37. *Industrial Association of San Francisco, et al. v. United States* 268 U.S. 64 (1925), at 64.

38. Ibid., at 75–76.

39. Ibid., at 84.

40. Ibid., at 69–70, 84.

41. San Francisco Building Trades Council. Boosters' Committee. *A Message of Vital Importance to Businessmen and All Loyal San Franciscans*, pamphlet dated July 15, 1922, in the "American Plan" files, Carton 27, SFLC Records.

42. AFL Executive Council, "Use of the Injunction by Labor a Snare and a Delusion," in *Organized Labor* June 17, 1922.

CONCLUSION

1. John Frey, "Labor and Politics," *American Federationist*, April, 1919, pp. 324f. The movement within the AFL for independent political action was strongest in Chicago and New York, and was part of a more general plan for postwar "Reconstruction." See Samuel Gompers, "Political Labor Party— Reconstruction—Social Insurance," *American Federationist*, January, 1919, pp. 33f. See also Joseph McCartin, *Labor's Great War: The Struggle for Industrial Democracy and the Origins of Modern Industrial Labor Relations, 1912–1921* (Chapel Hill: University of North Carolina Press, 1997), Chapter 7, especially pp. 202–205.

2. Louis Hartz, *The Liberal Tradition in America* (New York: Harcourt, Brace, 1955).

3. Karen Orren, "Organized Labor and the Invention of Modern Liberalism in America," *Studies in American Political Development* 2 (1987): 317–336, quote at p. 317.
4. Frey, "Labor and Politics," pp. 324–328. For more recent comparisons of the impact of the law on labor politics in Great Britain and the United States, see Victoria Hattam, *Labor Visions and State Power: The Origins of Business Unionism in the United States* (NJ: Princeton University Press,: 1993); and William Forbath, "Courts, Constitutions, and Labor Politics in England and the United States: A Study of the Constitutive Power of the Law," *Law and Social Inquiry* 16 (1991): 1–34. The AFL campaign to elect members to Congress between 1906 and 1909 has been meticulously covered by Julie Greene, *Pure and Simple Politics: The American Federation of Labor and Political Activism, 1881–1916* (New York: Cambridge University Press, 1998), Chapters 4–6; and idem., "The Strike at the Ballot Box: The American Federation of Labor's Entrance into Politics, 1906–1909," *Labor History* 32 (1991): 165–192.
5. Frey, "Labor and Politics," p. 325.
6. Ibid., pp. 327–328.
7. John Shover and Michael Rogin, *Political Change in California: Critical Elections and Social Movements, 1896–1966* (Westport, CT: Greenwood Press, 1970), Chapters 2–3, quote at p. 85. These chapters were slightly revised versions of Michael Rogin, "Progressivism and the California Electorate," *Journal of American History* 55 (1968): 297–314; and John Shover, "The Progressives and the Working Class Vote in California," *Labor History* 10 (1969): 584–601.

EPILOGUE

1. Quoted in Robert Zieger, *American Workers, American Unions, 1920–1985* (Baltimore: Johns Hopkins University Press, 1986), p. 29.
2. For a recent overview that stresses the galvanizing effect of both section 7(a) of the NIRA and the Wagner Act, see Melvyn Dubofsky, *The State and Labor in Modern America* (Chapel Hill: University of North Carolina Press, 1994), Chapters 5–6. Historians and political scientists do not always agree on whether labor unrest in the 1930s was a cause or consequence of New Deal labor policy. For a sample of this debate see Michael Goldfield, "Worker Insurgency, Radical Organization, and New Deal Labor Legislation," *American Political Science Review* 83 (December 1989): 1257–1282, and Theda Skocpol and Kenneth Finegold, "Explaining New Deal Labor Policy," ibid., 84 (December 1990): 1297–1304, and Goldfield's rebuttal, ibid., pp. 1304–1312. For an overview that suggests the interactive and mutually reinforcing aspects of labor militancy and New Deal labor policy, see Zieger, *American Workers, American Unions*, Chapter 2.

3. For a classic statement of the liberal view of the Wagner Act (and the New Deal more generally), see Arthur Schlesinger's contribution to Grob and Billias, *Interpretations of American History: Patterns and Perspectives* 4th ed. (New York: Free Press, 1982), Chapter 8. See also Carl Degler, *Out of Our Past* (New York: Harper, 1959), pp. 390–391, 413; and William Leuchtenberg, *Franklin Roosevelt and the New Deal, 1932–1940* (New York: Harper and Row, 1963), pp. 150–152, 326–348. On the New Left view, see Ronald Radosh, "The Corporate Ideology of American Labor Leaders from Gompers to Hillman," in Milton Mankoff, ed., *The Poverty of Progress: The Political Economy of American Social Problems* (New York: Holt, Rinehart, and Winston, 1972). For a critique of both schools from a "state-centered" perspective, see Theda Skocpol, "Political Response to Capitalist Crisis: Neo-Marxist Theories of the State and the Case of the New Deal," *Politics and Society* 10 (1980): 155–201. For a work that blends elements of pluralist, state-centered, and elite models in a persuasive manner, see David Plotke, "The Wagner Act, Again: Politics and Labor, 1935–1937," *Studies in American Political Development* 3 (1989): 105–156.

4. Tomlins, *The State and the Unions: Labor Relations, Law, and the Organized Labor Movement in America* (New York: Cambridge University Press, 1985), especially pp. xi–xiv, 95.

5. Ibid., Chapter 4, passim; Zieger, pp. 35–41.

6. *NLRB v. Jones & Laughlin Steel Co., et al.* 301 U.S. 1. Karl Klare, "Judicial De-Radicalization of the Wagner Act and Modern Legal Consciousness, 1937–1941," in Alan Hutchinson, ed., *Critical Legal Studies* (Totowa, NJ: Rowman and Littlefield, 1989), pp. 229–255 (originally published in *Minnesota Law Review* 62 [1978]). On employer resistance, see Zieger, pp. 39–41; Dubofsky, *The State and Labor in Modern America*, 131–135, 142–146.

7. Dubofsky, *The State and Labor in Modern America*, pp. 133–135. On the relationship between two important CIO leaders and the labor-Democratic alliance, see Melvyn Dubofsky and Warren Van Tine, *John L. Lewis: A Biography* (New York: Quadrangle, 1977), pp. 210–253; and Steve Fraser, *Labor Will Rule: Sidney Hillman and the Rise of American Labor* (New York: Free Press, 1991), passim; and idem., "The 'Labor Question,'" in Steve Fraser and Gary Gerstle, eds., *Rise and Fall of the New Deal Order, 1930–1980* (NJ: Princeton University Press,: 1989), pp. 67–78.

8. Robert Cherny and William Issel, *San Francisco, 1865–1932: Politics, Power, and Urban Development* (Berkeley: University of California Press, 1986), p. 214.

9. J. W. Buzzell, "An Open Shop Citadel Falls," *American Federationist* April, 1941. Estimates on union membership in Los Angeles drawn from Richard Perry and Louis Perry, *A History of the Los Angeles Labor Movement, 1911–1941* (Berkeley: University of California Press, 1963), passim.

10. Mike Davis, *Prisoners of the American Dream: Politics and Economy in the History of the United States Working Class* (New York: Verso Press, 1986), Chapter 2.

11. On labor's organizational and political woes in the 1980s, see Zieger, pp. 193–199, and David Brody, *In Labor's Cause: Main Themes on the History of the American Worker* (New York: Oxford University Press, 1993), pp. 74–76. Gary Hart as quoted in E. J. Dionne, "Unions Still Count," *Omaha World-Herald* October 15, 1999. Dionne recounted Hart's comment in an editorial on Al Gore's ability to outmaneuver Bill Bradley for the AFL-CIO endorsement for the Democratic nomination for the 2000 presidential race. With cautious optimism, Dionne argued that Gore's decision to "fight so fiercely" for labor's endorsement "suggests that if the unions aren't what they were in their heydey—Big Labor sounds antique—they still count for something." Dionne's optimism is refreshing; how realistic it is remains to be seen.

Index

AFL-CIO, 229. *See also* American Federation of Labor

African-American workers, 53, 135, 157; as strikebreakers, 53, 157; as victims of strike of strike violence 157, 194

Alameda County, 215

Alexander, George, 59–60, 64; policing policy of, 59–63

Alien Land Act, 136, 206, 275n.13

Amalgamated Association of Street Railway Employees (AASRE), 51–54, 181–83

American Anti-Boycott Association (AABA), 81, 208

American Bakers' Union, 85, 86

American Exceptionalism, 16, 17–18, 219, 232–33n. 12

American Federation of Labor (AFL): and anti-injunction bills, 87, 207; compared to IWW, 27; compared to state and local labor federations, 24, 128, 131, 132, 139, 141–43, 192; mentioned, 31; opposition to labor's use of the injunction, 212, 216; opposition to third party politics in Los Angeles, 57; political methods of, 14, 18–20, 40, 56, 64–65, 141–43, 192, 207, 219–23; and Red Scare, 191, and syndicalism, 27; and World War I, 183. *See also* Gompers, Samuel

American Federationist, 219, 229, 244n. 1

American Plan, 202–3, 207, 208–13, 214–15, 222

American Revolution: labor's collective action compared to, 32, 42–43

American Steel Foundries vs. Tri-City Trades Council (1921), 204–5

Anderson, Frank, 153

Angelotti, Justice Frank M., 98

Anti-Asian Movements, 23, 24, 83, 135–39, 143–44, 206, 260n. 86

Anti-Boycott bill, 163–64

Anti-Citizen's Alliance, 55

Anti-Injunction Legislation: 1903 anti-injunction law, 4, 86–89, 90–92, 98, 104, 107; 1917 Bill, 148, 162–66; 1919 Bill, 190–92; AFL and federal legislation, 87, 207, 221 (*see also* Clayton Act); Arizona law, 204, 206 (*see also*

281